Italian Days, Arabian Nights

Coming of Age in the Shadow of Mussolini

VITTORIO PALUMBO

Story Trust®
Story Trust Publishing, LLC
storytrust.com

Copyright © 2011 Vittorio Palumbo

All rights reserved. No part of this book may be used or reproduced by any means, graphic, electronic, or mechanical, including photocopying, recording, or taping, or by any information storage retrieval system without the written permission of the author.

Photos Credits

Family photos courtesy of the author; school photos courtesy of Fiera di Primiero town archives; postcard image by Brunner & C., Como, Italy; back cover photo of author courtesy of David G. O'Neil.

To contact the author about speaking engagements or for educational discounts on books, please send an email to palumbostory@gmail.com.

Produced and Published by
Story Trust Publishing, LLC
36 Floral Street
Newton, MA 02461
www.storytrust.com

Printed in the United States of America

ISBN: 978-1-937228-00-2
Library of Congress Control Number: 2011929627

For Cristina and Steven
You are very special and precious to your mother and me.

Family Tree

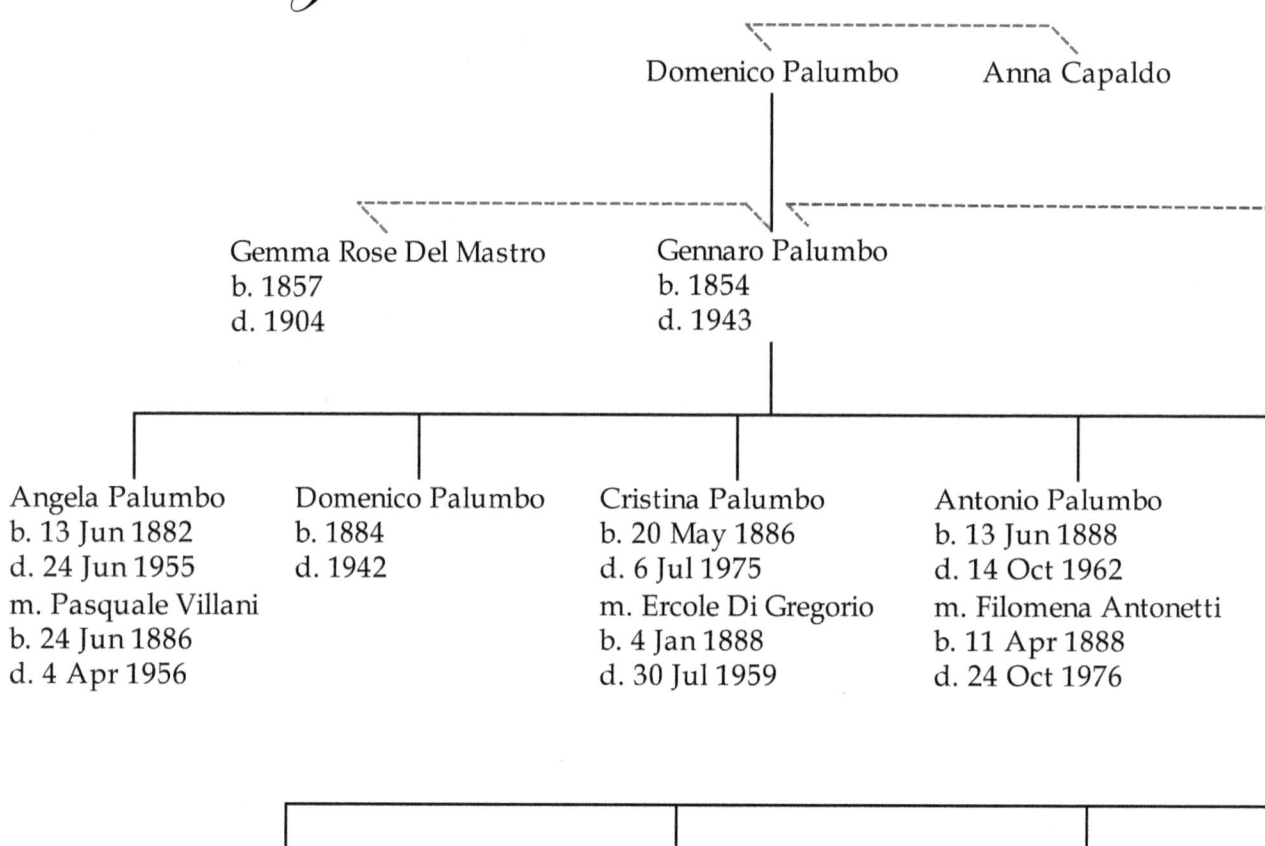

Domenico Palumbo — Anna Capaldo

Gemma Rose Del Mastro
b. 1857
d. 1904

Gennaro Palumbo
b. 1854
d. 1943

Angela Palumbo
b. 13 Jun 1882
d. 24 Jun 1955
m. Pasquale Villani
b. 24 Jun 1886
d. 4 Apr 1956

Domenico Palumbo
b. 1884
d. 1942

Cristina Palumbo
b. 20 May 1886
d. 6 Jul 1975
m. Ercole Di Gregorio
b. 4 Jan 1888
d. 30 Jul 1959

Antonio Palumbo
b. 13 Jun 1888
d. 14 Oct 1962
m. Filomena Antonetti
b. 11 Apr 1888
d. 24 Oct 1976

Gennaro Palumbo
b. 20 Sep 1920
d. 1 Nov 1987
m. Ilde Colelli
b. 18 Nov 1933

Giovanna Palumbo
b. 22 Jan 1924
m. Salvatore Del Mastro
b. 30 Jan 1921
d. 17 Jan 1989

Guerino Palumbo
b. 10 Mar 1926
d. 8 Dec 1972
m. Giuseppina Guzzon
b. 16 Mar 1932
d. 20 Jun 2000

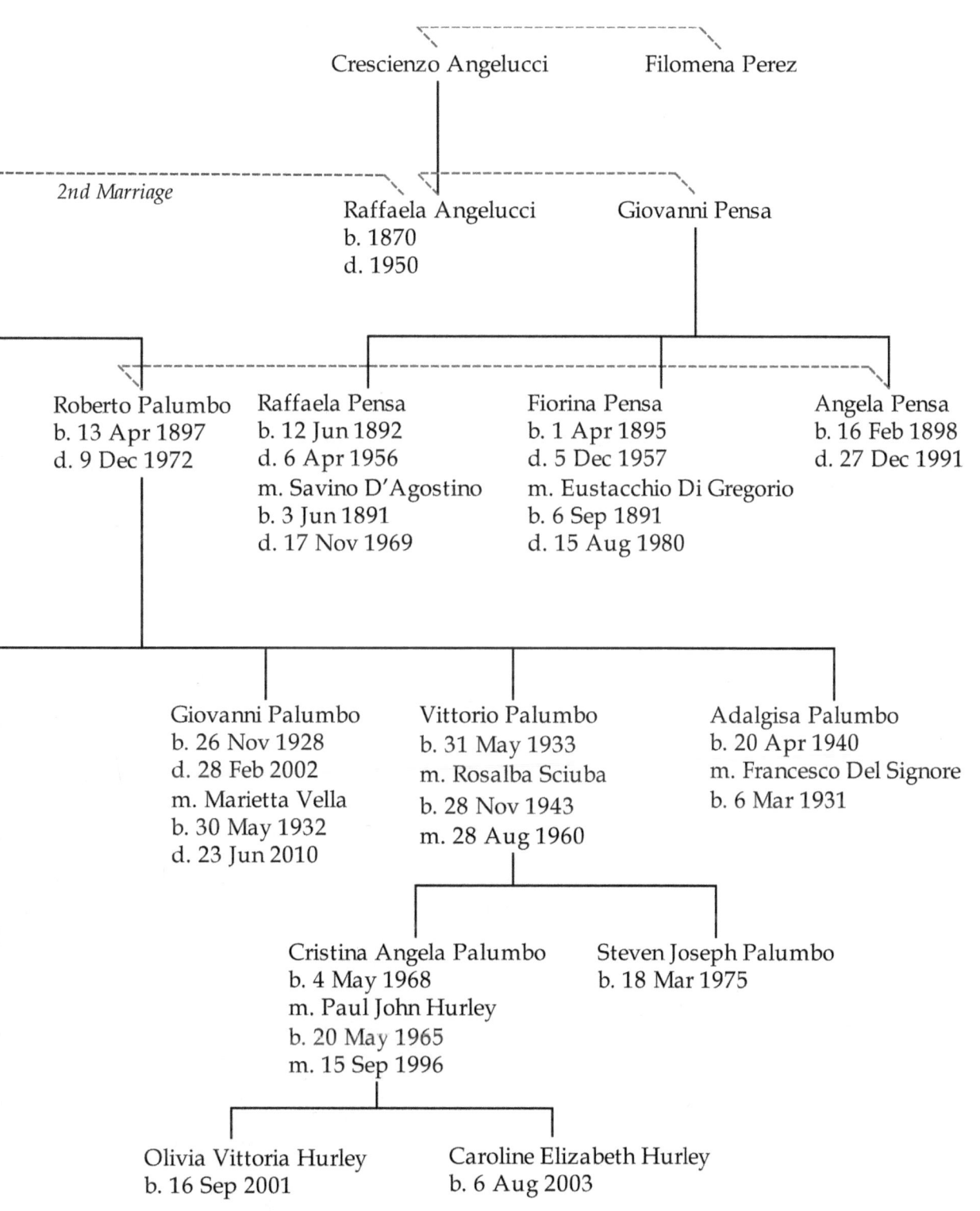

Acknowledgments

This book would not have been possible without the effort and skill of a team of supportive and devoted people.

Over the years, I have told many people parts of my unusual life story, but this is the first time all the stories are collected together in one place. I want to thank Margherita Simion, my godfather's daughter, for inspiring me to write down the memories from my childhood.

Initially, I wrote my stories in Italian and had them translated into English. I felt that something was missing from the translation. That's when in 2008, my dear friend, Donna Zlotnick, offered to help me write my stories in English. Over many, many hours I told Donna about my experiences and she patiently and diligently took notes on her laptop computer. In addition to putting my words to paper, Donna has devoted many hours digitizing and organizing the photos that appear in these pages.

It was then that my son-in-law, Paul Hurley, introduced me to David O'Neil and his company Story Trust. David helps families record and preserve their stories for future generations. David recorded interviews with me that enhanced and expanded upon Donna's notes. David then brought in his colleague, Heather Remoff, an accomplished writer and editor, to bring my stories to life. Heather's skill and devotion to my story have resulted in a memoir that I am very proud to share with my family and friends.

I am grateful to have these friends, both old and new, who have helped me fulfill a lifelong dream—to tell my story so that my grandchildren will know about their forebearers—their hopes and dreams, their struggles and accomplishments, and their devotion and sacrifice—all for the sake of their family. I hope, by knowing my story, that they will gain inspiration and seek to fulfill their dreams.

Contents

1. Down from the Majella Mountain 3
2. Campo di Giove 6
3. Pasta and Politics 14
4. A New Home Far from Home 24
5. "My Italian Vacation" 33
6. Return to Snow-Capped Peaks 42
7. A Song for Fiera di Primiero 49
8. 1942 on the Italian Riviera 55
9. The Fading Italian Summer 63
10. Not in Kansas 67
11. Fire and Steel 77
12. A *Capanna* in Winter 87
13. Polenta and Prayers 94
14. Picking Up the Pieces 100
15. Finding Our Way 108
16. My Life in Pictures 116
17. So, You Want to Be a *Sarto*? 125

18. Of Bread and Cigarettes.. 132
19. Reunion in Libya.. 141
20. Tailoring a New Life 151
21. School Days.. 162
22. Together Again 172
23. A Few Tales Short of a Thousand and One...................... 184
24. Arabian Nights.. 194
25. Farewell... 204

Epilogue

1. America: Land of Opportunity and Ice Cream 219
2. Letters Across an Ocean 230
3. Tears and Laughter... 239
4. Pieces of the Dream.. 244
5. Parents and Children 248
6. Tailor Made 258

Afterword

Return to Libya... 265

Italian Days, Arabian Nights

CHAPTER ONE

Down from the Majella Mountain

My name is Vittorio Palumbo and I am a tailor. Not famous in the way I had once hoped. You won't find my name stitched in silk inside a gentleman's fine jacket, but those dreams all happened so long ago, and Mussolini had other plans for me. Still, I continue, at age seventy-seven, to work at making patterns. Designing the prototype for a military uniform is not so different from telling a story. Whether one is clothing a man or spinning the tale of his years, it all begins with small pieces. Bits of fabric. Scraps of memory. One must know how to stitch them together to make a coherent whole. And just as any garment is dictated by the fashion of its time, so is my narrative set against the larger backdrop of a world heading into war.

The loom on which my story is woven has been shuttling the threads of my ancestral history back and forth for hundreds of years. My family home in Campo di Giove, Italy, was built in the twelfth century. My father and his father before him—back through too many generations to count—guided flocks of sheep down from the high pastures of the Majella Mountain, driven by the first howling snows, all the way across the southern provinces into Roman country until they came to a place where the winter weather was more mild. Urging a couple hundred sheep into a bleating flock that moved as one, they would walk or follow on horseback for maybe a month, stopping only at night to sleep, covering a hundred miles or more, seeking still-green pasture on paths that cut through the *trattoro*, as we called land held by the government. During the day, as long as they kept moving, they could travel across the *trattoro* land with no fear of trespass, all the way to Puglia where there was winter grazing. Their destination was a place my forebears called the *conte*, for the contessa, who had maybe 5,000 sheep. My grandfather and the others would take care of her large flock in exchange for grazing rights for their few hundred until April, when it was time to begin the journey back to our mountain pasture. The sheep all mixed together, but each family's ewes and rams were marked in such a way that there was no question of which ones belonged to which family. Palumbo. D'Agostino. Angelucci. It was never a problem. Each sheep carried on its rump the coded symbol of the family that claimed it.

The brands were iron, shaped into fancy designs with the initials of the owners. My grandfather's animals bore the mark GP, Gennaro Palumbo. When the first warm breezes signaled the return of spring, the men did the shearing before heading back to the Abruzzo region we called home. Holding a big pair of steel clippers in one hand, a man would catch and hold a sheep with his legs while he worked one blade against the other, in close against the skin, and quickly removed the lanolin-rich wool. It stayed together, almost as if it were being rolled off the animal in one piece. Everyone helped each other, not worrying about whose sheep was being clipped, but always keeping track of which fleece belonged to which family. The young animals that had been born since the last branding received the mark of their owners right there in the field before their wool had grown too thick.

As soon as the shearing was finished, agents came by, and, after a respectable amount of dickering, established a price per kilo. Once they shook hands on the agreement, they hauled the wool to the industrial mills spread throughout the region. In Campo di Giove most business was done by barter, no money changed hands. However, money was necessary when our people needed to make transactions with the outside world, so my ancestors came home with their flocks and with some cash that could be used to purchase the items we couldn't grow or build ourselves.

Campo di Giove—perched over a thousand meters above sea level, almost a mile higher than the ocean waters of the Tyrrhenian and sixty or more miles removed from it, even if the path had been direct—adhered to a way of life that for centuries had been dictated by the rhythms of nature and the ties of family. We lived in the midst of architectural records of the region's past, without realizing the part our family would soon play in Italy's turbulent entry into the Second World War. The history books tell of battles and politics, kings and prime ministers, but the actual events are shaped by individuals. Who has not heard of Mussolini? But his grand plans to build an Italy that commanded the respect of the major players on the world stage depended on the movement of people with names that are never mentioned. So many names. Too many to count, but I can tell the story of Roberto, Angela, Gennaro, Guerino, Giovanni, Giovanna, and, yes, Vittorio.

Our lives and the lives of thousands of other Italians were forever changed by events as much beyond our control as those first swirling snowflakes that warned of winter coming on and told my grandfather it was time to move the sheep down into the broad, flat plains of the *conte*. It's not that the families in Campo di Giove had not previously been touched by the wider world. After all, my own maternal great-grandfather was married to a woman whose people came from Puglia. When the flocks returned in April, sometimes more than sheep made the long journey back. Even my name paid tribute to our King, Vittorio Emanuele III, grandson of Vittorio Emanuele II, the Father of the Fatherlands, the man who had forged a united Italy out of all the scattered states and regions that were once fractured by a succession of influences: Greek, Austro-Hungarian, Austro-German, Slavic, and, of course, Italian. Vittorio was a common name in my generation, as was Benito. Italy's wider borders gave us winter grazing and a place to sell our wool. Sometimes it gave a man a wife or small boys the names they would carry all their lives, but I'm not sure anyone from Campo di Giove fully understood the forces already in motion. Did even my parents know that the past was no longer a reliable predictor of the future?

CHAPTER TWO

Campo di Giove

Because Italy was a new nation as judged by the standards of those countries that surrounded us, it remained a geography characterized by regional dialects and a sense of local distinction that was often stronger than any unified identity could be. Wars and military service sometimes pulled the adult males away from their homes (and provided another source of cash), but they returned ever more sure of who they were and where they belonged. My own father, Roberto Palumbo, had served in the Bersaglieri, the elite mountain corps of the Italian Army. Famous for their marksmanship and physical stamina, the Bersaglieri were troops whose high morale and aggressive spirits were instrumental in challenging traditional methods of warfare. In parades they were known for their stylized fashion of jogging, so different from the more usual soldier's march. Since my father's service ended when he was forty and I was only three or four, I don't remember his absence; but the *vaira*, broad-brimmed black hats with a cascade of capercaillie feathers, and the tasseled purple-red fezzes that were a trademark of these celebrated fighters, made a big impression on me as a little boy.

My affection for those hats caused me some momentary trouble when I was small, but others must have found the story amusing because it became one of those oft-repeated tales that bind a family together in shared laughter. In addition to working with the sheep, the people of Campo di Giove cultivated small holdings of land. These plots were scattered, some close to town, some a mile, some three miles, a few as far as five miles away. My family owned such a piece of land and had a plow and a horse and a mule with which to cultivate it. The soil is thin and rocky halfway up the Majella Mountain, not fertile like in the valleys below. The crops we raised—potatoes, corn, wheat, beans—stored well and could be dried to feed us in the winter. Our harvests were strictly for family use and trade; we couldn't grow enough to sell. We had no lemon trees. No olives. All those things came from Sulmona. Oh, and in Pescara, the figs. Unbelievable! But we were too high up the mountain. No figs. No tomatoes. No grapes. Maybe here and there a pear tree would find a way to flourish. Our summers were too short. The sun too fickle.

How did my father come to own a plow? I think, perhaps, with the money from his service with the Bersaglieri. At any rate, he had a small stable in town where he kept the horse and mule and some other animals, a few goats, maybe a dozen chickens. When he had finished plowing his own field, he would lash the plow to one side of the mule and, on the other side, balance the load with the picks and shovels needed to work mountain fields. Then he would either walk or ride the horse until he came to the fields of those who wanted him to turn the earth for them. There was no pay. No money for the work he did. Instead, someone would divvy up the yield. Potatoes, maybe, or some corn. It was an exchange—my father owned the plow—the others shared what they grew when he helped them out.

I loved to go with him. Over the years, the rocks pulled from the alpine tracts and tossed to the edge of the land had formed stone walls that surrounded each small holding. Boys like to hide behind such barriers. Filled with visions of imaginary battles, I frisked about like a little goat as my father tended to the field work. Perhaps it was the heat of the midday sun that caused him to remove the red fez he still wore, a remnant from his days in the corps, and plop it down on top of my own head. Or perhaps his action was prompted by some unexpected burst of affection. Whatever the reason, I immediately felt the glory his gesture conveyed. Crowned with the sign of the Bersaglieri, I became as brave as my father. I was a fabled marksman, peeking just high enough above the wall to target the enemy below. Here and there I dashed, tossing my head in such a way as to send the long blue tassel that hung down the back whipping about. What does it take to startle a horse? A red hat popping up from behind a wall? The sudden snap of a tassel? Whatever it takes, I did it that day. The horse, already hitched to the plow and hard at work, went berserk, rearing, bucking and neighing while my father struggled mightily to bring it under control. "Whoa! Hey! Whoa." The plow, the horse, my father were all a blur of potential disaster. "Vittorio!," he cried. "Whoa, stop, hey, Vittorio! Stop. Whoa! Stop." And then it was over. All the commotion ceased as suddenly as it had begun. I stood frozen in my spot behind the wall. The horse's sides were heaving. My father was also breathing hard and not just from the exertion.

Roberto Palumbo was known for being quick to anger. Quickly come and just as quickly gone. Crushed to have let him down, shame tied my tongue. The hurt was doubled by what I couldn't express: I was only trying to *be* him. I never meant to cause such harm and disappointment. He angrily snatched the offending hat from my head. However, not more than an hour later, he silently placed it back on again. He didn't have to say anything. I knew all was forgiven. I found my father's meteoric explosions easier to endure than my mother's response to any sort of disagreement. She would silently let something fester for days, filling the home with tension until the burden of that quiet fury finally became too much for even her to bear and life returned to normal.

Campo di Giove's town center boasts medieval architecture and a beautiful cast-iron fountain, but when you are a child you live with those things without really seeing them or understanding all they tell you of what has gone before. The women came to the fountain every day with large copper urns, which they used to haul water up into their kitchens. Metalsmiths pounded sheets of copper over a mold until they achieved the desired shape, large at the bottom, tapered in at the top, and then flaring just slightly into two handles. The construction guaranteed that nothing would splash out as our mothers and grandmothers transported seventy-five pounds of water on their heads up many flights of worn stone steps. Since the base of the container was cushioned with a border of sheep's wool and designed to fit snugly, they didn't even need to use their hands to balance the vessel. Mountain water was sweet and pure. We used it for everything: drinking, cooking, washing. Precious. How did the women have the strength to carry such a load? As a boy, I gave it no thought. It was just something the women did.

Huge stone walls formed a fortress around our town, enclosing it almost as if the whole town were a castle. Four heavy doors of planked wood once held Campo di Giove safe from the *briganti*, bandits who, in my grandfather's time, lived in the wildest reaches of the mountain range. I was born in 1933 and, although the wooden doors were no longer latched at night, my world was contained within the shelter of these walls. The days of robbers were behind us. I knew only the tumble of a sister and brothers, parents and grandparents, all living on the single floor of a tall row house that had four or five floors, each one holding a different family.

Built in the 1100s, our home, my grandparents' home, consisted of two large rooms halfway up a much taller building. The kitchen wasn't like the kitchens we know now. It was three, four times as big. An enormous fireplace covered one entire wall, and it was there that the women did all the cooking. To the right of this fireplace was the brick oven where every other week my grandmother baked bread. In front of the fireplace, reaching the full length of the room, was a bench large enough to hold everybody, not just the immediate family members but neighbors as well. I remember the women, and the men too, all gathering there to say the rosary. Those times were more religious. The women went to church maybe a couple times a day. The fireplace heated the entire room and served as a gathering place whenever friends and relatives paid a visit.

In one corner of the kitchen, my grandparents' big, very high bed was surrounded by *Nonna's* trinkets and treasures, all the fancy things we children weren't supposed to touch. Set in the heart of our home, it was their special place. The rest of the room was for everyone. The women cooked there. We ate there. Prayed there. Chatted with neighbors there. The other room, which was divided into partitions by heavy sheets of canvas, was where everyone else in the family slept. My parents and my brothers Gennaro, Guerino, Giovanni, my sister Giovanna, and I all shared the second room.

When I was a young boy, I was intrigued by the stories of the old days, days when each floor of that dark stone building was defended by windows with a succession of shutters that could be snapped closed, one after the other, until the only opening left was just large enough to enable the barrel of a gun to poke through and drive off any marauders. It didn't matter that the barricade against *briganti* was no longer necessary, the telescoping shutters of the kitchen window held even imaginary dangers at bay and secured my world.

After a quick breakfast of hard bread soaked in either warm sheep or goat's milk and eaten with a spoon, I filled the hours playing with my friends. We scampered up and down the stone steps that linked one family's dwelling with another. We spilled into the narrow cobblestone streets. My cousins lived just across the way in that same square. Our grandmothers were busy doing the things that grandmothers do—mending, cooking, baking bread, going to church—and we found ways to get into minor mischief, unhampered by too much supervision. Our fathers' and grandfathers' capes were trimmed with brass buttons that we boys coveted for use in one of our favorite games. Whenever we found a moment when no one was looking, we would pull these buttons off the cape and dash outside, enriched by a secret fistful. Our mothers and fathers could never find where their buttons went. I don't think we fully understood the monetary worth of our theft, but we did understand that our status was immeasurably enhanced by the treasure we now commanded. One of our favorite games employed rules similar to bocce. We had two bricks, one whole, one broken in half. We would set the first brick upright with the brass buttons arranged on top. The half-brick was our throwing stone. We took turns aiming at the standing brick from maybe twenty feet away. When we hit it, the buttons would go flying in all directions, and the ones that landed closer to you were yours.

Another favorite game was soccer. The empty, many-layered paper bags that had once held dry cement were a highly valued resource. We'd form those empty bags into a round ball, over which we tightly wound a very strong twine made from goat hair. There was a skill to wrapping the string around the ball, many overlapping layers guided the shape into a fairly symmetrical orb. Done right, the strength of the ball was such that it withstood many spirited games between boys who prided themselves on the power and accuracy of their kicks.

Sometimes the older boys got to go with the sheep, but the boys I played with and I were still too young. Not just the men traveled out; the women did as well. Wives often accompanied their husbands in the movement of the sheep. Sometimes they went all the way to Puglia, but it was more usual for the women to go to the summer pasture, the one closer to home, where they would work beside the men—being gone for maybe a week or two—sometimes more. Our parents periodically came home for supplies or clean clothing. We children were raised by grandmothers, by aunts, by the town. All the families lived so close. Complicated ties of relationship bound most of the people of Campo di Giove one to the other. Not much was made of the difference between friend and relative, as the two were often the same. The whole town could be viewed as a complicated network of family connections. Bewildering to the outsider, but easily understood by those who lived there.

My grandfather, Gennaro Palumbo, was a handsome man. Even when he was in his eighties, he was trim and stately, no belly on him. He told me, "You have to live healthy if you want to live to be eighty-nine." That's how old he was when he died. He always looked good in his clothes. Working with the animals, working with the sheep—it never mattered. It's like no dirt got on him. He dressed in a coat and pants and the pants were always sharp, not with the crease like they do now, but always elegant. He and my father were the same in that way. Men with a dashing air about them. My father wore his hat at an angle, much like that favored by the Bersaglieri. He had a look of pride. People noticed him. My father and his father had the same slim build. The same straight posture. They worked with the plowing and the farming, moving the animals about, up in the mountains with the sheep but, even so, they always had a natural kind of style. Sharp. Dignified. My grandfather was always with the coat and pants. It mattered how he looked.

My grandmother, Raffaela, the one I remember, was my grandfather Gennaro Palumbo's second wife and was sixteen years younger. His first wife, Gemma Del Mastro, my father's mother, died when he was only seven. My father never told me how she died, what illness took her. Being so young perhaps he never knew. Gemma left five children behind. My father, Roberto, was the youngest. His sister, Angela, was twenty-two when her mother died; fifteen years older than my father and, even many years later, she looked out for him, much as a mother might do. There was an older brother as well, Domenico; and, in between, Cristina and Antonio. In those days, not everyone lived to a healthy old age like my grandfather. Those five children lost their mother. Their father lost his wife.

Because my father's mother had died so young, Raffaela is the only grandmother I ever knew. It becomes a complicated story. Her husband had died in the prime of his life, leaving her with three daughters: Raffaela, named for her mother, was born in 1892; Fiorina, the middle one, was born in 1895; and Angela, who would one day become my mother, was born in 1898. Giovanni Pensa, my grandmother Raffaela's first husband, fell from a horse and broke his leg. He'd been out working in the fields and was riding the horse back into town when something spooked it. It reared

11

up and he crashed to the ground. Today a broken leg is not such a big deal, but then it was. There were no doctors. No penicillin. So, they did the best they could with that leg, but the gangrene set in, and he fell ill and died from the fevers and infection. He was only thirty-three when he passed away. Such a loss. That history makes my father's anger over my spooking the horse more understandable.

Can you guess where this story is headed? The widower, Gennaro Palumbo, married the widow, Raffaela Angelucci Pensa, and their two families with children of assorted ages became one. A big family of eight children, not all of them living together, and not all of them related by any scrap of blood. The union between my grandfather, Gennaro Palumbo, and my grandmother, Raffaela Pensa, produced no children in common. Their hands were full enough with the ones they already had. Remember, times were hard. The newly formed couple lived together with the children each had brought to the marriage in those two rooms where I was later born.

Grandmother Raffaela's youngest daughter, Angela, the one who would become my mother, was, as I have said, born in 1898. Grandfather Gennaro Palumbo's youngest child Roberto, the one who would become my father, was born in 1897. The result of earlier unions, each with a parent now deceased, those two had not spent their tender years being raised together. However, born just a year apart, they suddenly found themselves cast in the role of stepbrother and stepsister. My father was nine. My mother was eight. You know how it is with boys and girls that age. They don't play the same games and don't want much to do with each other. Kids that age, boys and girls, they're like magnets forced against the opposite pole. That natural resistance was probably even stronger between young Roberto and Angela. After all, they were still sad about the parents they had so recently lost and may not have been too keen about having substitute families thrust on them. So that's how it was until they grew to marrying age.

In 1915, my father, Roberto Palumbo, had to go to war; and after being gone for three years, came back a little bit of a different man. He had developed a more independent streak. When he returned, he was twenty-one and had a girlfriend, Anna-Rosa. I've heard that story many times. He had Anna-Rosa, and my mother had a boyfriend by the name of Eustacchio, a very popular name at that time. So these little romances are happening and their parents, my grandparents, aren't too happy about the whole thing. Because at that time, when you go to marry somebody out of the house, you have to give a dowry. A sheep. Other stuff. You have to give all the things the bride needs. So, my grandfather, he just kept saying over and over, "Why bring somebody from outside when you have somebody inside here, she is so nice, we get along so fine." He kept saying it. "She's no sister, nothing to you, and we get along so fine. Why bring somebody from outside?"

That's how it went. Times were hard. It wasn't easy to put a proper dowry together. My grandparents, their parents, put a lot of pressure on them. So, one day my mother and father were away from the house, out working in the fields together. I don't know what happened, not really. Perhaps they just looked and saw each other in a different way, maybe like seeing someone for the first time. I can't tell why, but my father suddenly said to her, "Let's just do it. Let's go and get married. That's all. Let's just get married." And so they did.

The dowry sheep remained in the family, and my parents continued to live in the same house they had shared ever since the two families came together. They ended up being very happy together. They stayed married and had six kids; all but one of them, little Ada, born in that house. From 1906, until my father died in 1972, they were together. All those years they knew each other. Married for over fifty of them. A strong bond. They went through a lot, helping each other, working side by side. The glue that held them held them firmly.

Years later, when I was fully grown, women would come up to me and say, "Your father was such a good-looking guy. He could have had any girlfriend he wanted, so why?" Even after I came to America, I met a woman from our town. Same story. "Your father was the best looking man in town," she told me. "He could have married any of the girls from Campo di Giove, but, instead, he picked someone very close to home." The truth is, at that time, the parents used to rule the situation. But they got it right, didn't they? My parents were very happy together for all those years.

CHAPTER THREE

Pasta and Politics

Our days had a pattern, a rhythm. When the talk in the kitchen grew too loud, I ran outside and found my cousin Pasquale Palumbo, and all the boys my age—Rinaldo, Domenico, and the others. Sometimes we ran to the fields closest to the square and played wild games of hide-and-seek. But no amount of hiding stopped the talk.

Giacomo Matteotti. My grandparents had favored this popular Socialist member of Parliament. When he was kidnapped and murdered in 1924, they felt certain Benito Mussolini's secret police were responsible. Socialists. Anarchists. Fascists. Divisions within our household reflected debates playing out across Italy. A combination of chaos and poverty paved the way for the support my father gave to *Il Duce*, but my grandparents remembered their former loyalty to Matteotti and could not commit to the level of allegiance Mussolini required. It's hard to change old ways.

My grandmother Raffaela's style of dress did not reflect her Puglia country roots, but her style of cooking was pure Puglia. Grandmother Raffaela's father, Crescienzo Angelucci, had married my great-grandmother, Filomena Perez, there on one of the trips taking the sheep to winter pasture. How many years had my great-grandmother lived in Campo di Giove? Long enough to see children, grandchildren, and great-grandchildren born. Even after all that time, the local women remembered her origins elsewhere and would ask what the women in the Puglia were like. "*Carne osse*," she would tell them. That meant skin and bones, like you. But despite her insistence that they were the same, my great-grandmother held to some differences that set the women of the two regions apart. She wore the long skirts and sleeves of the Puglia region. Her blouse was white, until later circumstances forced the change to black, but, before then, always white, very blousy, coming all the way down to the hands. And on top, the outside corset, velveteen, tied right up to the bust with decorated string to make the corset nice. The inside corset was the tight one, laced up the back. "Tighter, tighter," my Aunt Cristina, used to say. Sometimes she got a kid to pull on those strings, but I was little and not so strong. The outside corset was the fancy one, more loose. On her head she wore a white kerchief, all embroidered in lace scallops around the edge. The hair was pulled up, very neat, with a pin in the middle.

Having learned from her mother, Filomena Perez, my grandmother Raffaela still cooked in the Puglia way, even making a different kind of pasta, *fusilli*. She'd put a piece of iron on the pasta mill to make a small hole through the middle of the dough. And *orecchiette*, little ears. The Campo di Giove women didn't make those kind of noodles. Ravioli stuffed with fresh cheese and eggs was what Campo di Giove women served for special Sunday dinners. Not much meat. We didn't kill the sheep and goats to eat. Not so much. They were for the milk. Goats gave us the soft cheese. Sheep, the hard kind to grate. All those years, my grandmother kept the influences of her region. Pasta and politics. Two hard things to change.

Talk. Talk. Talk. What did any of it have to do with us? What did any of it have to do with Campo di Giove? "Pasquale, Pasquale," I called. "Come play leapfrog with Rinaldo, Domenico, and me." More boys fell into our game and we formed a curving line around the fountain. Back to front we flew, propelled by the thrust of our feet and the push of our arms. If we weren't careful a wayward foot might catch the head of the boy who stooped beneath us. As the fury of the talk around us grew, so did the intensity of our games.

And while I called to Pasquale, my father called to Uncle Savino. He was married to my mother's sister, Raffaela. The two sisters were six years apart in age, but never apart in their affection for each other. Where one went, the other liked to go. It was almost the same between Uncle Savino and my father. Whatever my father said to Uncle Savino, Uncle Savino would agree to do. Nodding their heads in shared thought, Roberto Palumbo and Savino D'Agostino talked about the progress Mussolini was finally bringing to our country. They sat on the stone steps not far from where we children laughed and called to each other. Too much of such talk inside the house could make my grandmother fold her arms and stare silently at them. But in the square, conversation was freely shared between the men. Further south, in and around Rome, the swamps had been drained, the strikes that had crippled everything were under control. The economy was growing faster than the economies of the countries that bordered us. It wasn't just the industries that benefitted. There was to be a place for those who worked with sheep as well. What did we children hear? Did we comprehend the ideas that mingled with the splashing of the fountain and formed a kind of background music to our games? We absorbed the admiration, I think. My grandparents had memories of another time, but for the younger generations this new pride held a kind of promise. I don't remember talk of war.

Besides, what did a six-year-old child know of war? All that talk of politics was a mere buzz droning above the always chattering, sometimes laughing, warmth of family. Fascism was just a word to a boy from Campo di Giove, this small town in Abruzzo in the Province of L'Aquila. But it *was* 1939, and even I could detect a new sense of urgency and excitement in the adult voices that drifted in and out of my awareness as I played with the other children of our village. Something was about to happen. I sensed possibility and swelling hope in the adult discussions and debate. But, I was still a boy, one who was mostly concerned with finding time to simply romp across the cobblestones with his friends. Did we seize sticks and engage in imaginary battle as we darted between the stone walls that separated one field from the next? Of course. We were boys. The burden of worrying about survival fell to our parents, to our mothers and grandmothers struggling to find ways to feed their families and to the men caught up in mapping a brave way forward.

Was it war my father and a small cluster of other men from our village planned? No. It was dreams of a peaceful harvest. They were being given a chance to serve in a way that would employ their skills as farmers, tillers of the soil, herders of sheep. They would bring a desert to life and in the process rescue us from the economic hardship which gripped so much of southern Italy in those years. We were desperately poor. Everyone was. Jobs were scarce. Food was scarce. Only the large landowners and those with specialized skills seemed able to survive. "Hey, Savino," my father called across the square. "Want to go to Libya?"

"Sure, Roberto, sure," Uncle Savino agreed. "We'll go to Libya." He was all the time agreeing with my father.

When they applied to be a part of the wave of Italians sent to settle Italy's *la Quarta Sponda,* the Fourth Shore of Mussolini's Greater *Italia,* did they question their chances of being selected, or were they both infected by my father's Bersaglieri-like confidence? So many wanted this opportunity. Out of all the hundreds of thousands who applied, only a few families would be selected from each town. It was understood that a Fascist loyalty was required. If chosen, we would have to leave my grandparents behind. They were perhaps too old to be able to bend to the hard work necessary to build an Italian Libya, but it was also understood that their political reluctance ruled them out.

I remember the heightened tension of the times, but the wait between application and notification was probably more difficult for the men who had seized on this path to building better lives for their families than it was for us children who waited for nothing more than the start of another game. However, once we learned that three families from Campo di Giove were suddenly being offered new homes and an opportunity to enjoy the benefits that come with claim to a piece of land, my joy erupted. Both our family and Uncle Savino's and Aunt Raffaela's would be going. So would the Del Mastros. We had all been selected to be part of Prime Minister Benito Mussolini's planned return to the splendors of our Roman past. Italy has a proud history. Had I not been born filled with a love of my land, I would have quickly learned it in a country overflowing with the dazzling array of arts associated with the Renaissance, with the architectural traces of the Roman Empire. Of course, much of what I now know, I know as a man looking back. What I knew as a boy was that I was cocooned in a reliable cushion of family and friends, some of whom would join my parents in this adventure. We would not be entirely alone. The applications to participate in the colonization of Libya had been approved for three families—a total of twenty-one people—from Campo di Giove! The excitement on learning of our acceptance allowed no room for regret. True, I would be leaving my grandparents, aunts, uncles, cousins, and friends behind, but surely with fewer mouths to feed, they would be safe in the shelter of the Apennine Mountain range that watches over Campo di Giove.

It was October 28, 1939. We were going to Libya. Once a part of the Roman Empire, the Libyan economy had recently flourished as a result of Italian investment in roads, ports, hospitals, schools and other public works. By January of 1939, the colony of Libya had been officially incorporated into Italy and was considered an integral part of the Italian state. Old Arab villages had been razed and bulldozed away. In their place, Mussolini had built compounds of new homes in preparation for the Italian settlements deemed necessary to address the burden of overpopulation blamed for much of the economic crisis in Italy.

Africa. Libya. Those words had a foreign ring. However, the Fourth Shore of Italy was a phrase that promised the comfort of a known world. We would be going by ship through the Tyrrhenian Sea and across the Mediterranean, our sea, to build a new life in the village of Garibaldi. Those were not unfamiliar words. Garibaldi rolled off the tongue with a comforting cadence and offered the promise of home. We would be settlers, cultivating an arid land and raising the standard of living, not just for us, but for the people of Libya as well. Our dreams were splendid. Hope, held so long in check, was allowed to flourish under the sudden shower of our good fortune.

We were all going—my father Roberto, my mother Angela, my sixteen-year-old sister Giovanna, and my brothers: Gennaro, at eighteen almost a man; Guerino, then fourteen; Giovanni, eleven; and me. At age six, I was the youngest in my family. We would travel with the D'Agostinos and the Del Mastros to L'Aquila, a city just north of us. Once there, we would connect up with hundreds of others who were part of this mass emigration to Libya. Italian development policy was focused on capital-intensive economic colonization. Libya's governor, Italo Balbo, brought the first settlers to Libya's shores in 1938. These 20,000 Italians, the *ventimila*, arrived in a single convoy. We would be part of the second wave. By 1940, 110,000 Italians would constitute twelve percent of the Libyan population. We weren't leaving Italy behind. We were taking her with us.

But we were leaving Campo di Giove. The sun burned through the copper-colored beech leaves on the day of our departure. Our goodbye waves felt no more final than their quivering flutter. It was as if we were simply off on an adventure, a picnic perhaps, or an extended camping trip. We took very little with us. We had very little to take. A trunk or two. That was all. My grandmother hugged me tightly and then turned quickly away. "I'll see you soon," I cried after her. And that part was true. I would see her again later in the day. L'Aquila was only two hours by train from our village. I had never been on a train! Once we got to L'Aquila, there would be a big celebration as we joined with the many hundreds of others from our region who were privileged to participate in Mussolini's Libyan Relocation Program. A larger, fancier train carrying all the excited patriots headed for the Port of Naples would travel back down through Campo di Giove on its way south. The entire town planned to gather on the platform of the railroad station to cheer us on our journey. How could a boy's imagination not be fired by the mental picture of our extended families celebrating us almost as heroes carrying all the pride of Italy on our shoulders?

When we joined the milling crowds of others gathered at the train in L'Aquila, the festival-like excitement mounted. The cars of the trains were draped in three-colored Italian flags bearing the emblems of both King Vittorio Emanuele II, the first king of a united Italy and proudly called Father of the Fatherlands, and of our current King, his grandson, Vittorio Emanuele III. In the economic depression and instability that had followed the First World War, the very unity Vittorio Emanuele II had overseen during his reign (1820–1878) was threatened. When anarchists assassinated Vittorio Emanuele II's son, Umberto I, Vittorio Emanuele III assumed the monarch's role. In the midst of the ensuing political turmoil, the new king had turned to Benito Mussolini for help in rescuing the young nation from chaos. I know how the post–World War II history books portray these events: Prime Minister Mussolini pursued his dream of a united and expanded Italy with a ruthlessness not always apparent to a population who saw only the results, not the process. It is said of *Il Duce* that he made the trains run on time. Such a simple thing, but the predictability of ordered lives was a relief after decades of upheaval. Credited with having saved Italy from Bolshevism, support for him approached a level almost of worship. People cut his photographs from the newspapers and pasted them on their walls. Granting him almost mystical powers, some claimed those who kissed his hands would die in peace; others said his embrace could cure the blind.

He gave the women of Campo di Giove kerchiefs to wear over their shoulders. All the matrons setting forth to colonize the new land were so honored. My mother touched hers shyly. Any former concern about the shabbiness of her garb vanished and she stood just a bit taller, clothed in pride. "Silk," I heard the women say. "Fine cotton, woven through with silk." They ran their fingers around the deep bronze braid that bordered each scarf. Mother bent over to show me the pattern. "See, Vittorio," she said. "This brown braid is for the richness of the soil that awaits us." She touched the golden symbol of wheat in the center of the scarf. "And this is the harvest. This is the wheat whose grains will fall through our fingers once we bring the desert to life." So many dreams. We were all filled with so many dreams.

The excited crowd waited anxiously for the signal to board the trains. Our family stayed close to the D'Agostinos. My mother and Aunt Raffaela moved almost as a single person. Savino and my father laughed with pride. So much had happened since the day my father called across the town square, "Hey, Savino, want to go to Libya?" The D'Agostinos had a daughter and three sons, my cousins. My brothers, being close in age, laughed and joked with nineteen-year-old Filippo, fourteen-year-old Umberto, and eleven-year-old Antonio. Caterina, a young woman of twenty-four, stood just slightly apart from the good-natured jostling of the boys.

I looked around the square. Where were the Del Mastros? And then I saw them moving toward us. They had eight children, but only six were making the journey with them. Daughter Rosina was the twenty-four-year-old wife of Umberto Di Capito. Rosina and her husband had established a home in Campo di Giove and would remain there. Olindo Del Mastro, at seventeen, was of an age to accompany his family to Libya, but was forced by frail health to stay behind in Campo di Giove with his Aunt Eugenia.

Valerino Del Mastro, the father of the family, cut through the crowd with his wife Antonia close behind him. She and her twenty-year-old daughter, Elisena, were clearly in charge of the little ones. Five-year-old Carmela rode on her mother's hip. Elisena held her ten-year-old sister Aquilina's hand. Salvatore was, to my young eyes, fully grown at nineteen. He spotted my brothers and cousins and, followed closely by *his* brothers—fourteen-year-old Enrico and Vittorio who shared my name but, being five years older, had not many interests in common with me—moved toward our little group.

The three families gathered together in anticipation of the moment of departure. Why among all these children was there no boy my age? Only Carmela was close and she was a girl. Besides, there was something too babyish about the way she clung to her mother. I edged nearer to my brother Giovanni, but he, engaged in some story he shared with our cousin Antonio, acted as if I wasn't even there.

I leaned my head back and studied the snow-capped peaks of the mountains overlooking L'Aquila. Would there be such vistas in Libya?

L'Aquila was not my home, but it shared a mountain range with the place of my birth. Would I miss the alpine meadows that pressed against the granite base? Lacking a map, I had no sense of how long a journey the trip to Naples would be. Could I expect to see exotic terrain as we approached the ocean? Abruzzo is in the geographical center of Italy, but its landscape, cut through by tall mountains, has more in common with parts of northern Italy. My town, Campo di Giove, is considered part of southern Italy, not so much for its location but for the reputed Sicilian nature of its origins. I did not know all these things as a boy, but perhaps, in some way, the geography and history of the place can explain how easily I embraced the pride of a larger Italy.

At last everyone was accounted for, and we pressed toward the train. Our three families were eager to position themselves on the side that would offer the clearest view of Campo di Giove. Suddenly it dawned on me that the flags, the fanfare, the cheers were for us. I wasn't sure what it all meant, but my heart beat with pride. I looked at my father, the man who had guided us to this point, and wanted everyone to know I was his son. Being one of the youngest in our group, I was granted a place near a window, the grownups making sure that no one blocked my view of the countryside. The train traveled along the base of the Apennine mountains. The jutting peaks, snow-covered all year, stood starkly white against a blue Italian sky; the woodlands were caught in a mix of fir, bare branches, and the colors of late October. The high plains. The valleys. The dry beds of small streams. This was the landscape of home.

I don't remember if I asked that question so common to childhood, *Are we there yet?*, but as the train made its approach to Campo di Giove, even my parents and older siblings leaned forward to wave and call out to dear ones. Watching my friends race beside the tracks, I read both pride and longing in their farewell cries. I knew they would have loved to have been on our magnificent train, all draped in the royal flags. We had the blessing of kings. I saw my grandparents only too briefly, and then the town and its people faded from view. And, as they did, I felt my first pang of yearning for the friendship of all those I was leaving behind. Glancing at my brothers, I envied them the intimate bond they shared with the cousins and other boys their ages, a bond that would be forged into even stronger metal by this shared experience.

A trio of huge ships—the *Piemonte*, the *Lombardia*, and the *Toscana*—was waiting for us in Naples. Even as an air of festive confusion carried us through the process of registering for our further travel information, I could not take my eyes from the boats. Rising so high above us, they challenged every image my young mind held of boats. How excited we were to realize that the three families from Campo di Giove were all assigned to the *Piemonte*. We were traveling in a style unheard of in the small town we had left behind. No ordinary transport ships for us. We were being carried to our new home aboard former luxury liners. When the depression that gripped Italy impacted even the privileged classes, the state took over these ships, and now we would head out to sea surrounded by reminders of our special status.

It was a carnival of happy faces, announcements, lines, and holding areas. Every mother anxiously counted heads. The fathers gathered the badges that identified the towns where we would begin building our new lives. As they pinned them on we said the names aloud over and over, "Garibaldi. Garibaldi." Our family, the Palumbo family, was assigned to Garibaldi. My mother and her sister, Raffaela D'Agostino, happily hugged one another. The Palumbos and D'Agostinos would remain together to establish roots in this newly constructed compound located somewhere between Tripolitania and Cyrenaica. The Del Mastros were bound for Giordani. But, for now, the three groups from Campo di Giove moved together toward the dock where the *Piemonte* waited to carry us to Libya.

As we made our way up the gangplank, my father's hand pushed against my shoulder and guided me into the care of my mother. Vast blue seas stretched between us and the coast of Africa. The adventure already was more than living up to its promise. I hesitated briefly, then stepped on board and immediately could feel the ship's engines rumbling beneath me like a living thing. After exchanging a few words with my father, my mother took my hand, and I was passed from the world of men into the world of women. All the men and older boys were assigned to one side of the vessel, all the women and young children to the other. Staring after the retreating backs of my father, Uncle Savino, Mr. Del Mastro, and their cluster of young men and growing boys, I felt myself branded even by the passenger list as somehow apart from the responsibilities the others were about to assume. When I pulled my hand away from my mother's, she rested hers on my shoulder. "You'll see," she murmured. "You'll see." I wasn't quite sure what she meant, but on a sudden impulse, I reached up and touched the bronze trim that bordered the scarf she still wore around her shoulders. Feeding it between my thumb and forefinger, I felt the promise braided into those silken cables. Italy was bound together in that promise. Our families were bound together in that promise. The threads of each cord were as separate as one person from another, but we would work together to bring *Il Duce*'s vision into being. In the meantime, on this leg of our journey, I would enjoy my elevated status as one of the oldest of the boys on our side of the boat. Taking my father's place, I would watch out for my mother and sister.

CHAPTER FOUR

A New Home Far from Home

Despite my plan to stand in for my father, the excitement of our journey finally caught up with me. I collapsed into the luxury of the *Piemonte* and slept my way through a couple of days and across the better part of two oceans. As I drifted in and out of sleep, my mind replayed snatches of conversation between my father and Uncle Savino on the train to Naples. "Everything first-rate. Mussolini has that pride." My father had run his hand along the upholstered seats of the train. "He wants nothing but the best for his people." The grandeur of the train had inspired that observation; the accommodations on the former cruise ship reinforced it.

When the ship docked in Tripoli, the magnitude of Mussolini's undertaking became clear. Hundreds of trucks snaked in long convoys around the unloading area and pointed in the direction of the recently paved road leading from the port city. Everything was new construction. A world had been created, waiting only for the people to fill it. Not that Libya was without a population of its own. In fact, hoping to assimilate the Arab people, Mussolini called them "Muslim Italians"; and prior to our arrival there had built ten villages, complete with mosques, schools, social centers, and hospitals. It is only much later that I learned that the new communities waiting for *us*, the Italian settlers, had been constructed on land from which the indigenous Arabs had been forcibly evicted during the colonial war in 1920, *their* homes razed in the process of preparing for *ours*. But now it was 1939, and we were thinking only of how we would grow crops where none had grown before—for them, for us, for everyone. Two years before our arrival, Mussolini himself had visited Libya to celebrate

24

the opening of the *Via Balbo*, the military highway that ran the entire length of the colony and would provide the route by which we'd be transported to our assigned farms. In encouraging the Arab nationalist movement, Mussolini may have been looking ahead and hoping for Muslim support should he one day end up confronting Britain and France over control of the African territories. During his 1937 visit, he declared himself "Protector of Islam" and local dignitaries presented him with a ceremonial sword symbolizing the gratitude of those he vowed to safeguard.

Two hundred and twelve houses had been constructed in the new community of Garibaldi. Since the settlers came with many children, only two families could fit in the back of each of the trucks scheduled to carry us there. A hundred and six trucks just for those of us who would be going to Garibaldi. Of course, there were also convoys waiting to take other settlers to Giordani, a town much closer to Tripoli and where the Del Mastro family would be living. Here I was, a little boy who had considered it an adventure to make the five-mile trip with my father to plow a neighbor's field, and now I had spent a day on a train and several more crossing waters so wide that no land was visible. Even so, we still had not arrived at our destination. I suddenly understood that I was headed off to help my family turn fields that were too far away for even a mule to walk. Not worrying about whether or not I appeared to be a baby, I turned and clung to my mother's hand.

The two or three soldiers assigned to each truck helped us up into the back where we arranged ourselves on benches in anticipation of a long trip. Headed to farm #32, my family shared the truck with the seven members of the Garavello family who hailed from the Friuli region. Since we spoke different dialects, conversation was difficult, but we soon learned enough to figure out that they would be our neighbors at farm #31. The D'Agostinos got into a different vehicle because, although they were going to the same village, their farm, #125, was not in the same estate as ours. As we said our good-byes, I felt a small tremor of anxiety at yet another separation from my known world. I wasn't frightened by the black-shirted soldiers. After all, we too were Fascists or we wouldn't be here. These were our soldiers. There was even some comfort in the uniform. What was frightening was the vastness of the landscape. There were no trees. No mountains. Nothing. Just that long stretch of road that seemed to lead to nowhere.

We were no sooner headed out on the road when a strong wind of the kind we Italians call the *ghibli* seemed to seize the very desert and hurl it at us. It was as if the Sahara itself pounded across the highway in blinding waves. Not only had my old world vanished, but the new one was also suddenly gone. It was impossible to see anything but the flying granules of sand that lashed against the truck. Much as I had been frightened by my first sight of our new land, I was even more terrified by its abrupt disappearance. The road ahead of us was quickly buried.

I had experienced snowstorms back home in the Abruzzo region. They blew down from the mountain passes of the Majella in drifts so deep that we sometimes could get into the house only by marching across five feet of snow to enter through the second floor. In Campo di Giove, as soon as the blizzard stopped, we would tunnel in through the wind-packed snow to reach the front door. But this sandstorm had a shifting shape. I immediately sensed there was no solid place where one could hope to gain a foothold.

The soldiers seemed unfazed by the delay. Grabbing shovels and sheets of chicken wire from the back of the truck, they moved with practiced efficiency. My father and Mr. Primo Garavello didn't need to use words in order to understand what was going on. The two of them and the seven older boys jumped out to help. Not knowing what to expect, the women and girls huddled together. This was obviously something that happened often, because the soldiers had a system. Shoveling sand off the road, they quickly placed wire mesh in front of the tires. This gave enough traction that we could slowly move forward, the whole process repeated once the truck had managed to cross the strips of wire. And so we began the halting journey across Arab land. It was midnight, maybe one o'clock in the morning, before we arrived.

The winds had stopped. A bright moon ruled the cloudless sky and illuminated the clusters of houses that waited in readiness. The soldiers helped us down from the trucks, but we stood at first almost as if waiting for permission to move forward. Finally, Mr. Garavello reached for a cigarette and asked my father for a *fulminante*, a light. Given that the Garavellos were from Friuli, we couldn't understand what he was saying. My parents became immediately alarmed because in Abruzzese the word means "light from the sky." After the violence of the sandstorm, they wondered at the madness of a man who was now asking, please, to be struck by lightning! After much laughter, it all got straightened out. "Come," my father said. "Let's have a look at our new home." And so, as a group, we tentatively moved forward, growing more excited and separating into individual families only when we identified the houses that would be our own.

In an unsuccessful effort to contain her joy, my mother pressed her hands against her mouth. "Oh, oh. Everything is so elegant." She reached her hand toward the arched front entryway but stopped just short of touching it. My father led the way to our dining room. A special room for dining! Just beyond it, the kitchen contained a fireplace and a marble slab designed for kneading dough. My mother would bake the bread in a brick oven just outside the back door. There would be no more baking done inside. We hadn't yet felt the intense blaze of the Libyan sun, but we had heard enough to know our days of using a kitchen fireplace for heat were behind us. Three bedrooms. No canvas dividers. Real walls. The two bedrooms for the kids were on the same side of the house, while my parents would sleep on the opposite end in the very front of the house. Although it had no plumbing such as we know now, we were excited to find a bathroom attached to the outside of the house. Everything we needed—furniture, dishes, pots and pans—everything was waiting for us in that house. So much care and planning had gone into making our new home ready for us. Even the cupboards were stocked with enough food to last us for two weeks. After that, we would rely on a ration book that could be used at the village store, a kind of cooperative, where we could purchase what we needed with coupons until the farms became self-sufficient.

Forgetting the hour, once we'd dashed through the interior, we spilled out to look again at the exterior of the house and to inspect the landscape. There were no trees. No flowers. Nothing grew. That part of the deal fell to us. We turned again to study our new shelter. White stucco walls gleamed in the moonlight. The roof was flat and painted white to reflect the heat. Dark green shutters framed each window and could be closed, not against *briganti*, but against this same heat. There were four homes in every estate, each built in an identical style. The front doors faced each other, one house on each side, all centered around a small plot of ground in the middle. Each family was responsible for its own parcel, two square miles of as yet untilled soil. Plot #29 Uliani, #30 Onorato, #31 Garavello, and plot #32 Palumbo. We were lucky, in a land with so little water, that the windmill that pumped the water up from thirty feet in the ground was right in our back yard. One did not have to drill too deep to hit sea level here, and since the water was filtered through so much sand, it was sweet and pure. Most of the people in the village of Garibaldi had to travel some distance in order to haul the water they needed for their family's use back to their homes in barrels. All the irrigating would be done from huge pressurized tanks filled from the well just behind our house.

About one hundred feet from the house was a barn and stables. Everything was painted green. Inside the double doors we discovered farming tools: shovels and picks; plows; a two-wheel buggy with inflated rubber tires, which made it easy to travel across sand; an irrigation cart that held a large barrel. A new mule was waiting for us in the stable that held all the creatures that were part of our new farm. As I gently stroked its soft grey flanks, I proudly announced, "A beautiful face, the most beautiful face I ever saw on a mule."

My father laughed. "Well, Vittorio, a mule is a cross between a donkey and a horse. This one must have had a donkey for a father. All its good looks come from the mother's side of the family." We not only got the mule, we also got yokes and harnesses and all the other things we would need to establish a productive farm.

We weren't as used to cows as we were to sheep and goats, and it's a good thing one of our two new cows had horns and one did not. In the beginning, that was the way we told them apart. They were milking cows. The idea being that they would have enough calves to keep the milk flowing and the size of our herd increasing. That night, I fell asleep listening to my brothers and sister chatter about the seemingly endless bounty of our new lives. We were a farm with everything but crops. The empty fields stood as a reminder of what was expected. The last thing I heard was Gennaro laughing. "If we can grow potatoes and wheat in the barren soil of the Majella Mountain, we can grow anything here in this land of endless sun."

Every village consisted of fifty-three estates, each estate was composed of four houses. That meant two hundred and twelve farms in Garibaldi alone. And this area of Libya contained many such villages: Bianchi, Crispi, Micca, Tazzoli, Tigrina, Taruna, Oliveti, Breviglieri, Garian, Corradino, Marcone, and Giordani. So many villages. So many people. The Fourth Shore of Italy was, indeed, in the process of being established here in Libya, on the northern coast of Africa.

But there were still no kids my age nearby. Traveling by the main road that went right by our house, we had to cover four miles just to get to the next estate. The villages themselves were even further apart. In order to get from one to the other, it might take a full day and required hitching up a horse and buggy. Everything was laid out in a precise plan. Mussolini seemed to have thought of everything, except he'd forgotten to put some kids my age in our estate.

The sun had barely risen above the horizon, when we sensed its ferocious heat. It's a good thing we arrived in October, when temperatures mostly stayed below 100 degrees. The Libyan winter gave us time to adapt to our new climate. By summer, it would be nothing for it to hit 120 or 130 degrees. Despite that, my mother never changed her way of dress. Not even fourteen years in the Libyan sun could force her to abandon the long skirts and long-sleeved blouses of the region where she was born. However, we adapted in other ways, learning to tackle the hardest physical work in the early morning or after the sun had set. Relying on huge electric floodlights run by generators, we often worked the fields until nine o'clock at night or later. And when the moon was full, we needed nothing more than its broad face in order to work, freed from the day's heat.

But in those first days, my biggest problem was finding someone to take the place of Domenico, Rinaldo, and cousin Pasquale. Therefore, I was delighted to learn that I would be going to a school that had been set up in part of the stable behind house #23. The teacher, Mariadonata, lived on this farm, and spent her days watching over the youngest children, while the older ones worked beside their parents. Was it some shyness on my part or did I perhaps sense that my time in Libya would be short? I don't know, but I don't remember any of those kids I so much wanted to find in my new home. It was cousin Pasquale who occupied my thoughts. He is still my friend. Even now, here in America, where I am a grown man—an old man some might say—I go from Boston to New York, to Long Island, to see my cousin Pasquale Palumbo.

Five months after we arrived, on a day in March already so warm that we had come inside and shuttered the windows to keep out the blistering rays, we heard a sharp knock on the door. Not like the gentle tap a neighbor might make, no quiet calling of my father's name, "Roberto, Roberto," just an insistent sort of rapping. My parents glanced across the table at each other. They weren't expecting anyone. Who could it be? My mother hung back while my father answered. "Yes, yes, of course, come in," we heard him say.

I was more fascinated by the soldiers than frightened of them. My father shook hands all around and proudly introduced his family. In only five month's time, our farm was beginning to show the results of our labor, the first green shoots already breaking through the irrigated soil. The small trees we had planted were taking root. We had much to display and nothing to hide. These were our soldiers. We were all part of the same ambitious plan. I stood beside my mother while my father and the soldiers exchanged small talk.

"We're just taking a census," they explained. "We need to identify all the children of the settlers. Mussolini knows the future rests with our young people and wants to make sure they are enrolled in proper schools."

My mother stroked her hand against her swollen belly. When I had told my father the new land must agree with her because she was growing fat, he had laughed and explained I would be getting a little brother or sister soon. She stopped rubbing her belly and reached for my hand. "Vittorio is already in school with Mariadonata."

The soldiers smiled at me. "Good boy. And are you the smartest in your class?"

Uncomfortable with being the focus of their inquiry, I simply shrugged and slipped a little further behind my mother.

They laughed and chatted while they wrote down the names and ages of all the kids in our family. Before leaving, they lightly rumpled my hair and that of Giovanni, who, next in line to me, was five years older. Then they shook hands again with my father. After they left, Giovanni turned to our parents, "Do you think they might be planning to build us a proper schoolhouse?" He was not much taken with the classes in the stable.

A few weeks later, an official-looking letter arrived. My mother set it on the table. "We'll wait and let your father open this."

When he came in for the noonday break, he read it with a solemn face. "It's about the schools." My mother reached over to read for herself, but my father hesitated before handing her the letter. "I think there might be some mistake here. Vittorio is still so young."

"This can't be," she said, scanning quickly through the letter. "You have to write to them. Six is too young. You must explain that six is too young. There must be a mistake. Perhaps they meant Giovanni and Guerino."

This was how we learned of the way in which Mussolini intended to educate the next generation of proud Italians. *Gioventù Italiana del Littorio.* The *GIL* schools, as they were called, reflected Mussolini's recognition of the importance of education in creating the next generation of Fascists. These schools were essentially schools of indoctrination and were established throughout Italy. However, most of them were day schools, whereas Mussolini wanted all the Libyan settlers' children who were between the ages of five and fourteen to return to Italy to be enrolled in special *GIL* boarding schools. Drafting a carefully worded letter, offering to send my fourteen-year-old brother Guerino in my place, my parents politely protested the decision.

The authorities weren't convinced by my parents' arguments. Even five-year-olds were going. Guerino would soon be fifteen and would find other ways to serve his country. My father could see the logic in that. "He's a good worker. I need him here to help Gennaro and me with the harvest. Besides, look at what it says." He pointed to the closing paragraph in the letter. "This is not a permanent assignment. Think of it as a vacation, just a short vacation back to the mainland."

After only five months in Libya, Giovanni and I were scheduled to return to Italy. How was it that the boy who had been too young to be separated from his mother on the *Piemonte* was now old enough to sail back through those same waters accompanied by no immediate family member other than an eleven-year-old brother?

Six *is* very young. A child doesn't understand that. All a child knows is that he is the oldest he has ever been. At the time, I felt myself to be quite grown-up, and, compared to what I'd been before, I was. But when I actually grew to be a man and had, first, children, and, then, grandchildren, I'd study them on their sixth birthdays and think, "So young. They are still so very young." The full import of what had happened to me came only many years later when I looked at my own family at that same age and felt a fierce urge to keep them safe.

The letter assigning us to the schools came in early April. By Saint Adalgisa Day, April 20th, my mother had a new baby to occupy her thoughts and time. Because my parents were so busy raising crops of another sort, other sort, they hadn't given much consideration as to what to name the newest arrival. On the day she was born, my father glanced at the calendar and said, "We'll name her Adalgisa." And Adalgisa it was, although when she was small, no one ever called her anything but Ada. I was fascinated by how tiny she was. Pressing her little hand against my palm, my own grip seemed so large that I felt I suddenly had the hands of a man. Perhaps my mother saw me in the same way, or perhaps she felt that she had tried her best and could do no more. Whatever the reason, no one talked much about the fact that my brother and I would be leaving sometime that summer.

In July of 1940, Giovanni and I, Vittorio Del Mastro, and my two cousins Umberto and Antonio D'Agostino, joined hundreds of other boys and girls who were traveling in a convoy of military transport trucks to the port of Tripoli in preparation for a return to the Italian mainland and enrollment in the newly established schools. What a different journey this was from the one that first brought us to Libya. There were no trains draped in festive buntings, no waiting luxury liners. Italy was now at war with England. Responding to pressure from Great Britain, the League of Nations had censured Italian imperialism in Ethiopia. Mussolini, stung by this perceived betrayal and counting on an Axis victory (in hindsight, a terrible miscalculation), had recently joined forces with Hitler's Germany. The only flags flying in our honor were those of the Italian Red Cross. They fluttered above the two battleships on which the young children of the Italian settlers in Libya were scheduled to make their way through mine-infested waters back to more familiar soil. According to the Geneva Conventions, no ship traveling under the protection of the Red Cross could be fired upon. The battleship Giulio Cesare had the solid feel of a military vessel, but instead of offering comfort, it served only to remind Giovanni, our cousins, and me that we could be in danger. The future patriots of Italy were strangely silent. I guess boys find excitement in the stuff of battles, but my memories of the trip are so foggy that I suspect I was more afraid than I was perhaps willing to admit. I later met a man who had been on the same battleship with me. How is it that he has such clear recall of being delayed in the sea near Malta, where we were forced to wait while demolition experts exploded the mines networked through the waters all around us? How is it that I have no memory at all of the hold-up, the excitement, the sharp bursts of fire, and finally of the way in which the captain—tentatively at first, then with more confidence—resumed our journey and guided the ship forward?

CHAPTER FIVE

"My Italian Vacation"

"Naples," my older brother pointed excitedly toward the first mirage-like glimpse of land. "I can see Naples. We are almost home." Responding to his cries, other children happily crowded against the rail, each claiming to see some identifying landmark long before it became visible to anyone else. But Giovanni had been right. We were steadily streaming closer and closer to that busy Italian port city. Chaperones with bullhorns directed us to line up in the appropriate groups and told us where to gather once we had disembarked. Happy to leave the battleship, Giovanni, Umberto, Antonio, and I pushed our way toward the man issuing assignments to various platforms at the rail station. "We'll stay together," I told my brother. "They won't separate relatives now."

They had already divided relatives by gender. Just as the men and women had been assigned to different sections of the ship on our way to Libya, so were boys and girls billeted in their own quarters on the *Giulio Cesare*. It made sense that the boys and girls would be educated in separate schools. I expected that, but surely brothers and cousins would remain in the same group. Even so, I was already feeling set apart from the three older boys. Busy with their own exchanges, they didn't even seem to hear me. As the names were called out—"D'Agostino, Umberto;" "D'Agostino, Antonio;" "Palumbo, Giovanni"—it was quickly apparent that I was wrong. Relatives weren't automatically kept together. The officials in charge were sorting us by age. Trying hard not to show my disappointment, I sadly climbed onto a car filled with kids who looked to be about as old as I was. After scanning the crowd, I shook my head. Not a familiar face in sight. Hesitating, I ran my hand along the top of the upholstered seats. The movement reminded me of the gesture my father had made on the trip from Campo di Giove just ten months earlier. And suddenly it was as if I could hear his very words in my head. "Everything first-rate. Mussolini has that pride. He wants nothing but the best for his people."

I would be all right. I was in good hands. Feeling more confident, I glanced around in search of an unoccupied place. Three boys had adjusted the backs of the seats so that they were facing each other, two on one seat, the other just across the way. "Is someone sitting there?" I asked. They smiled at me and one patted the empty spot beside him. In what I thought was a very grown-up fashion, we exchanged last names only. "Brisolin," said the boy who'd indicated a place for me. "Palumbo," I declared and reached out my hand as I had seen my father do. The other two quickly followed our example. "Airo." "la Morgia." The four of us forged a friendship in that moment. We stayed together until 1943, and in all that time never called each other by anything but our last names.

As the train turned from the coast, headed inland, and began rattling its way through Italy, I leaned across Brisolin to catch a glimpse of any countryside that might look familiar. "Where are we going?" I asked, hoping that my companions might have some information that I, having been too concentrated on where my brother and cousins were headed, might have missed. They simply shrugged their shoulders. After our initial introductions, conversation was halting. There was, of course, the problem of regional differences in dialect. However, during my ten months in Libya, my exposure to other children in Mariadonata's school had given me a proficiency that even my parents occasionally relied on. It wasn't so much a language barrier that held me back, as it was a sudden wave of homesickness. Shutting my eyes against any onslaught of tears, I pretended to sleep. And with the world around me temporarily blocked out, I tried to focus my longing on a physical place. Garibaldi held my parents; my brothers Gennaro, Guerino; and my sister Giovanna, as well as baby Ada; but Libya still had a foreign feel. I can't say I missed the hot dry climate. Was it Campo di Giove that was pulling on my heart? Certainly the sights and smells of Italy, the return to Naples, made me recall standing on the dock looking up at the vastness of the cruise ships. And I'd felt such pride watching Pasquale, Domenico, and Rinaldo race beside the train waving their farewells as we'd traveled back down through the place of my birth at the start of this grand adventure. How would I feel if I returned to my town now? I'd love to see my grandparents, aunts and uncles, cousins and friends again, but coming back so soon after leaving would lack the triumph I'd imagined.

I still had things to do. This trip, on this train, was my personal contribution to the cause of Italy's brave future. I opened my eyes and glanced over at Airo. He nodded solemnly. It was as if we'd exchanged a secret signal. We were the chosen ones. The landscape had changed during my pretense of sleep. Lemon groves, the fruit already streaked with yellow, flashed by the windows. When Brisolin moved past me on his way to the toilet facilities that had been pointed out to us as we'd boarded, I slipped over and took his place beside the window. When he came back, his failure to offer protest over being usurped was so different from the way my brothers would have responded that I nodded at him in appreciation. The smallest movements seemed to bind us in a pact of solidarity and fair play. As the train traveled from the coast, the flat plains gave way to rolling hills and, finally, to mountains. Just as the railroad car that had carried us to Naples ten months before had done, so did this one suddenly head into one of the long tunnels that cut beneath the mountains. Transported from the southwest slope of the Alpine range to the northeast, my friends and I quickly traveled through geographies. The more dislocating the swift passage from one place to another became, the more firmly we clung to each other. We may have been between homes, but in this enclosed space a new sense of home, of family, was beginning to flourish.

Between two and three thousand boys were headed to the Province of Rovigo, in northwest Italy. Our destination there was the small town of Corbola, which was caught between the horseshoe curves of the slow-moving Po River. Not even the train could travel directly to Corbola, and a caravan of buses carried us on the last leg of our journey. Airo, Brisolin, la Morgia and I raced to the long back seat, so that the four of us could remain together. As we disembarked in Corbola, our luck held, and we found ourselves assigned to the same squadron of thirty boys. It dawns on me now that there was no accident in the original divisions at the railway station. From the very first, we must have been sorted according to squadrons of similarly aged children. There would be almost one hundred such squadrons in Corbola alone, each one named for an Italian hero. My friends and I would be the boys of Guido Pallotta. As we left the buses, I quickly scanned the crowds of other children, hoping to somehow spot

Giovanni, Umberto, and Antonio. But since they'd been pointed in the direction of a different train, leaving from a different platform in Naples, I knew better than to hope. It was, nonetheless, a hope I silently held close to my heart, but many months would pass before it was answered.

Before being seized by Mussolini's government, our new home had been a large medical facility for therapeutic massage. Tall cedar trees lined the driveway leading up to it. We climbed off the buses and milled anxiously about on a vast reach of lawn. Once all the names had been called and we were properly sorted, two official-looking gentlemen held the elaborately carved entry doors open, and we filed through them and made our way down a gleaming hallway and into an enormous auditorium. The director marched confidently to the center of the stage. Standing behind a lectern, he paused, making eye contact with individual students in each corner of the assembly until we had all quieted down. "Welcome, welcome *Figli della Lupa*." Children of the she wolf? Was he talking about us? We must have all had puzzled expressions on our faces, because he smiled broadly before continuing. "What do I mean by that? I mean that you boys have a proud Roman tradition behind you. Just as Romulus founded the city that is symbolic of our fatherland, so will you found a brave new Italy. Through your adventures and courage you will extend and consolidate Italy's influence in a world built on the valor you will learn in Mussolini's schools." My grandfather had told me about Romulus and Remus and I found that part really interesting, but as the director's voice droned on and on explaining that we would be taught in a new way, my mind began to wander. I tried hard to pay attention, but the excitement of the journey had tired me out. Every time I started to doze, la Morgia would give me a little kick. I nodded gratefully at him, as I was terrified of getting off on the wrong foot my first day in school. How could the future of Italy be so disrespectful as I fall asleep while being addressed by the director?

Filing out of the auditorium squadron by squadron, we followed the lead of two women who had been introduced as our guardian and our supervisor. As they escorted us to our rooms, they explained that they would oversee our care while we were in Corbola. All the children living here were between the ages of six and eight. As the youngest in the three-tiered program of education, we were officially the *Figli della Lupa*. I had had a birthday that spring and was now seven—not the youngest, not the oldest, but right in the middle. Before stepping through the doorway into what would be my home for the next year, I studied a series of cots arranged at right angles to the wall, each one with a small locker positioned at the foot. I'd no sooner begun to wonder how I would ever figure out which space was mine, when my guardian rested her hand between my shoulder blades and rather gently guided me to my place. "Here, Vittorio, you'll be sleeping here. These are your clothes." She gestured toward a small pile of garments neatly folded at the foot of my bed. I looked at her in astonishment and hesitantly shook my head. I had brought no clothing with me. How could these be mine? She smiled. "Your mother told us what size you wear." At the mention of my mother, a lump rose in my throat. Quickly changing course, my guardian picked up a little garrison-type cap. "Just like a soldier's." She looked around the room. "All of Guido Pallotta's boys are in the same unit. You'll look quite fine in uniform." Across the way, Brisolin had already tried his cap on. He gave me a little salute as I shyly positioned my own cap on an angle that I thought might make my father proud. I reached my hand out and tentatively explored the rest of my uniform. The black cotton shirt reminded me of our soldiers. It even contained the official emblem, the fascio, a symbol depicting a bundle of rods wrapped around an ax in such a way as to bind them all together under one authority. I put my finger on the insignia and felt the promise reflected back from the scarf Mussolini had given my mother when we first began our journey to the Fourth Shore. The supervisor saw us holding up various pieces of the uniform. One of the boys had already slipped the white canvas bandolier over his head and was successfully arranging it so that it formed an X across his chest. "Stop!" The supervisor's voice was sharp, but she softened it when she saw she had our attention. "Please. Wait until morning before trying on the full regimentals. For now, pay close attention as we instruct you on their proper care and keeping." Our guardian was moving between the other boys, and I watched and imitated as she demonstrated how we were to fold and store our new clothes. Carefully, I arranged my things in the foot locker. Shirt. Green woolen pants. The royal blue neckerchief made me hesitate. I was afraid I would be unable to tie it in the proper fashion when it was time to get dressed in the morning. Next to the cap, the thing I treasured most was the dark green woolen *mantellina*. Since I knew this was for winter wear and would be unnecessary now in late July, I should have put the cape underneath everything else in the bottom of my trunk, but I was not yet willing to relinquish it. How it reminded me of my grandfather's cape. It sported a convertible collar held together by a little chain with brass buttons at either end, brass buttons each imprinted with the head of a lion. Hoping the supervisor wasn't looking, I pressed my thumb hard into one, determined the brand of the lion would remain with me even after the cape was stowed away. Remembering how keen a throwing arm Pasquale Palumbo had, I knew I would *never* give him a chance to send these gleaming buttons bouncing across the cobblestones of Campo di Giove.

Once we were all tucked into our beds, the supervisor stood in the aisle between us and explained the rules necessary to keep everything running smoothly. Her posture was very straight, her voice firm and loud. "You will be out of bed at six a.m. sharp. As soon as your feet hit the floor, you will make your beds. After making your beds, head straight for the wash room." She paused and looked up and down the rows of boys, mere bumps under army-issue blankets, as if to be certain we all understood. "Once you've washed, head back here to get dressed. Breakfast is at 6:15 sharp. Don't make your squadron late, or you may all go hungry." I was so worried about not being fast enough, that I found it hard to fall asleep that night. Whatever had happened to the insistent drowsiness that had required kicks from la Morgia in order to stay awake in the auditorium? It had been replaced by images of Romulus and Remus, but instead of focusing on their bravery, all I could think of was that they had been abandoned by their mother and that one would end up killing the other in a struggle for power.

It was a long night, and I felt as if I'd no sooner fallen asleep than a sharp whistle blasted me awake. The other boys all did seem much speedier than I was. With mounting frustration, I pulled at bedcovers that bore testimony to a night of dark dreams filled with thrashing and kicking. The more I rushed, the more the tangle of covers resisted my efforts. Suddenly I felt a soft hand on my shoulder. "Go get washed with your group, Vittorio." I looked up and saw my guardian smiling at me. "We'll sort these covers out when you return."

I raced after the others into the army-like lavatory. Splashing water from the marble wash basins onto my face, I could feel it hit my bare toes and knew more had spilled down onto the tiled floor than had found its intended target. In our haste, we were fairly quiet that morning, but soon enough, we would discover the way those walls could echo. We all learned not to laugh or talk too loudly in the washroom or we'd bring the supervisor on the run. "What's going on in here? Those who aren't dressed in fifteen minutes will find themselves with no breakfast."

Adhering to this schedule would not have been possible without the assistance of the our guardian. By the time I got back to our sleeping quarters, my tangle of covers required little more than a final straightening. Signorina Guardian was already a few beds over showing one of the other boys how to fasten his scarf in the appropriate fashion. Happy not to be the only one with a fear of knots, I pulled the pants and shirt on with confidence. By the time I'd positioned the troublesome kerchief about my neck, the competent hands I'd come to rely on were twisting and arranging. "It isn't difficult. Once you get the hang of it, you'll need no help at all."

Our schedule never varied. After the shock of the first few days, I caught on quickly and was always one of the first in line. As soon as we had wolfed down breakfast, we joined the other squadrons on the wide lawns behind the building. Our formations were precision-smooth but not straight in the way of a measuring rule. Lining up exactly as we'd been instructed on our very first morning, we became experts at spelling out formations of giant "M"s. Only when our Prime Minister was so honored, did we, still in position, raise the flag. In forming his coalition government, Mussolini had won the Catholic Church to his side by declaring it the official Church of Italy and by recognizing papal sovereignty over the Vatican City. In short, the Vatican was granted status as a city-state with full diplomatic rights. As a kid I never understood the compulsory moment of silence that followed every flag-raising, but it must have been a way of honoring the government's agreement with the Church. Still in formation, we ended the silence by extending our right arms stiffly in front of us and shouting in unison, "*Viva il Duce! Viva il Re!*" *Il Re* was a reference to the King of Italy at the time, Vittorio Emanuele III, for whom I had been named.

Physical fitness was a large part of our training. We practiced military-type maneuvers. During these exercises, we were armed with scaled-down replicas of the Royal Italian service rifle, the *Moschetto Balilla*. This felt more like play than work for young boys, but we had to be careful to follow orders exactly. Horsing around was not allowed, and we learned to handle our rifles as if they were the real thing. In the classroom, I became quite familiar with the number of horses in Mussolini's stable. "If *Il Duce* had seven horses in his pasture when he got up in the morning and only four were there when he returned that night, how many had jumped over the fence while he was gone?" We were sent, one by one, to the blackboard to do our sums. Our days followed a strict routine, and blended pretty much into each other. My memories of this first school are not as clear as those of the two I would attend later, but one day stands out.

We had just slid our tablets into our desks, when there was a knock at the classroom door. I could hear Signorina Supervisor's voice explaining something to the teacher. "Vittorio Palumbo." My teacher called my name and signaled that I was to step forward. As I slowly made my way to the door, all the kids turned around in their seats to stare at me. I wondered if I'd forgotten to make my bed in the proper fashion, or if I was going to be blamed for not cleaning the long breakfast table well enough that no stickiness remained. "There is someone here to see you," the Supervisor explained as she led me out into the garden.

Visitors were unheard of and I don't know how they got permission, but my mother's sister, my aunt Fiorina Di Gregorio, stood there with her son, my fourteen-year-old cousin Vittorio. And just beside her was Aunt Cristina Di Gregorio, my favorite aunt, my father's sister. These two aunts were stepsisters who had married brothers. Both their husbands worked for the railroad. Aunt Cristina and Uncle Ercole lived along the railroad tracks in a house just outside Campo di Giove. Aunt Cristina's son, my older cousin Tonino, was with them as well. Knowing that Tonino was soon going to be a priest and still caught in the fearful state in which I'd been called from the classroom, I thought at first that something must be wrong, perhaps someone had died. Worry must have clouded my face, because Aunt Cristina spread her arms, "Vittorio, aren't you glad to see us?"

Those words were precisely the release I needed, and I rushed into her embrace. Of all my relatives, she was the one quickest with a hug. It was Aunt Cristina who, when I grew tired on the long walk back from her home, would hoist me on her shoulders and carry me in a way no one else in the family ever considered. In my Aunt Cristina's arms, I could smell the aromas of home. The mountain air. The bread. The smoke from the fireplace that lined the wall of the home the government provided to those who kept the tracks in repair. All the tears I hadn't shed and still forced myself to contain formed a dam in the back of my throat that kept words from spilling out as well. Aunt Cristina held me away from herself as if to take another look, as if to make sure it was really me after almost a year apart. Then she gathered me back in and I felt truly safe. "So big," she murmured. "You've grown so tall."

I finally managed an answer. "I'm seven now," I said as if that explained everything.

She squeezed my shoulders. "We can't stay long. Only an hour they told us."

"Let's sit on the bench where we all can see him," Aunt Fiorina said. Once we were settled near the cedar trees, everyone talked at once and I didn't have to say too much. They were on their way to the San Antonio Sanctuary in Padua. Padua is not far from the Rovigo region. Since their husbands worked for the train lines, they had been able to arrange the trip. Aunt Cristina patted her son Tonino on the leg. "It won't be long, Vittorio. It won't be long until your cousin is a priest." Her eyes shone with pride, but Tonino just shifted uncomfortably and had even less to say than I did.

As it happened, Tonino never did become a priest. His refusal broke my Aunt Cristina's heart. Unable to absolve herself of responsibility for this perceived maternal failure, from that point on, she was certain all family tragedies were somehow linked to her son's unwillingness to follow the path she had envisioned for him. Looking back now and knowing how all that turned out, I wonder if the trip to the San Antonio Sanctuary had more to do with attempting to hold my cousin Tonino to his commitment than it did with making sure that I was all right. But, back then, I only knew that I had seen and heard and smelled the world of Campo di Giove. I fell asleep that night with an image of home that filled the empty place that had previously held only unspecified longing. Now I saw Aunt Cristina's terra-cotta-colored house in my mind's eye. It was positioned on a small rise not too far from the railroad track, but up high enough to offer a clear view of the Majella Mountain with its gleaming crown of snow. Just across the track, Uncle Ercole's garden was filled with flowers no one else could grow. He watered everything from a pure spring that bubbled down from the mountain. Sweet mountain water. No pumping, no well required, just water making its own little fountain. I heard its happy song even in my dreams.

CHAPTER SIX

Return to Snow-Capped Peaks

As Brisolin, Airo, la Morgia, and I climbed on the bus that would take us from Corbola, I can't say I felt any regret at leaving the austere-looking massage therapy building behind. I was growing used to this soldier's life and felt, as long as I had my comrades at my side, change was just another word for adventure. We were headed to a region whose name promised beauty. Given that I was a child of the mountains, my heart raced faster as our bus headed northeast and I caught my first glimpse of the jagged limestone and rock pinnacles that loomed over the town of Fiera di Primiero. The town itself is nestled at the foot of the Dolomites, an alpine outcropping known for the orange-pink hue of its stone. We pulled up to the Hotel Orsingher, where we would be housed during the early part of our stay in the Province of Trento, and I breathed in the mountain air and felt I had returned home. Set in a broad valley at the confluence of two mountain streams, the Cismon and the Canali, Fiera di Primiero itself is 730 meters above sea level—not as high as the 1,111 of my home, but I immediately sensed a kinship with the alpine meadows which reached higher still and framed the town. Completely taken with the landscape, I didn't at first notice the unusual architecture of our hotel. In fact, it was only when Brisolin poked me in the back that I forced myself to turn from the mountains and actually look at the building where we would be staying.

Although the hotel was at least five stories high, it was so completely surrounded by the snow-covered granite peaks that not even its imposing bulk could block them from view. They rose into the sky, above the sky. In places, clouds hung just below their pinnacles. "It's like looking into heaven," I told la Morgia. All around me my friends were gathering their things from the bus, but I was dumbstruck and could scarcely move. Finally I inhaled deeply. I had spent my early years breathing mountain air and, despite the Teutonic nature of the buildings, the air told me I was home.

A slim young woman was smiling at us from the front steps of the hotel. With wavy hair that fell to her shoulders, her slender grace made even the Fascist uniform she wore look as if it had been designed just for her. Can an eight-year-old boy fall in love? Perhaps I'd already fallen in love with the Dolomites and from there it was but a short step to noticing a woman's beauty for the first time. As this lovely person made her way toward us, she extended both hands. "My name is Signorina Turra." She seemed genuinely glad to see us. "I'll be your teacher and guardian while you are here with us in Fiera di Primiero." She waited until our group of thirty was gathered around her and then she continued. "You must be very tired after your long trip. First I'll show you to your rooms." We were following her up the stairs. I felt I would have followed her anywhere. "There will be four boys in each room. After you've had a chance to get settled in, we'll see that you get something to eat."

Every room had doors that opened to a small balcony. As soon as I'd put my things away, I went and stood looking out at the Alpine landscape. The town seemed caught in a wide bowl formed by the jutting granite boulders that framed it. I saw meadows surrounded by pine and larch trees. In the middle of each field, tiny farm buildings claimed their place. Constructed of whitewashed stone on the bottom and dark wood on the top, some had roofs that sloped almost to the ground. I knew that a steeply pitched roof was better able to withstand the weight of heavy snow and hoped we would still be here when winter came. The voices that drifted up from the street below seemed more influenced by Austria than Italy. And while I studied the voices and the landscape, the voice of Signorina Turra, as she had asked us to call her, was the backdrop against which all else played out.

Brisolin joined me. "Our guardian seems nice, doesn't she?"

Afraid to reveal the depth of my agreement, I only nodded my head. After all, I saw no point in alerting my companions to my feelings. More than that, I didn't really want to share Signorina Turra with anyone quite yet.

I slept more peacefully that night than I had in a long time. We were soldiers well-drilled in routine. Although the building was not yet familiar, our schedule for waking, washing up, and eating breakfast was unchanged. After the morning meal, we lined up behind Signorina Turra, who had lost none of her beauty during the night, and marched out into the courtyard. How good to have cobblestones beneath my feet once more. I liked the synchronized ringing noise our boots made as we so effortlessly positioned ourselves into the proudest letter in the Mussolini alphabet. Our flag, the one used by the schools, had the familiar vertical bands of green, white, and red, but the central white band also contained the emblem of King Vittorio Emanuele. Our early lessons in Corbola interpreted the meaning of each color. Green sang the praises of our landscape, white the snow-capped Alps, and red the bloodshed that our brave soldiers had shed in the making of a unified nation.

Years later, someone would tell me that green was for hope, white for faith, and red for charity. And someone else more versed in history would explain that the colors were really borrowed from Napoleon I, when he declared control of Northern Italy. Who knows what gives an object meaning? Who can really say what makes something true? We were told so many things during my years in school. We were told we were winning the war.

So, on that first sunlit morning in Fiera di Primiero, I knew only the pride of the green alpine meadows, the beauty of the white veins of snow that traced through the Dolomites even on a summer day, and the glory of the bloody sacrifices others before me had made. The flag fluttered against a backdrop of mountains in a town so peaceful it was as if the war had never happened or was at least already won, already finished, our expanded borders reaching all the way to Libya, strong and secure. With an enthusiasm inspired by the innocence of pure belief, a hundred young voices thrust their right arms forward and cried out, *"Viva il Duce! Viva il Re!"*

This was a ritual we followed both morning and night. As soon as it was over, we marched behind Signorina Turra—our teacher, guardian, and surrogate mother—into our designated schools. With the exception of a short break for lunch, our lessons continued until two in the afternoon. We finished our homework assignments as soon as the formal school day was over. All those who tended to us were women. Our director, la Rossi, and our supervisor, la Benvolo, were more concerned with enforcing discipline and keeping the schools running in an orderly fashion. Their memory fades from me. It is Signorina Turra who stays as strong in my heart as if I saw her only yesterday. It was her compassion that made the rigors of our training bearable.

Early on a Saturday morning only two days after my arrival in Fiera di Primiero, my squadron was getting ready to board the buses that were to take us for a bit of recreation in the mountain woods and fields. Just across the street, a similar group of older boys was also lining up in preparation for a day's adventure away from the town. As they fell in behind the young man who was their guardian—boys aged twelve to fourteen were all managed by gentlemen in their mid-twenties—I thought I saw a familiar face. Startled, I looked again. I was right. This was no dream. My brother Giovanni was among those getting ready to climb on board. "Signorina Turra, please, Signorina Turra," I broke from the line and ran to her. "I see my brother!" I pointed across the street. "I see Giovanni. Please, Signorina Turra, please."

She dropped to her knees, so that we were face to face. "You see your brother in that group of young boys?"

"Hurry, Hurry," I told her. "Before his bus pulls away."

Turning to my companions, she said, "Stay in line. Wait until Vittorio and I return before climbing on the bus." Then she took my hand and we quickly made our way over to the other bus. She said a few words to the driver and he motioned us on board. Their guardian was just getting ready to take attendance when Signorina Turra tapped him on the back and asked to see the list of names. I didn't need a list of names to know Giovanni Palumbo when I saw him. And right beside him were my cousins Umberto and Antonio D'Agostino! I started to move toward them as they stood in their seats, but Signorina Turra held me back. "Not now, Vittorio." She looked as disappointed as I felt. "Your squadron is waiting for us, but don't worry, I've made arrangements. You'll see you brother…"

"And my cousins," I interrupted.

She smiled. "You'll see your brother and your cousins this evening after we return." She turned to leave, and I backed out after her, still looking at faces both familiar and strangely older. "I've made arrangements," she told me. "They are staying in the Hotel Roma just across the street." We were back on the pavement. "You'll see them tonight," she said as I slipped into line beside Brisolin. "But for now, we're all going to the mountains."

The weekends were the only time we had to play, the only time we were really allowed to run free and just be boys. As it turned out, this first trip to the San Martino di Castrozza mountains was unusual in that we traveled by bus. As long as we contented ourselves with scenery in the foothills of the range, we could hike to our destinations on a series of well-worn trails that began just outside town. But on this day, our excursion served two purposes: an introduction to Fiera di Primiero, and transport to the higher reaches of the landscape.

A boy named Savino raised his hand, "This sure doesn't look like Italy." The others laughed and he grew a bit defensive. Pointing out the window to a chalet-style cottage with window boxes spilling over with geraniums, he said, "We don't have those kind of houses at home."

"Savino is correct." How swiftly Signorina Turra had learned all our names. "This region of Italy was occupied by Austria from around 1880 until 1915. It wasn't fully recognized as a rightful part of Italy until 1917." Ever the teacher, she asked if any of us had noticed other differences in the area.

I shyly raised my hand. For reasons I can't explain—maybe because of how my great-grandmother's dress bore the mark of her family's roots in the Puglia and set her just a bit apart, or maybe because I somehow was born almost with a tailor's instinct for fabric, I can't say why—but I always saw the clothes, the material, the pattern beneath the style. Signorina Turra nodded at me. "Yes, Vittorio?"

"The people wear unusual clothing. Colorful embroidery," I cautiously began. When no one laughed, I continued. "If the fabric is dark, the women cover it with bright embroidery. Lots of bright colors. The men wear red woolen socks that come all the way to their knees. They have patterns in them." At that point, la Morgia poked me with his elbow, and I sensed my enthusiasm was turning the bus ride into too much of a classroom. I stopped talking and when no one, not even Signorina Turra urged me to continue, I turned my attention to the window. However, I had stopped noticing the outside world. In the silence that followed our impromptu instruction, thoughts of Giovanni, Umberto, and Antonio drove all else from my head.

At last the bus pulled off the dirt lane we'd been following and parked in a tunnel of shade formed by trees that arched over it from both sides and tangled their branches together at midpoint. We lined up as Signorina Turra explained the rules. "When I blow the whistle once, you are free to run and play at whatever games you devise." She looked down at our small feet already agitating for the release that single whistle blast would bring, and bit her lips together, almost as if holding back a smile. "However, when you hear me blow twice, you are to return and *immediately* fall into formation." Then she did smile, broadly, and in a slow and teasing fashion brought the whistle to her lips. She drew a deep breath and suddenly the sweet sound of our release cut through the air! My squadron raced off through flower-filled fields. However, as used as we were to regimentation, the first game we played was one that required us to form a line. Leapfrog. It was only after the game grew wild and fast and we grew silly, knocking each other down and tumbling about in the sweet-scented grass like puppies, that we finally gave in to a day devoted to running and tagging and hiding from each other in small gullies here and there. On those Saturdays we became boys like any other boys, but as soon as we heard the double note of Signorina Turra's whistle, we quickly returned to formation and to our lives as soldiers in Mussolini's schools.

As promised, that evening Signorina Turra walked me into the lobby of the Hotel Roma, just across the street from the Orsingher. After our day in the meadows, I felt proud of the Austrian sound of my new home and couldn't wait to share all that I had learned with my brother. "I'll return for you in an hour, Vittorio," my guardian explained after I'd managed to introduce her to my family.

Giovanni, Antonio, Umberto and I stood awkwardly looking at each other. Finally, Giovanni stepped forward. He reached both hands out almost as if to hug me, but our family was not much for hugging. Then I went to shake his right hand just at the moment he dropped it to his side. Umberto laughed and broke the silence. "So. Vittorio, how have you been?"

I shrugged my shoulders and took a deep breath. "Fine." I tried hard to think of something else to say, when, in a single instant, the four of us all asked the same question. We went from total silence to a jumble of words none of us could understand. We began laughing and finally established that my brother and cousins had arrived in Fiera di Primiero just a few days ahead of me. That said, there seemed to be little else to talk about.

"Have you three been together the whole time?" I asked, trying hard to keep a note of longing from my voice.

They nodded in unison and went on to explain the routine in the school they'd recently left. Except for the difficulty of the lessons and the fact that they had all male guardians and supervisors, our training seemed much the same. "The little kids have ladies to take care of them," Antonio told me.

"We don't need taking care of," I shot back, drawing myself up to my full height.

Giovanni must have sensed the hurt in my voice, because he softened Antonio's remark by saying, "Your guardian is very pretty." The three older boys all admitted that they would not mind having her for their teacher, and I hoped that in their enthusiasm no one noticed the fire I could feel growing in my cheeks.

Then out of nowhere and eager to impress them with all I'd learned, I announced, "The Province of Trento wasn't part of greater Italy until 1917."

"We know that," Umberto told me, as if my proud knowledge was common information. "It was Austrian. That's why they dress so funny."

Giovanni moved to my side. "We just have an hour. Why don't we all sit down?"

It was only after we had stiffly arranged ourselves on the edge of a formal settee that stretched along one wall of the lobby that I found the magic words that could command the respect of my relatives. "I saw Aunt Cristina and Tonino. They visited me in Corbola. Aunt Fiorina and cousin Vittorio came too."

Suddenly the questions flew too fast for me to answer all at once. And that's how Signorina Turra found us when she came back to claim me, lost in talk of Campo di Giove.

CHAPTER SEVEN

A Song for Fiera di Primiero

During the weeks that followed, we were all so busy in our different schools and with our training that I caught only fleeting glimpses of my brother and cousins. The exception to that was in church. As part of Mussolini's agreement with Pope Pius XII, we were required to attend Mass on Sundays. Giovanni and I were both assigned to the same church in a small section of Fiera di Primiero called Transaqua. By September of 1941, we were scheduled to receive our First Communion and Confirmation. This is a significant event for Catholic children and their families, and as soon as I learned the date, I felt a renewed longing for home. Remembering how Aunt Cristina had managed to travel to Corbola, I wondered if something similar might be possible now. However, before my dreams had a chance to run too far ahead, Signorina Turra told me that since the children in the schools were without nearby relatives, the *podestà* or selectman from Fiera di Primiero was in charge of finding a godfather or godmother for each of us.

On the morning of September 20, 1941, we marched into the courtyard of the Orsingher for the ceremony that would pair us with our godparents. Instead of the usual military attire, we were dressed entirely in white. Our clothing alone marked this as an important event. Fidgeting with the cuff of my short pants, I secretly studied the faces of the adults lined up on one side. Anxious about who my godfather would be, I found it hard to assume an appropriately devout posture. Palumbo comes near the end of the alphabet. Would all the best godfathers be assigned to someone else? Might I get stuck with that thin, bald-headed man whose face seemed frozen in a permanent frown? What a relief when he was paired with someone else early in the ceremony. There was one man who seemed to me to be all that anyone could ask in a godfather. Perhaps I felt drawn to him because he was apparently having as much trouble standing with head bowed as I was. Whenever I looked at him, he seemed to be looking at me. When that happened, his eyes held mine briefly and flickered with almost the beginning of a smile. Keeping careful track of our progress through the alphabet, I knew it was time for my name to be called. "Vittorio Palumbo." The gentleman I had been watching paused just long enough to let the smile that had been held only in his eyes spread across his whole face. Then he stepped toward me grinning so happily that I could hardly believe my luck. Everything in Mr. Gino Simion's posture radiated kindness. One could say he was the answer to my prayers.

Almost 300 boys and girls from the *Gioventù Italiana del Littorio* were to participate in our First Communion on that day. Walking beside our newly appointed godparents, we made our way to the church and waited our turn to approach the altar. The Confirmation ceremony was celebrated by Bishop Facchinetti, then the Archbishop of Tripoli, and a very well-known authority in the region. The line was so long that not all of us could fit into the church at the same time. The little girls, their dresses forming a fluttering ribbon of white, went first. Standing beside Mr. Gino Simion, I felt already touched by good fortune in the form of the reassuring man next to me. Impressed by the gravity of this day, all of the children were unnaturally quiet, but when my godfather and I finally passed through the two large doors leading to the foyer, it was as if some stillness entered my heart. Walking by the marble basins on either side of the entry and into the cool hush of the cathedral, I was overcome by the sense that I was now embraced by the Church. I was about to join the generations of Italians who had worshipped here before me and whose feet had worn the stone floor to a smooth, shiny surface. There were three rows of pews—left, right, and center. Two large devotional paintings hung behind the altar. As my godfather and I drew close to the bishop, awe washed the last trace of anxiety from me, and I received my First Communion with reverent joy. On turning to make way for the next child in line, I noticed the enormous organ housed in a balcony over the front entrance. My heart was making its own music.

After all the anticipation, my Confirmation and First Communion were suddenly over, and I walked from the church proud and happy to share this milestone with Mr. Gino Simion. He gave me a beautiful fountain pen, engraved with gold. Memories of that day are a flickering burst of shadow and light: I missed my parents, I worried that I would forget some part of my response, I felt humbled and very small before the glory of the Church, but mostly I rejoiced in having a godfather such as Mr. Simion.

When I heard his friends and relatives call him by his nickname, "Espedito, aren't you going to introduce me to that handsome godson of yours?" or "Espedito, how did you get so lucky?" I was even more certain that good fortune had blessed me all around. Espedito. What an elegant name. What a perfect name for this man who seemed able to make all the happiness of a real home available to me. From that day on, my Sundays were filled with the potential for magic. Mr. Simion obtained a permit to take both me and my brother Giovanni from our hotels, not every Sunday, but often enough that we quickly felt welcomed as a part of his family.

Those golden days with the Simion family capture the blaze of happiness that warms memories of my time in Fiera di Primiero. Mr. Simion and his relatives were surrounded by so many children that I've forgotten many of the names. But I clearly recall that the affection with which everyone treated them was extended equally to me and Giovanni. The dress of the women my guardian's age featured the bright colors and crewel-like embroidery typical of the Trentino region and seemed almost a reflection of their cheerful temperaments.

I can still hear the echoes of that laughter. No wonder it was so easy to fall into the habit of calling my godfather Espedito. "Vittorio, Vittorio, aren't we friends enough that you can call me by the same name everyone in the family uses?" I loved the feel of that name rolling off my tongue so much that it didn't take much persuading. Sometimes he was accompanied by a lovely young woman, Signorina Dellazzeri, who seemed to take as much pleasure from hearing his name spoken as I took in saying it. The way they smiled at each other made me suspect she fancied him. Feeling it would be rude to ask, I just quietly made note of the sentiment between them.

Espedito and his brother Carlo both wore the dark grey woolen *zuara* trousers, called knickers in America, that were so common in Fiera di Primiero. These were always accompanied by patterned red knee socks and brown mountain shoes, equipped with special spikes that enabled one to hike up icy slopes in the snow. I loved those shoes and felt that by wearing them a person announced a certain readiness for adventure.

At first I imagined that Espedito and his brother had jobs that required mountain climbing, and was a bit disappointed to find out that Carlo ran a general store, a food cooperative. In fact, the boots were necessary mostly for recreation, and I quickly learned that that type of fun seemed as much a part of life in this big family as did more ordinary work. One of Espedito's sisters was so strong-willed that the others were forever tormenting her. It was as hard to get Romina to back down as it was easy to get her to laugh. In my memories, playful banter accompanied every meal and was as nourishing as the food itself.

Mr. Simion's mother, Antonia, who was the matriarch of the family, did the cooking for those special Sundays. She wore long black dresses covered with white aprons that came all the way to the hem. A favorite meal was polenta with meat from Capriolo goats, special goats that are raised in the mountain country. My mouth watered as I watched Antonia ladle abundant amounts of sauce over her savory creation. Giovanni and I felt like kings and, when those magical Sundays drew to a close, rejoined our classmates filled with both food and love.

It didn't matter what hotel they moved us to, my godfather always managed to find us. I have never understood why they moved us so often, but there seemed to be some unwritten law that we weren't to stay in any one place very long. During our stay in the Province of Trento, I lived in three different hotels but never shared one with my brother and cousins. The age groups were kept as segregated as the sexes, the differences between the older boys and the younger marked by variations in the uniforms we wore. Regardless of which hotel we occupied, Signorina Turra always came with us. Sleeping, waking, day and night, she was there. After only a few months in the Hotel Orsingher, my squadron relocated to the Villa Trieste Hotel. Later destroyed by an avalanche, the Villa Trieste is no longer standing. Even the things one loves, such as deep snow and a mountain climate, can cause damage. I was much older when I learned the ultimate fate of the hotel where I once lived, but nothing in that knowledge altered my affection for the Dolomites. Weather contains its own truth and the sometimes treacherous shifting of temperature and wind generates destruction for which no person can be held accountable.

Although not within formal borders of the municipality of Fiera di Primiero, Siror is such a near neighbor that when we relocated to its Brewery Hotel, named for the building's original use, it was as if we had never left the *comune* that first claimed my heart. The landscape around us was unchanged. Signorina Turra was still our guardian. The people greeted us with the same open friendliness. And at night, after all our studies, exercises, formations, homework, and meals were finished, I would find a place to stand and watch the sunset ignite the already pink limestone of my beloved mountains with deeper shades of rose and gold. As the sun dropped from view, the snow-covered peaks held all that was left of the fading light. White church spires pierced the growing darkness and finally, first one star and then another, claimed the night as their own, and I made my way to bed.

I was not alone in feeling that the time my companions and I spent in the Province of Trento was almost a pause, an interruption, a reprieve from all that had been so difficult in our young lives. Our parents were far away in Libya, a place we hadn't lived in long enough to really call home. Italy was at war. We had no communication with our families. We were still terribly young, children, mere children who had been asked to march into history wearing the outsized dreams of leaders whose visions for our country we embraced and, yet, the weight of those dreams was sometimes too heavy to expect our slight frames to bear. But in Fiera di Primiero the warmth of the people and the beauty of the scenery salvaged a bit of childhood we might otherwise have lost. It is no wonder that we composed a song that expressed our gratitude. It is no wonder that I remember it still.

>Primiero sei Bella, sei Cara
>Fra monti prati e boschi
>É sorta una colonia
>che accoglie un be migliaio
>Di libici bambin
>Lieta si quella balda schiera,
>marcia ben, saluntando con amor
>il vessillo tricolour
>
>Primiero sei bella, sei cara ed ospital!
>Tua gente ci accolse con simpatia cordial!

Italian Days, Arabian Nights

Ed anche i villegianti
con noi tanto gentili
ammirano entusiasti
L'allegra gioventú
E l'eco dei canti risuona nella Val
inneggiando al Duce, all'Italia immortal
Tra marce studio e giochi
e qualche passeggiata passiamo la giornata
in gran serenitá
Pavione, Canali e Gruppo Sass Maor
o roccie trentine, vi porteremo nel cuor
con l'Itala Vittoria
in Libia ritornati
La mamma tanto cara felici abbraccerem.
Di Libia, o Duce, seguendo il tuo voler.

The following is a translation of this anthem of appreciation sung by the children of the *GIL* schools.

Between mountains, prairies, and forests
there grew a colony
hosting a thousand Libyan children.
The rank is happy, it marches very well greeting with love the
  three-color flag.
Primiero: you are beautiful, you are dear and hospitable!
Your people welcomed us with heartfelt sympathy!
And even the tourists were so friendly with us,
and enthusiastically admired the cheerful young people.
And the sound of the songs echoed in the Valley
praising the Duce and immortal Italy.
We spent all day on marches, in study, games,
and on a few serene walks
Pavione, Canali and Group Sass Maor (mountain groups),
Oh Trentino rocks, we will keep you in our hearts
  with the Italian victory.
We will happily hug our dear Mother,
Belonging to Libya, oh Duce, following your wish.

CHAPTER EIGHT

1942 on the Italian Riviera

We'd moved so often that I should have been prepared for Signorina Turra's announcement at the end of class on a beautiful afternoon in May of 1942. "I have some exciting news," she told us. "You've done so well in your studies that you've been recognized for relocation to San Remo."

I turned to la Morgia. "What did she say? Where's San Remo?"

Signorina Turra lightly clapped her hands together and looked at me more in disappointment than in anger. "Class, quiet, please. This is a great honour. Give me time to explain before you ask questions."

I tried to listen, but once she reached the part where she told us she would not be travelling with us, I found it hard to pay attention. When she'd finished talking, others raised their hands. The questions flew at her. "When do we leave?" "How long is the journey?" "Where will we stay?" "Who will be our new guardian?"

I guess the answers flew back as rapidly as the questions, but I didn't hear any of them. I didn't care about the questions. I didn't care about the answers. I had already heard the only part that mattered to me: Signorina Turra would remain behind in Fiera di Primiero.

I was unable to eat my evening meal. At one point, Signorina Turra walked behind my seat and rested her hand lightly against my back. "Aren't you feeling well, Vittorio?"

I just shrugged my shoulders and waited for her to leave. After a few quiet moments she did. When the tables were cleared, Signorina Turra stood in the doorway and released us group by group. As my squadron filed past, she pulled me aside. "I'd like to talk to you before you join the others."

Embarrassed by the curiosity with which the other boys looked at me, I stood as far from her as I could without appearing to be disobedient. As soon as we were alone, she dropped to her knees so that we were face to face. "I can tell something is bothering you."

I just shook my head.

"Vittorio, you and I know each other too well for me to believe that nothing is wrong."

A long silence stood between us. I examined my feet, knowing that if I looked in her eyes, all the sadness that was bottled up inside me might escape.

"Guardians are assigned to one location," she said as if reading my thoughts.

"You came with us to Siror," I blurted out.

"Yes, I did. But Siror is still in the Province of Trento. San Remo, on the other hand, is in the Province of Imperia, in the region of Liguria." She sighed. "I have a job here. You and I share a loyalty to the same cause. My job is to help the next class that is assigned to me."

At that, I lifted my head to study her expression and was relieved to see that she wasn't smiling.

"Oh, Vittorio, saying good-bye is always hard." Then she rushed ahead, "But you know I'll never forget you."

Once again, the study of my feet saved me from embarrassment. How I regret that I didn't tell her that she would always remain in my heart. She *has* always remained in my heart. There really aren't words to say some things. I guess I didn't need to say them. I guess she knew.

We both took deeps breaths, and then she continued in a more professional manner. "The scenery in San Remo is very beautiful. By the ocean! Have you ever lived where you could watch the sea?" Not waiting for an answer, she leaned a little closer to me. "And there's one thing I haven't told anyone else. This time you and Giovanni will be staying in the same hotel."

At that I raised my head. As it was clear there would be no persuading her to change her plans, there was nothing to do but move forward.

Taking encouragement from my change in attitude, she pressed on. "San Remo is called the Italian Riviera. You've heard of the Riviera, haven't you? It's a narrow slice of land caught between the Mediterranean and the Alps. A beautiful spot. You and your brother are assigned to the London Hotel; it's a very fancy place and used to be a casino where all the rich people came to play." She stood up. "Now, go catch up to your friends. You'll be leaving together right after breakfast, and you have some packing to do."

Of the many places I have lived in my seventy-seven years, Fiera di Primiero is the one that most truly feels like home. Not since my time there have I ever been in a spot so filled with beauty. Of course, that was all before I had met and married Rosalba, before our children and grandchildren were born. I suppose if it were just the two of us, Rosalba and me, looking for a spot to live out our years, then there would be no finer location than there in the foothills of the Dolomites. However, home is more than a piece of geography. Home is also a place in your heart. And here in America my heart is filled with the love of my family. How could I ever move away from the pride I feel in my children and grandchildren? In the end, it is love that makes a home. So, my home is here now, with Rosalba and with those we love. But those days in the Province of Trento will always be remembered with deep affection.

I wish I could say my fears about leaving Fiera di Primiero proved to be groundless, but from the very first, I sensed a change. First of all, San Remo was a much larger city than anywhere we previously had stayed. Although Signorina Turra had not exaggerated its beauty, not even the natural wonder of the Alps rising just behind the municipal limits offered much comfort. I could see those mountains, but there didn't seem to be a way to reach them. Too many streets, too many buildings blocked my access. In the end, they felt more like a barrier than a destination.

The sea was closer and more available. *Had I ever lived near the ocean,* Signorina Turra had asked. No, of course not, not lived there, but I had sailed across its wide waters on my way to and from Libya. All the children in Mussolini's schools for the children of the settlers had. My guardian and I both knew that I had never lived on the coast. I'd always called the mountains home and, until now, found comfort in their shelter. But the sea? The sea served mostly as a reminder of something that separated me from family. I watched its waves cresting and crashing, was interested in following the pattern with which the tides turned, and, in time, my friends and I would occasionally run on its beaches on Saturdays devoted to recreation. But the sea never offered the reliable comfort of a mountain that refused to change, that stood for something I could count on always finding.

In Fiera di Primiero, the children of the *GIL* schools seemed to be recognized and welcomed by all. Here we did not seem so set apart, so special. Mussolini had claimed our hearts, excited our imaginations. From there it was but an easy step to capture our minds. On entering our school on my first day in San Remo, I saw a poster describing the philosophy of our education: "Book and Musket Make the Perfect Fascist." An elaborate etching featured the open pages of a book containing those words. A drawing of the fasces with a crucifix strapped tightly to it stretched across the binding and covered two pages. We were told Fascism and the Church were naturally connected. Although the lessons we learned within the classroom continued to carry the same stirring messages of pride and victory, I sensed a subtle change in the way the world outside the walls of the school saw us. In San Remo, more than the tides of the Mediterranean were turning. As I walked from my school back to the hotel, I could no longer be certain my uniform would be greeted with a smile. For all the hours we devoted to our studies, there were things we still did not know.

By 1942, the so-called Italian empire was in a shambles. Italy had been driven out of Greece in a humiliating setback for Mussolini, who had boasted that he would resign from being Italian if his forces had any difficulty achieving victory there. Despite his other efforts to demonstrate the importance of Italian military prowess to the German alliance, any victory that Italy might want to claim was, in fact, due more to the superior weaponry of the German forces than it was to any strength found in Italian troops.

Looking back, trying to puzzle it all out, I know that those in the Italian military were as capable of fierce and brave defense as were soldiers anywhere. After all, the marksmen I knew best, the Bersaglieri, were recognized worldwide for their superior skills. Where along the way had Italy lost its spirit? Mussolini rose to power from Socialist roots that embraced egalitarianism for women, Jews, the poor and oppressed. The move to Fascism was made easy by the fears many Italians had of following what, to many in my parents' generation, looked to be the frightening outcome of the Bolshevik Revolution in Russia. We craved strong leadership that could forge a united Italy from all the feuding political factions. Mussolini had that vision. His speeches excited crowds. Everywhere we turned, he was celebrated in posters and in the newsreels that were shown prior to every feature film in the Italian cinema. Our country seemed to flourish under his guidance, but no country operates in a vacuum.

When a person is hailed by cheering masses lining whatever route he travels, perhaps it becomes too easy to believe that mistakes are impossible. While Mussolini's faith in his own infallibility grew, the rest of the world was choosing up sides. He had no special admiration for Hitler and once had privately mocked him as "a silly little monkey," but when Mussolini's dream of returning Italy to borders reflecting the Roman tradition seemed to get a more sympathetic hearing from the German Axis, the resultant compromise with that force began to tarnish his formerly grand vision. Once the choice was made, a simple desire to reclaim territory gradually drifted toward something that the Italian people found less compelling. I suspect our soldiers were beginning to question the turn their dreams had taken.

As early in the conflict as late 1940, Italy's invasion of Egypt had been reversed by British Commonwealth forces that drove it far back into Libya. Libya! Italy's Fourth Shore. The colony my family now called home. We had failed to claim Egypt, but in the battle to drive Allied forces back out of Libya, the Axis could claim at least temporary victory. However, not even in Libya, did the praise go to Italian forces. All the glory went to General Erwin Rommel, the Desert Fox. In 1940 and 1941, German and Italian forces pushed the British troops out of Libya and into central Egypt. By 1942, Italy officially controlled large amounts of territory along the coast of north Africa. However, credit for the victory Mussolini claimed was described in the worldwide press as due to superior German tanks and other weapons under the experienced command of Rommel.

Despite the success in Libya, and no matter who claimed the credit, by 1942 the war was not going well for the Axis forces anywhere. At one time, Italy had the fourth largest navy in the world, but British airstrikes crippled Italy's major warships in a surprise attack at Taranto. The Italian economy failed to adapt to wartime demands, and its citizens grew impatient when the growing prosperity promised by Mussolini couldn't satisfy even the most basic of their everyday needs. Allied bombs were beginning to fall on Italian cities.

But they had not fallen on San Remo, and our new guardian, Signorina Fogliadella, greeted us in our first assembly with every confidence in the rightness of the path before us. Her words were not unfamiliar, "You are the future of the Fascist State. You, unlike less-privileged others, understand that all human and spiritual values are encompassed by the state." She turned to survey the children now under her care. "You are the true Italians, the complete citizens, and the face of *il Duce's* grand vision."

I did not doubt her, but something in her manner frightened me. Perhaps it was my still fresh memory of being greeted by Signorina Turra, who had worn her uniform with such slender grace. The uniform hadn't changed, but on Signorina Fogliadella it assumed a military aspect that made me uncomfortable. Proud of my father's history, I liked being a soldier for Mussolini. So why did our new guardian's manner of dressing make me afraid? Because for the first time, I sensed that she could use her authority against us. From the very beginning, it was apparent that she was a strict disciplinarian. A stocky woman, she never softened the set of her jaw with a smile. Her posture was rigidly straight, her legs like posts jammed into clunky black shoes that laced up tight. White blouse, black skirt, coat, and stockings. More than her clothes, her hair conveyed an attitude that would not yield to any excuse or influence. When Signorina Turra leaned down to better hear what a shy classmate was trying to express, her shoulder-length waves fell forward as well. Signorina Fogliadella's hair was bound in braids that wrapped so snugly around her head that I imagined even she must feel some pain from this no-nonsense approach to grooming.

San Remo may have been caught in a perpetual spring of warm days and cool nights, her trademark carnations may have filled the air with the sweetly spicy aroma of cloves, the London Hotel may have been surrounded by palm trees, but I sensed some chilly uneasiness in the local population. Kids don't talk about things like that. I told myself everything was okay, that I was just afraid of attracting the attention of Signorina Fogliadella. My cousins, Umberto and Antonio, were assigned to the Mira Mare Hotel just across the street from us. When I caught sight of them, rather than calling out a greeting as I might have done in Fiera di Primiero, I simply gave a curt nod of my head and, keeping my arms still at my side, managed a wave so small that I could have denied the intent had I been challenged.

Our familiar routine needed no explaining. By now I was so accustomed to waking at six, making my bed, washing, getting dressed, and lining up ready for breakfast in fifteen minutes that it seemed almost as if I had time to spare. It was as if nothing had changed, but then one day our already strict schedule became even more tightly focused. For weeks, every inspection demanded a meticulous attention to detail. Every hair had to be in place. Every bandolier exact in the cross it formed across our chest. The covers on our beds had to be tucked in as tightly as the skin on a drum. The courtyard where we performed our drills and exercises was swept so clean that not even the smallest of stray leaves escaped notice. Every march had to be in precision step. Our legs moved in such regimented formation, it was as if we were formed of a single body. In saluting, our right arms rose rigid as steel from our shoulders. No voice could falter in our loud praise. *"Viva il Duce! Viva il Re!"*

What was driving this push for near-impossible perfection? We were told the reason only on the morning of the event which had put even our director and supervisor in a frenzy for weeks. Mussolini himself was coming to review our squadrons. As soon as the director made the announcement, we burst into excited applause. "Quiet. Quiet," he commanded. "Today more than any other, we must demonstrate our devotion to discipline." We fell immediately silent. He glared sternly around the auditorium before continuing. "Obey because you must obey." We had heard this quote from Mussolini a great many times. After a significant pause that gave all he had said time to sink in, the director continued. "With our obedience, we give to *il Duce* the gift of our hardened will."

We needed no further reminders. Once outside, we lined up in tight and flawless formation in front of the London Hotel. We could hear the hoof beats of *il Duce*'s horse even before the first of his retinue turned the corner. I stood as tall and straight as it was possible to stand without going on tiptoe. The instant the officers surrounding him began to march in our direction, it was as if an electric current filled the air. The director stood in front of us, with his head turned just slightly to one side. By the time he gave the signal, Mussolini had turned his horse so that he and the gelding were directly facing us. *"Viva il Duce! Viva il Re!"* we cried in proud unison. The horse's grey flanks quivered as its skin rippled over muscles frozen into a stiff posture almost as erect as my own. Its nostrils flared. Mussolini sat straight in the saddle and returned the salute in a simultaneous acknowledgment of his worth and ours. The horse now pranced in place and turned just enough to one side that I could see the gleam of

Mussolini's polished, mirror-smooth, knee-high boots. He rode with his heels pressed downward and his head raised. It was as if his gaze were focused on a distant mountain, and then he lowered it and scanned the assembled boy soldiers before him. Each one of us left the event convinced that *il Duce* had made brief, but nonetheless individual, eye contact. I felt certain he had seen directly into the devotion that filled my heart.

CHAPTER NINE

The Fading Italian Summer

School was not all drudgery. Anxious to reduce the rate of illiteracy, Mussolini had always been interested in education. In the early days of *il Duce*'s power, his Secretary for Youth Physical Education, Renato Ricci, sought out those with special expertise in how to shape the moral and physical development of young people. Ricci traveled to England to meet with Robert Baden-Powell, the founder of Scouting. Baden-Powell's ideas on the importance of exercise and physical fitness were incorporated into the curriculum. Ricci also met with Bauhaus artists in Germany. This emphasis on the importance of the arts as an influence on a society's way of life no doubt was responsible for the trips the children in the *GIL* schools made on weekends.

Looking back, it's tempting to believe that our exposure to painting, music, and sculpture was carefully orchestrated to enhance our appreciation of Fascist values. However, I remember little of what we actually saw once we arrived at our destination museums and theatres. Sometimes we went to the nearby city of Imperia, sometimes we traveled to Mentona, close to the border with France. It didn't matter where we were headed, getting there was the most exciting part. Brisolin, la Morgia, Airo and I had first bonded on a train ride, and our friendship seemed to find its highest expression when riding together on a bus. We laughed and bantered as boys do, the actual conversation mattering less than the relaxed spirit of our chatter. The one film that made a real impression on all of us was *The Wizard of Oz*. For weeks afterward, we risked incurring the wrath of Signorina Fogliadella by exchanging a secret signal whenever we thought we had the opportunity to do so unobserved. All it took was the quick exchange of a surreptitious click of the heels and we were transported, if not back to Kansas, at least back to the glory of that day and to Dorothy's happy ending. Why had our supervisors selected that particular film? What possible conclusion could they have expected us to draw from the exposure of the man behind the curtain? I guess they were more focused on the newsreels that preceded the film. I loved those as well. I'd now seen Mussolini in the flesh and never tired of hearing vast crowds roaring back in approval of his every word. I felt no envy for the masses of adoring followers. After all, those people were positioned far from the actual man, whereas I had been close enough to almost touch his horse.

In September of 1942, something happened that made me feel as if I might actually have the power to click my heels, make a wish, and end up back home with a new appreciation of all that had been left behind. From out of nowhere, my adult cousin Rocco Di Gregorio, Aunt Fiorina's son, suddenly appeared with all the paperwork needed to take Giovanni and me back to Campo di Giove to see my grandparents. I'm not sure how Rocco obtained the permits. There may have been some concern about how long my grandfather had to live; he did, in fact, die just five months after our visit, but no one told us at the time that his health was failing.

"Your permit is for exactly two weeks." Signorina Fogliadella did not seem happy about the unexpected turn of events. "Make sure that you report back here not one minute later than the time and date stamped on this document."

As I hastily gathered a few personal items to carry with me, Fogliadella's words meant almost nothing to me. I was going home. It didn't matter for how long. She would have no control over me once I was gone. Giovanni seemed as stunned by this turn of events as I was. Rocco was vague when we asked him how it was that we had been granted this return to our family. I suspected he didn't want to reveal too much while we were still near school property. However, even after we had reached the train station, he was similarly brief. When Giovanni and I pressed him about how things were in Campo di Giove, he said only, "The same, much the same." As we climbed on the train, I wondered who had secured our tickets. Probably Rocco's father, my uncle Eustacchio. He would have been able to arrange things because of his employment with the railroad, but by now I thought better of asking Rocco any more questions.

Giovanni finally gave voice to what was worrying me. "Is everyone all right?"

"Yes. All right." Rocco looked out the train window. "Times are hard. As always, times are hard." He scratched the back of his hand and I noticed how thin his wrists were. "Always hard, but with the war and all, harder still."

I pulled my sleeve down over my own wrist, suddenly aware that I had grown taller and stronger since Rocco had last seen me. I had inherited the lean figure of my father and grandfather, but, even so, I was uncomfortable that Giovanni and I appeared robust in comparison to our fully grown cousin.

At last I could see my mountains, the Apennine range. "We're almost home," I said.

When he heard my words, Rocco smiled at me in the old way. "It's good to see you again, Vittorio." He glanced from me to Giovanni. "Remember, no talk of politics. Even more than before. No talk of politics." He laughed softly, mostly to himself, and patted me lightly on the chest. "Pasquale is about your size. Best you borrow a shirt from him."

Giovanni raised his eyebrows. "And how about me?"

"Not to worry. Something of cousin Luciano's will fit you."

Suddenly I remembered how it had been before. How any talk against *il Duce* had to be spoken only behind closed doors. People had been arrested simply for challenging his vision. Not anybody in my town (we lived too far up in the mountains), but even my grandparents had expressed their reservations in quiet voices and never outdoors. Did they still feel the same? Hadn't Mussolini made things better for them now? Couldn't they see the wisdom of his path? But Rocco had said *No talk of politics*, and I heard the concern in his voice and knew Giovanni and I would honor his request.

Campo di Giove seemed strange without my parents in it. Even our home was too large, too quiet. My grandfather was much older than I'd remembered. When I first walked through the door, he beckoned me over to where he sat in the corner. "Ah, Vittó." He smiled. "Ah, Vittó, it is good to have you back." My grandfather was the only one who called me by this diminutive, and hearing the name of my childhood spoken in his now whispery voice made me long for all that I'd had and for all that was now missing.

Everyone was eager for news of our family in Libya, but we could tell them only a bit from the brief time we had spent there in 1939 and early 1940, and that felt like a lifetime ago. I found it hard to describe the fine home and well-stocked cupboards that had been waiting for us in Garibaldi, when it was clear that things in Campo di Giove were even more difficult than they had been before we left. I found myself focusing on the birth of Ada and the smallness of her hands.

Suddenly I understood why Rocco's answers had been so short. Conversation did not flow with the old ease. When our two weeks were up, after we'd dressed once again in our uniforms and were ready to return to school in San Remo, a photographer took a picture of Giovanni and me standing with our grandparents. It's the only time my grandfather ever had his picture taken, the only likeness of him we have. I have given it to my son Steven for safekeeping. It's very precious, the four of us looking at the camera. That silent image holds much of what was true about our two weeks at home in September of 1942.

CHAPTER TEN

Not in Kansas

Typical of the nature of our education in Mussolini's boarding schools for the children of Libya, we didn't stay in San Remo long. In late April and early May of 1943, we moved to Igea Marina, a county in the Province of Rimini, on the east coast of Northern Italy. Giovanni, Umberto, Antonio, Brisolin, la Morgia, Airo and I gathered our few possessions and climbed on the bus with hundreds of other children. Signorina Fogliadella was coming with us. As I studied her stern face, I remembered Signorina Turra's inability to travel with our squadron from Fiera di Primiero, and I wondered for the first time if it was really official duty that kept her there or if she had more personal reasons.

Built close to the ocean, the building that housed our new school had once been a naval hospital, and its grand structure reflected the proud glory of Italy's maritime history. I was fascinated by the architecture. Who would have thought that four floors could be connected without the use of stairs to join them anywhere? Huge spiraling ramps were obviously designed to make it easy to push someone in a wheelchair—or even a bed—from floor to floor. It would have been just as easy and a lot more fun for us kids to run up and down them, but we were too disciplined to risk trying.

As part of its conversion to a school, the hospital had been renamed *Ventotto Ottobre*, Twenty-eight October, a tribute to the date when Mussolini first took power. Everything associated with the schools—our lessons, our uniforms, the songs we sang, the posters in the halls and classrooms, the slogans we repeated—everything served to reflect the glory of *il Duce*'s Fascist plan for Italy. Above the front door of the school, a beautiful marble carving of the *fascio* (the bunch, the very same symbol that was embroidered on the badge that was stitched to the front of our shirts), reminded us that many pieces of wood bound tightly together around the authority of the ax were stronger than any individual alone could be. It was everything I had been taught; it was everything I had learned; it was everything we children still believed. However, not even marble can hold an ideal in place when the people it represents begin to question what it stands for, what it really means.

*

Five years later, I would learn from my sister Giovanna what had happened to my family in Garibaldi in the very month when the children of Libya traveled from San Remo to their new school in Igea Marina. My mother and father and two sisters were also moving in May of 1943, but theirs was a far more desperate and violent relocation.

I didn't find out what really went on in Libya until after my return to that country in 1948. The fighting was over. We had all suffered much. I knew my parents were no longer living on the farm in Garibaldi. They had lost their first home during the war. I had heard the rough outline, but I still had not grasped the full story.

On May 10, 1943, the fragile claim Italy had had along the Mediterranean in Libya was shattered by revitalized British forces. The English were forcing a retreat of the German and Italian troops in the area. How strange war is. All that my family had worked so hard to build in our first settlement, now our own soldiers and German allies rushed to destroy in order to keep the homes, crops, land, even the water from offering any kind of support or shelter to our enemies. The wonderful well that once stood behind our first Libyan home—gone. Everything trampled, demolished.

My father's main concern was to get what was left of his family to safety. Only my father and mother and two sisters remained in Libya. Giovanni and I were enrolled in the *GIL* school in Igea Marina. Guerino was off serving as a telegraph operator for the Italian army in an area somewhere between Sudan and Nigeria. Gennaro had been recruited by the military not long after war was declared and, at the time of the retreat, no one knew of his whereabouts. In fact, he had been captured by the Americans and was detained as a prisoner of war at Camp Stanley in Taunton, Massachusetts.

My sister Giovanna remembers our father standing in the middle of the road trying to flag down the fleeing troops, pleading with them to take his family to Tripoli where things were rumored to be still quiet. Trucks and tanks swerved to pass him on either side. Their tires sent dust and gravel flying as they veered off into the berm in an effort to avoid running over my family.

"We could hear the bombs exploding," Giovanna told me. "Could see the hot flashes of fire and light not far from where we stood." She paused in her story. "It got so bad that we were dodging shrapnel, and still no one stopped. Only when little Ada caught a piece of flying metal in her finger did our father's despair grow so evident that a truck filled with Italian soldiers hit the brakes and pulled us in with them."

Ada was only three years old and her finger was so badly damaged that it never grew to its full length. My parents and two sisters rode to a military camp in Tripoli with the soldiers who had rescued them. While staying there, my family became quick friends, in the way that you do in the midst of war, with an Italian soldier, Mario, from Rome. On learning that my father hoped to reach Giordani, Mario told him he was headed to Azzizia, a city halfway there, and could take them that far. My father quickly agreed, since finding transportation of any kind was hard. He had hoped that the fighting would be less intense around Azzizia and that it would be easier to hitch a ride from there. However, he was wrong.

"I have seen our father cry only two times," Giovanna told me. "And both of them were when he was pleading for his family's safety." She paused before continuing. "Mario was authorized to go only as far as he had promised and then he had to return to the military camp. Once again, we were left in the middle of the road." Giovanna is ten years older than I am, but as I watched her tell the tale, I could see how terrifying it must have been for a young woman to sense her father's inability to do the one thing all fathers feel bound to do: keep their loved ones from harm.

In Azzizia it proved even more difficult to get someone to stop than it had been in Garibaldi. "The Italian soldiers wouldn't even glance in our direction," Giovanna told me. "All of us were waving. Ada's entire arm was already beginning to swell as a result of her wound. Má steadied little Ada on her hip with one hand while trying to hail someone down with the other. The retreating vehicles had raised so much dust that the history of our father's tears was clearly written on his cheeks."

"Finally a truck commanded by two blond German soldiers took pity on us." Giovanna's face softened at the memory. "They took us all the way to Giordani, where the Del Mastro family lived. It was as if there were no war there. All was quiet. How kind those two soldiers were. I can't remember their names, but they gave us a photograph of the two of them posing together." She shrugged her shoulders. "Do you think they remember that day as clearly as I do? I wonder if they even survived the war."

*

Although I was puzzled by the subtle shift in the way the students were treated by the population of San Remo, I was still able to convince myself that Mussolini's vision of a proud Italy, both united and expanded, continued to have the support of our people. However, by the time we arrived in Igea Marina, it was clear that something was very wrong. I just wasn't sure what. German planes flew over the city on their way south. This was a new development, and we wondered what sort of exercises they might be performing. Even when Signorina Fogliadella cautioned us to listen to her and ignore the aircraft, she spoke in a softer voice. We stayed close to the buildings where we slept and attended classes. Posters displaying a German soldier reaching out his hand—*"La Germania è Veramente Vostro Amica"*—were ripped from the walls where they had been nailed. It seemed no one any longer believed that Germany was truly our friend.

There were whispers among the students. When the bus transporting us to the west coast made what seemed to be an awkward detour, one of the older boys said something into the ear of his companion that quickly spread through the carriage. "They don't want us to see evidence of Allied bombing." We all wanted to blame Hitler. "He has betrayed us," we told each other after the lights had been turned out and we were tucked into our beds. It was all Hitler's fault. The war was never supposed to land on Italy's shores. Not one of us was willing to consider that *il Duce* had done anything to hurt his people. We'd all seen the films and knew we weren't alone in our adoration. Didn't everyone support him?

We learned the answer to that question early one morning in September of 1943, only a few months after our arrival in Igea Marina. We'd just finished breakfast and were on our way to class, when we heard what sounded like a large crowd of people shouting words we couldn't understand. As we turned the corner, we saw what all the commotion was about. An angry mob was attacking the marble fascio above the schoolhouse door with sledgehammers. The *Ventotto Ottobre* sign had already been ripped from its posts.

"Noooo," we began to wail. "No! No! Stop, please stop," we cried. Hundreds of young voices rose in anguished protest of the violence.

On hearing our screams, the mad herd turned and charged for us in the full fury of their rage. Children were pushed to the ground or fell in their attempts to escape this teeming onslaught. Some got stepped on. Most were crying. We had no understanding of what was happening to us or what we might have done to incur the wrath of all these people. It was as if they had been waiting for us to show up, because many in the crowd were armed with scissors and moved with such determination that it was clear what they planned to do with them. Grabbing us one by one, they pulled our shirts away from our bodies and furiously cut our beloved badges with the Fascist symbol from our shirts. I was just ten years old and was certain I would be killed before I found a way to escape. A pair of shears that showed so little hesitation in cutting away my clothing could just as easily be used to pierce my heart.

Suddenly we heard the repetitive beeping sound associated with police, but there were no police. Filled with anti-fascist contempt, these stewards of the state had weeks ago turned on their own government. All authority figures seemed to be gone except for a man with a loudspeaker who had run to the top of the steps and was shouting to the crowd. "Stop immediately. Stop immediately, or I will personally lock you up."

At first I thought he might be addressing the children of the school. Apparently I was not alone in my reaction; because accustomed as we were to obedience, there was a momentary pause as the students from my school looked to the man with the megaphone, waiting for his next command.

He had the attention of the crowd as well. As soon as everyone had quieted down enough for him to continue, I understood that he was here not to further harass us, but to protect us from the angry townspeople.

"What has Italy become when its people are reduced to attacking unarmed children?" He shook his head in disbelief. "These young people did not start the war. Don't turn your rage on them. They are mere children and as long as they are here in Igea Marina, they are under my protection as much as are any of the citizens I represent." I then realized that the gentleman who was bringing the riot to order was the local *podestà,* or selectman.

There was an almost stunned silence, which gave our guardian time to come forward and gather her charges together. "Follow me," she said briskly. "We will return to our building and wait there until your parents can be notified."

The townspeople let us go. Some of them were shaking their heads and looking at their hands as if they couldn't comprehend what they had done. Others continued muttering under their breath. We children all crowded together. The bigger boys helped the little ones who were still crying. Not able to grasp what had just happened, I felt very frightened. What had we done to make these people so angry?

Signorina Fogliadella demonstrated her loyalty to us in a way that I have come to view as heroic. She actually shed tears when she explained what had triggered the riot, but she vowed not to leave our sides until every single child from this one of Mussolini's schools had been picked up by relatives still remaining in Italy. She gave a list of all the names and addresses to the *podestà,* and the two of them combined efforts to locate family members. When no living relatives could be found, strangers sometimes volunteered to give the children shelter. Not all of the citizens of the town had been represented by that mob; others demonstrated extreme kindness. In the meantime, none of us was allowed to leave the building where we ate and slept.

In late July of 1943, King Vittorio Emanuele III (the one who inspired my name) had initiated a campaign to remove Mussolini from power. In this action, he was supported by even the Fascist Party's Grand Council. On July 26, Mussolini's ouster was official, and he was replaced by Marshall Pietro Badoglio. Immediately following the formation of the Badoglio government, the Fascist Party was outlawed and Mussolini was arrested. It was in telling this piece of the story that Signorina Fogliadella was unable to stop her tears. "We never wanted war," she told us. "This war was never in our plan." She turned her head and noisily blew her nose. "Look at what your parents have accomplished in Libya. This was the vision *il Duce* embraced. This was the vision we all embraced. Unity and a return to the glory of Roman days, for everyone, for the people of Italy and for the Italian Arabs, as well. Remember, they gave *il Duce* a ceremonial sword in appreciation for all he had done for them." We were somber. Kids aren't used to seeing grown-ups cry, especially not the stern Fogliadella. "This war is Hitler's doing."

No wonder the posters declaring that the Germans were truly our friends had been torn down. I think the older boys among us sensed, perhaps more clearly than even our guardian, that we could no longer call Mussolini "*il Duce*." He had been arrested. The Fascist Party was outlawed. Some sympathetic townspeople were donating clothing for us to wear, as our school uniforms would not be accepted anywhere.

It was only after we'd been attacked by the angry mob in early September, that anyone informed us of the momentous change of government that had occurred at least six weeks before. Why was there such a delay? Perhaps those dedicated to the Fascist Party were unable to grasp that this change was permanent. Whatever the reason, Signorina Fogliadella's words turned our young worlds upside down. Not only had we lost our leader, but the whole nature of the war had changed. On July 27, the Fascist Party was outlawed. On September 8, 1943, the Kingdom of Italy withdrew from the German Axis and joined forces with the Allies in their battle against Nazi Germany. On learning that the armistice with the Allies had been signed, people in Southern Italy where the German presence had been most brutal, took to the streets chanting, "*Viva la pace*." Long live the peace. It was a very different slogan than the one with which we were used to beginning and ending our days. It was a whole new war. With just a few quick strokes of the pen on a piece of paper, former friends became enemies, and the man who had marched through the newsreels accompanied by the sound of cheering crowds was imprisoned in a mountain hotel.

Uncle Ercole and Aunt Cristina came to get me and Giovanni almost immediately. She was the one person I could always count on, and this time when she opened her arms to us, I needed no urging before running into them. Umberto and Antonio seemed almost in shock as they walked to meet our cousin Rocco, who was coming to take them back to Campo di Giove, not for a two-week visit as he had done with my brother and me, but for good. Our grandfather had died since Giovanni and I had made the trip from San Remo to see him. Umberto and Antonio would be living with our seventy-five-year-old grandmother in the home where my family and I had once lived. I felt lucky that Aunt Cristina and Uncle Ercole were taking us back to their place. Hadn't that terra-cotta-colored dwelling positioned so prettily above the railroad tracks been the home I'd pictured in my dreams ever since the first time Aunt Cristina had visited me so long ago in that first school in Corbola?

As we were walking toward the train station with my aunt and uncle, Giovanni swooped down and picked up a weather-beaten flyer that had blown into the corner of a deserted doorstep. Uncle Ercole reached out his hand and took it from my brother. "It has become a war of paper dropped from the sky." He turned the tattered document over. "We'll read this after we get home." Folding it carefully, he stuffed the notice into his pocket.

He waited until we were on the train to tell us that, as of the end of July, all railway and post office employees had been militarized. Since Uncle Ercole worked for the railroad, keeping the two miles of track that ran in either direction from his cottage in good repair, he was unsure what impact this militarization would have on him. "Perhaps none," he laughed. "No one really seems to be in charge now, and we live so far in the mountains that I doubt government agents will come calling."

Suddenly I was very anxious to be back under the shelter of the Majella Mountains. I looked at my uncle. "The people attacked us," I told him. I opened my mouth to say more, but was stopped by the sorrowful shaking of Aunt Cristina's head.

"It wasn't you," said Uncle Ercole. "It wasn't meant for you." Ever the railroad man, he brushed some dust from the back of the seat in front of us. "It's happening all over Italy, in towns everywhere. Riots against the Fascists." The corners of his mouth pulled into a deep frown. "It wasn't you. It wasn't your fault." He reached out and patted my knee. "They just went nuts. People want something to blame. Crazy. Crazy. Picking on innocent children."

Before we went to bed that night, Uncle Ercole gathered us all together so he could read the leaflet Giovanni had picked up from the street. Aunt Cristina sat beside him and looked at Giovanni and me and at her two sons, Luciano and Tonino, the one who was going to become a priest. She started to speak, "Don't you think it's too soon..." When she hesitated before continuing Uncle Ercole cut in.

"It's the quickest way to bring them up-to-date." He didn't look happy. "Vittorio and Giovanni haven't really been told what is happening to our country." He gestured toward the mountain range behind him. "Tomorrow is time enough for some of it." He tapped his thigh decisively. "But tonight we'll read the message our new allies, the English, are sending to Italians everywhere."

He smoothed the wrinkles from the paper. "Here's the title: 'Out with the Germans—or Fire and Steel.' This was taken from one of Churchill's speeches." He looked at me. "Do you know who Churchill is?" When I nodded, he started reading. Everything was written in the Italian language. "The keystone of the Fascist Arch has fallen...we may reasonably expect very great changes...I cannot doubt that the main wish of the Italian people is to be rid of the Germans and restore their democratic institutions." At this point Uncle Ercole explained that, in fact, the people of Palermo had given a rousing welcome to the Allied troops when they marched into the city. He studied the words carefully. "The choice lies with the Italian people. If, however, the Italians have not the will or the courage to free themselves from Germany, we shall continue to make war against Italy from every corner, by land, air, sea...Italy will be covered with scars and bruises from end to end."

Uncle Ercole stood up and paced a bit. Then he looked at us and continued his explanation. "In this speech, Churchill told his parliament that when the Germans occupied a territory, they made the mistake of destroying all forms of local authority. So," Uncle Ercole said, referring to the words on the paper in front of him without really reading them, "Churchill says he doesn't want to reduce Italy to anarchy and have no authority left with which the English can deal."

He snorted a bit. "He wants an unconditional surrender. Unconditional! As if Italy has no pride and can be treated as a minor player, almost as a child."

Aunt Cristina stood up and walked over next to him. "The boys are tired. It has been a long day." She rested her hand on her husband's forearm. "Can't this wait until tomorrow?"

"I'm almost finished. Just a few more words." He looked at the flyer again. "Churchill tells us, 'the real enemy is Germany, the real point at issue is Hitler's destruction—and for this, unconditional surrender is necessary. The affairs of Italy must be handled with this supreme end constantly in view'."

(Note: The language quoted on the English flyer is as reported in *War in Val D'Orcia, an Italian War Diary: 1943–1944* by Iris Origo, © 1947. First published in the United States in 1984. David R. Godine, Inc., Boston.)

CHAPTER ELEVEN

Fire and Steel

Uncle Ercole and I were the first two up the next morning. I walked beside him to inspect what remained of his flower garden by the bubbling spring. September frosts were common at this altitude and only a few shriveled stalks were left. He crouched down on his haunches and with his head indicated the Majella range of the Apennine Mountains. "A lot has happened since we've last seen you, Vittorio." He rubbed his palms against his thighs as if cleaning off dirt, but there was nothing on them. "The Germans have occupied this portion of the mountain. Everything is fortified with cannons and machine guns."

I followed the direction of his glance, but could see nothing but the familiar fir trees and then the rock face of cliffs and deep ravines, above which towered the snow-covered peaks.

Uncle Ercole stood up and looked down the track toward the center of town. "It's a good thing Umberto and Antonio are staying with your grandmother." He shook his head. "She'd never seen an airplane before, and now fifty or more at a time go screaming overhead."

When he stopped talking long enough to massage the back of his neck, I interrupted, "Whose planes? The Germans?"

"No. The English. The fire and steel." He looked me solemnly in the eye. "The old people, the ones your grandmother's age, think the end of the world is coming." He gave up on the tendons in his neck. Raising one hand to his forehead, he moved his thumb and forefinger back and forth across it. "We all hear the bombs exploding and the gunfire hitting the ground when the bombs are dropped. So far no direct hits in the village, but the flying shrapnel is a threat, and the holes left in the ground can be even more dangerous." Again he paused to study me. "Be very careful, Vittorio. Be very careful."

"Do you think the Germans will come to hurt us?"

"They already have." He drew a deep breath. "Do you remember Matteo and Maria Di Marzio?"

Of course I remembered the Di Marzios. I knew everyone in Campo di Giove and hadn't been gone that long. "Sure. I know them. Why? Did something happen to them?"

Uncle Ercole nodded. "Almost." He pointed south. "The Germans have built a prisoner-of-war camp in Sulmona." Sulmona was a town about twenty miles from us.

"Are they locked up there? Did someone take them away?"

"No. But the English concentrate their bombing around that camp. They don't actually want to hit it. The prisoners are mostly English. The Allies don't want to kill their own countrymen, but when the bombing gets heavy the German and Italian guards fear for *their* lives and run to safety."

I broke in excitedly, "Why would the Germans punish the Di Marzios for giving shelter to the German and Italian guards?"

My uncle smiled a bit. "Whoa, Vittorio. You get ahead of the story. When the Italian and German patrols run from the bombs, they leave the camp unguarded, and it gives the British POWs time to escape."

Not quite able to believe what I was hearing, I asked, "Did the Di Marzios give comfort to our enemies?"

"It has all changed, Vittorio. Everything is topsy-turvy now." He reached to pat me on the shoulder. "The Germans have been very cruel. They don't have many friends left in Italy."

I remembered the posters of the German soldiers that had been ripped from the walls in Igea Marina and waited to hear the rest.

"Five English soldiers escaped the camp in Sulmona and headed for the mountains, but before they could reach their destination, daylight forced them to hide under a haystack in the barn with the Di Marzio animals." He looked at the rising sun as if to gauge whether or not he had time to finish his story before Aunt Cristina called us to breakfast. "Just a minute more. We'll sit on that little bench and enjoy the peaceful morning."

"Please tell me what happened," I urged.

"Well," he paused and looked puzzled. "Sides are changing up so fast that it's hard to know who you can trust. Somehow the German SS heard that Italians were hiding English soldiers in their home in Campo di Giove." He frowned. "They came straight to the Di Marzios' door, guns in hand, and didn't even bother to knock. They demanded to know where the English soldiers were. Matteo told them he had no idea, even though he knew full well they were in his barn!"

"Wasn't he afraid to get caught lying like that?"

"Well, it worked, at least for the moment. But the next day the Germans again came and again asked where the English soldiers were. Again Matteo told them he didn't know." Uncle Ercole stopped, and I leaned forward, afraid that Aunt Cristina would call before he finished.

"Uncle..." I prodded him.

He smiled just a bit, perhaps enjoying the suspense as much as I was suffering from it. "At that," he continued, "the soldiers grabbed Matteo, Maria, and Matteo's elderly parents and dragged them into the center of the town square. They lined them up and said, 'Tell us, or we will shoot you all, starting with her.' They pointed their guns at Matteo's mother. By now almost the whole village was watching and one brave youngster darted across the cobblestones and into the church to fetch the local priest, Don Vergilio."

"Who was the kid?" I asked.

Uncle Ercole just shrugged to indicate he didn't know and continued with the story. "As the priest slowly walked toward the SS, the commandant of the German troops came riding into town in the sidecar of a motorcycle. Putt, putt, putt. The sound of the engine turned everyone's attention from the imminent shooting to the approaching officer."

"And then?"

"And then the priest and the commandant had a discussion. No one could hear what they were saying, but after a few minutes, the officer spoke to his troops in German and they dropped their guns to their sides. As the officer climbed back into the sidecar, he addressed the town in halting Italian. 'We'll be back tomorrow.' However, by the time..."

Aunt Cristina stood in the doorway. "Come in now and get something to eat."

"Oh, Uncle, please..."

"Don't worry." He smiled at me as we walked across the tracks and up the little hill toward the house. "I'll tell you later. Everyone's all right. The Germans didn't shoot them. The Di Marzios are safe." Uncle Ercole put his arm around my shoulder. "And we'll be safe, too, Vittorio. I have made plans."

Breakfast was never a big meal in Campo di Giove, but I was surprised to notice how small the portions were. My aunt and uncle had always been better off than the rest of the family due to his regular employment by the railroad. Aunt Cristina had an oven for baking bread right outside her back door and, if I had expected the usual bounty, I was wrong.

"I don't bake as often," she explained, as she poured warm goat milk over the dry crusts. "Why alert the Germans to the fact that we have fresh loaves?" She smiled ruefully and glanced fondly at her husband. "Your uncle always loved the aroma of bread baking." She gave him a little nudge with her elbow. "In that at least, he is very like the Germans."

Aunt Cristina was almost like a mother to me. I also shared a special bond with Uncle Ercole, and now that I was living in their house, it naturally grew stronger. It wasn't just because I was the youngest. I don't know how to explain why some people are so drawn to each other. I was the youngest in the household, of course, but there was more to it than that. He was a man who used to yell at his sons, but he never yelled at me. He never yelled at me and he never yelled at my brother, Giovanni.

At night, even in that time of war, the older boys would have things they wanted to do as soon as it got dark. And Uncle Ercole would say to me, "Those guys, they all go out. Giovanni, Luciano, Tonino—they all go out, but you and me, we're going to go to sleep."

However, it usually was Aunt Cristina who went to bed first. Instead of going to sleep or at least instead of going to sleep right away, Uncle Ercole took that time to talk to me. It was after dark when I finally learned what happened to the Di Marzios. He picked up his story right where he had left off. "So, the Germans said they were coming back the next day." I nodded to let him know that I remembered and he didn't have to waste time telling me parts of the story I already knew. "Right," he said. "But that night, as soon as it got dark, Matteo and Maria crept out to their stable and loaded everything the soldiers had and every bit of food and supplies the Di Marzios could spare onto the back of a mule."

"Weren't they afraid the Germans would see them?" I asked. "Weren't they afraid that whoever had told the SS they were hiding English soldiers would see them?"

"Of course they were afraid, Vittorio. Of course they were. That's what makes what they did so very brave." He cleared his throat. "It doesn't take much courage to do something that has no risk." He looked at me to be sure I learned the lesson he was teaching, then he continued. "After helping her husband load the mule, Maria walked back to the house. The fewer people making this journey, the less attention they were likely to attract. And one thing about Matteo, he knows those mountains. No sheep under his watch ever got lost. He knows all the places where a sheep could hide. And he had an idea of a good spot where five Englishmen could find temporary shelter. So, he hid them right under the Germans' noses. They're still there and every two or three days someone from the Di Marzio family takes them food." My uncle shook his head. "It's not as if they have food to spare. It's not as if any of us have food to spare." He looked at me solemnly and put his finger to his lips. "Our secret, Vittorio. Careless words now have the power to end lives." He stood up. "Okay. Off to bed with you, Vittorio. Enough stories for one night."

*

It wasn't until after the war was over that I learned the full extent of the Di Marzio's courage. For a full year, they smuggled food enough to keep the English soldiers alive, smuggled it right past the German cannons and machine guns. In the summer of 1944, English troops occupied the other side of the Majella Mountain. German forces still held our side. When Matteo and Maria were certain the English presence was secure, they helped the five escaped prisoners of war climb up and over those snow-covered, Alpine-like peaks and reconnected them with their own people. Remember, these aren't small mountain ranges. Climbing them is dangerous in the best of times, but they smuggled the five men they had chosen to save through the German line, across unstable fields of snow, and guided them in their scramble up icy cliffs. It was always a compromise between the safest trail for climbing and the one that would best avoid the Germans.

In 1950, those five soldiers made their way back to Campo di Giove to personally thank the Di Marzios for what they had done. The British government honored them with the Gold Medal for Humanitarian Action. To this day, the Di Marzio family is remembered in every school child's curriculum as a proud example of Italian history.

*

Because of Uncle Ercole's position with the railroad, he was pretty good at sorting through the rumors that flew as frequently through town as the airplanes overhead. We heard so many things, most of them every bit as terrifying as the low-flying squadrons. It was still 1943, just a few weeks after Giovanni, my cousins, and I had been sent back from Mussolini's school, and the sense of imminent danger mounted every day. Uncle Ercole, some of his friends, and his brother Eustacchio would disappear at odd hours. When they didn't come back in time for Uncle Ercole to eat with the rest of us, Aunt Cristina would pace and look out the window, up toward the mountain.

"Where do you think he is?" I once ventured to ask.

"Shh, shh," she said, hushing me as if just asking the question somehow put us all in danger.

One day Uncle Ercole decided that the older boys—his two sons and my cousins, the ones who were living with my grandmother—should come with him when he went to whatever task was occupying him in the mountain range. We all knew the Germans were requiring Italian males of a suitable age to join the Axis forces in the battle against the Allies. We'd pretty much ignored those rumors since no one seemed inclined to enforce them in Campo di Giove. However, the reports were that if the Germans came to recruit a young man and he was missing, his parents could be shot. There were some places south of us where people swore this was true, swore it actually had happened. When Uncle Ercole tried to persuade Umberto to come work with him, my cousin refused, saying he didn't want his grandmother to suffer should the Germans come looking for him. Uncle Ercole tried to convince him that his grandmother was safe, since the records were so screwed up that as far as the Germans knew, he was still in Libya. But there was no persuading Umberto.

He should have listened. One day in October, Uncle Ercole came back from his trip to town with a grim face. "It has happened," he said, the anger bubbling just below the surface of a voice held in check by clenched teeth. "The SS officers came and recruited Umberto. They've taken him to serve with them in their war here in Italy."

There wasn't much food on the table that night, and it was just as well since no one had an appetite. Finally Uncle Ercole pushed his chair back. "We need to think about moving ahead with our plan."

"So soon?" Aunt Cristina questioned.

Uncle Ercole nodded. "The Germans are requisitioning the railroad houses in the towns below us." He walked to the door and stood looking out. "They'll fancy this location. We're on a hill with a good view of the mountains and surrounding areas." He inclined his head in the direction of the roof. "They'll install radio transmitters at the highest point."

Then he turned around and came back and sat down at the table with us. "You boys know where Pietransieri is, don't you?" We all assured him that we did, but he continued his explanation as if he hadn't heard us. "It's twenty-five miles from here, close to Roccaraso. About 1,000 people live there. Lived there," he corrected himself.

Aunt Cristina covered her ears with her hands, as if she knew what was coming and needed to be spared the details.

"Well, it seems three German soldiers were found shot dead just outside the town." He shook his head. "The work of partisans. They don't think about all the people they put at risk when they use retaliation to settle some score." He drew a deep breath, then slowly released it. "The next day German troops marched into town asking who had killed their comrades. No one knew. So they had all the townspeople line up outside in the main square and asked again who had been responsible. No one could answer their question. At that, they systematically began pulling every third person aside. Man, woman, child—it didn't matter. If you were third in line, they separated you out."

I felt like covering *my* ears, but it was too late. I knew what was going to happen next, and I'd already heard more than it was possible to comprehend.

"The Germans then shot to death three hundred people, right in front of their family members and friends." Uncle Ercole squeezed his eyes shut and waited a few minutes before continuing. "We know one family...I knew them. Both parents dead. Two kids under the age of nine left orphans. They watched their parents die. And when the Germans were finished with their carnage, they marched the remaining men at gunpoint and had them dig a mass grave, a trench large enough to bury three hundred people." He turned his hands palms-up. "Pietransieri is no more. Its people destroyed. And then it was bombed by planes, both German and English." He looked around the table. "There is no safe place. Not here. Not for us."

A week later, as if to prove the wisdom of Uncle Ercole's assessment of the situation, the top officers of the local German unit came strolling up to the door of the railroad house. We knew just what they wanted, didn't need to be told. They walked through the rooms as if we were already gone. They looked at us, and the commandant with one motion of the hand, almost as if brushing a troublesome fly from his path, said, "Away."

Aunt Cristina guided me and Giovanni upstairs. "Hurry. I know what you'll need. Just grab a few things."

The officer below repeated his command with more authority, "Away!"

Clutching almost nothing, we came back down. The commandant gestured to the front door. "Away."

I realized it was perhaps the only word of our language that he knew. As we joined Uncle Ercole outside, I looked back at the men who were laughing and joking as they picked up first one of Aunt Cristina's things and then another. How carelessly they tossed her treasures about. I could feel her stiffen beside me. "Come," Uncle Ercole turned her so that she could no longer see what they were doing. "We'll go stay with Grandmother Raffaela. She has only Antonio there with her now." In fact, and unbeknownst to me, Uncle Ercole had had the foresight to move some of their possessions down to the town center and up the stairs into the home where I had spent my childhood, a childhood already gone. I was now ten years old.

We were turned out of the railroad house in late October. In early November, German forces paid a visit to Campo di Giove. We could hear the convoy of trucks rumbling up the mountain. Even above the near-constant boom, boom, boom of bombs and cannon fire, we knew the trucks were coming for us. Twenty trucks at a time they came, surrounding the village, leaving no room for anyone to escape. The commandant traveled in the sidecar of a motorcycle just as he had done before, in the incident with the Di Marzios. Shouting orders in German, he directed his men to go through every house. Some were marked as suitable for German use for offices or storage space. Others they completely passed over, and they made no secret of their contempt for the ones they chose not to commandeer. I didn't need to understand German in order to read the body language of scorn. One of the officers who had a fair command of Italian stood with a megaphone in the town square and demanded that every family bring themselves and all personal belongings of any value and deposit them beside the fountain.

My uncle was not the only one who had seen trouble coming. Not far from us, whole villages had been destroyed, and everything the Germans thought they possibly could use had been seized. It had happened in other places. We had heard about such things going on in towns we knew. As a result, some folks had hidden the things they weren't willing to surrender to the Germans in hollow walls within their homes. The ruse didn't work for long. Any family whose contribution to the growing pile was suspiciously small was then accompanied back into the household by a German soldier. While the horrified folks who'd hoped to outsmart the Nazis watched, armed men made a great show of rapping on the walls to identify secret chambers. When the echoes were suspect, the Germans didn't hesitate before thrusting their bayonets through the walls. In the end, those guilty of trickery felt lucky that no family members had been hidden there, felt lucky to be getting away with their own lives. Suddenly, preventing a few precious keepsakes from falling into German hands did not seem as important as it once had.

They turned us out of our homes at gunpoint. Families clustered tightly together. I don't think I was the only one who wondered if we were going to be loaded into those trucks and hauled away to concentration camps, who wondered if we were going to die. Or would we be asked to line up and then pulled out—*every other person? every third?*—perhaps we would all be shot, no one spared. Aunt Cristina was doing her best to comfort my grandmother. The men stood stone-faced, humiliated by their inability to stop what was happening. Even above the muffled keening of the women, I could hear the clicking of rosary beads. The Germans must have heard it too, because they began laughing and calling to each other as they ran toward the little stables where we kept our animals and herded them out, a kind of reverse Noah's ark. What an odd assortment: a pig, a few goats, a sheep or two, squawking chickens, a cow, a mule that kicked when the Nazis slapped it on the rump. They took all those animals and drove them into the church, into our church, into our place of worship.

When they were finished, they turned to us and with the same *away* gesture the commandant had used at the railroad house, stood aside and let us pass through the town gate and into the fading light. What a pitiful-looking bunch we were. So shabbily dressed. Giovanni, my cousins—Tonino, Luciano, and Antonio—and I had followed Uncle Ercole's advice and pulled all the clothes we owned, not so very many, over our heads, one layer on top of the other. I looked at the German soldiers. Their uniforms were made of nice quality wool, their boots of fine leather. Boy, where did they get the money to outfit an army in that fashion? They had our houses. They had everything. We weren't allowed to take mattresses, bedding, clothing, cooking utensils. We were permitted to load only a few remaining personal items on the backs of a horse and a mule. Not one of us looked dressed to face the weather. It was November 11, 1943, and already snowflakes were swirling down. I wondered if the Germans would follow us to see where we were going. No one seemed to. I don't think they cared. I don't think they expected us to survive without food or shelter for long.

Once past the circled barricade of trucks, the population of Campo di Giove split into groups. Some had relatives they hoped to reach in nearby towns, assuming those towns were still standing. But a party of about five hundred people stayed together and followed my Uncle Ercole. The men talked to each other in hushed voices, occasionally glancing over their shoulders in the direction of our former home. Then Uncle Ercole dropped back to walk beside me. "It will be okay, Vittorio. Remember I once told you I had a plan to keep us safe."

CHAPTER TWELVE

A *Capanna* in Winter

At first we took the same path the sheep followed to their summer pasture, but as soon as we were out of sight of the town, we branched off. I shoved my hands in my pockets and, trying to keep the cold wind from finding its way inside my shirt, tucked my chin down close to my chest. Reassured by Uncle Ercole's words, I wasn't as afraid as I had been. The snow covered our tracks. No one would be able to follow us now. Suddenly, the well-trained soldier in me sensed the adventure in what we were doing. I was physically fit. Mussolini had seen to that. There was nothing in the cold and in the mountain that could stop me. Thinking of the Di Marzios, I was inspired by their bravery and knew that if five British soldiers could survive in the Majella range, I could too. This was, after all, my home. My father had enlisted in the Bersaglieri. The father of my great-grandmother (Filomena Perez) was a Spanish soldier who had served under Ferdinand II. Surely, the blood in my veins promised courage.

Hours passed. The mountain paths grew steeper. There was more snow in these higher elevations and walking became increasingly difficult. At times we had to bend very low to move under pine branches heavily burdened by the fresh flakes of the growing storm; but once we got under the trees, the ground was almost bare and it was easier to move forward. My cousins and I took turns helping our grandmother. When we hit a small break in the forest where the drifts were deep, Antonio and Luciano crossed their hands and gripped their own and each others' wrists in such a fashion as to form a seat on which she could ride. We thought of removing some of the items from the horse's back and having it carry our grandmother instead, but she seemed too frail to learn to ride now. We decided she was safer being supported by us. I had lost all sense of where we were. Was Uncle Ercole taking us into a part of the mountain where I'd never been before, or was it just that the snow had covered all the familiar landmarks?

Finally, the word traveled back to us. "We're almost there," Aunt Cristina said with relief. "Just a bit farther and we can stop." I felt proud of Aunt Cristina. Even the women in my family were capable of great strength when it was needed. She seemed to understand what was waiting.

Given the news that we'd reached our destination, I moved away from my grandmother and walked beside my cousin Pasquale. Anxious to see what was going on, we quickly made our way to the front of the weary travelers. There were a number of small clearings ahead, not natural clearings but ones that had been created by felling trees in the area. "Oh, boy," I said. "Now we know what Uncle Ercole and the other men have been busy doing."

Using logs from the harvested timber, the men had constructed an entire village of simple cabins. There were almost one hundred of these *capanne*. They were tucked under the remaining pines in such a way that nothing would be visible to planes flying overhead. Some of the buildings were large enough for several families to share, and some so small that only a few people would be able to inhabit them. Each shelter had a central beam with the canvas tarps used to cover the cargo on freight trains sloping down from it in a way designed to keep the buildup of snow from forcing its collapse. I clapped my hands in wonder at the foresight of my uncles who worked for the railroad. How long had it taken for the two of them to secure enough tarps to provide roofs for every hut in this new city in the mountains? Pasquale and I peeked inside one of the *capanna*. More heavy canvas borrowed from the freight cars covered the bare floor. In the center was an open fire-pit, already laid up with kindling and split logs. A wall of rocks surrounded the cooking area. It was clearly designed for cooking because someone had already constructed a tripod over it. I instinctively knew that this single pit would also serve as our only source of heat until it was safe for us to go back to Campo di Giove.

In peacetime, this wonderful hideout in the woods would have been a boy's dream. However, we were at war and this was clearly not a place for fun and games. "Wow," Pasquale said. "The men have thought of everything."

I nodded. They had. It was hard not to be impressed by the ingenuity of Uncle Ercole and the others. It was equally hard not to contrast the estate waiting for us here with the one Mussolini had prepared for my family in Libya. There were no stocked cupboards that I could see. No coupon books to use at the general store until the first crops came in. What would we eat? Just asking myself the question reminded my stomach that I was hungry. Almost as if he'd read my thoughts, Uncle Ercole led me to the large *capanna* that would be home to six families—the Palumbos, D'Agostinos, Di Marzios (close relatives of the ones hiding the British soldiers), Di Gregorios, and two branches of the Capaldos. "We've been smuggling supplies up here in anticipation of this day." He pointed to a series of containers lined up against one wall. "Corn meal, wheat flour, potatoes." Tucked in behind the provisions was a sixteen-gauge shotgun. "I've been known to hit a bull's-eye or two. There are rabbits and pheasants in the woods. A wild boar would feed us all for a while."

As the various families claimed their spots, Pasquale, Domenico, Rinaldo, and I set to exploring. The pride I felt in my uncle for being clever enough to arrange this *capanna* drove any comparison with the provisions in Libya into the background. My friends and I were caught up in the magic of discovering a little village created from out of nowhere. We followed a path leading from the circled clusters of cabins directly to a mountain spring. The spring's overflow fed into a stream that tumbled down from the higher elevation. "Water from a spring won't freeze," Domenico told us.

"The center of the earth is warmer than the surface," I continued Domenico's explanation.

Pasquale knelt down and dipped his hand into the water. "Vittorio's right. The water *is* warmer than the air." He started to dry his hands on his pants and then hesitated, knowing full well that wet clothing offers less protection from the cold than dry.

Rinaldo exhaled in such a way as to form a soft, grown-up sounding whistle. "They've thought of everything. We have our own little world here."

Just then cousin Tonino appeared on the path from the clearing. "Come on boys. We were looking for you. It will soon be dark. Time enough to explore tomorrow."

We went to bed without eating that night, but one of the women fetched water from the spring in a large pot. "Polenta in the morning," she said, pouring dry grain into the pot to soak overnight. "We'll put something in our stomachs when the sun comes up."

This became our pattern. Fires at night were too easily spotted and could invite airborne attack from either the Allies or the Germans. What little cooking there was would take place during the day when the scattered smoke could be confused with tendrils of fog rising from the mountain. Not knowing how long it would take for the war to end, we also didn't want to use wood unnecessarily. Although firewood had always been a commodity my family turned to when we needed to barter for wine or something we couldn't grow in the higher elevations, I was beginning to understand that it could be a scarce resource just like everything else.

That first night, Giovanni, Antonio, Luciano, Tonino, and I struggled to get comfortable on our canvas-covered floor. We heard the occasional echoes of cannon fire. Because it sounded far enough away to be of no immediate threat, I found myself more frightened by the rumbling of my stomach. Between that and the cold, I wondered how long we would be able to survive. Uncle Ercole seemed my most reliable source of heat; and, relieved that he offered no protest, I finally snuggled up against him and fell asleep.

The next morning, we studied each other as we groggily stood and watched the first flames give the reassuring pop and crackle that signaled that the fire had moved beyond the mere kindling stage and would soon start to build a steady heat strong enough to bring the water in the kettle suspended over it to boil. "Did you boys sleep?" Uncle Ercole asked.

It didn't seem like the time to complain about anything, so Giovanni and I both dutifully nodded yes.

Seeing through our pretense, he laughed. "It will get better. We'll get used to our new headquarters." He walked over and looked into the pot. It was just beginning to boil. "We'll all feel more awake when we've eaten something. In the meantime, there is this to say for our little *capanna*. I don't expect any German officers to turn us out so they can move in."

We tried to smile at his attempt at a joke, but there were still too many unanswered questions. Would the Germans come looking for us? Did they care that we were hiding out here? Would they leave us alone as long as we didn't bother them?

Domenico started to ask the question I most wanted answered, "How long...," but Uncle Ercole cut him off before he could finish.

"No one knows. We'll just have to wait and see how long it takes for the Allies to gain control."

I looked at him in astonishment. The Allies? Wasn't it their planes whose constant drone frightened my grandmother into thinking the world was coming to an end? "Whose side are we on now? Are we with the Allies?" I had heard the grown-ups talking about the fact that Mussolini had been rescued by German commando forces from the hotel where he had been under arrest. However, everyone seemed to agree that the newly established Italian Social Republic in Northern Italy was really just a puppet state, more under the command of Hitler than of Mussolini. Yesterday's still terrifying memory of being driven from our homes at gunpoint only made it clear to me why none of us could possibly join forces with the Germans. What was left of my once-glorious Mussolini dreams? They seemed to have evaporated and left nothing in their place. So much had gone wrong. Italy was in tatters.

"Four governments to choose from," Uncle Ercole said, "and not one I fully trust." He pushed his cap forward on his head. "The Badoglio government has let us down by agreeing to humiliating terms. Mussolini has only a few holdout supporters here and there. The rest of the country has turned against him. The Allies and Germans fight it out with little regard for those of us caught in the middle. I'll vote for whoever can end this bloody war."

Aunt Cristina was busy stirring the pot of polenta. "Politics is a luxury reserved for those with full stomachs," she said with a sharp note to her voice. "And that would not be us."

The other women murmured their agreement while one of them walked forward with a small pile of flat plates. The polenta was ready. As Uncle Ercole passed the portions of food around, he spoke almost under his breath. "Whose side are we on? Our own." He handed me a plate. "We watch out for each other now, Vittorio."

I nodded solemnly. "You've built a good hideout. The Germans won't find us here."

"Right," Pasquale agreed. "The Germans are the ones who can hurt us most."

And then we set to eating with a ferocious hunger that the amount of polenta on my plate did little to ease. Uncle Ercole watched us. When we were finished scraping our plates, he said, "In the future, eat more slowly. Your stomachs will learn to be satisfied."

After we'd eaten, the women cleaned up and prayed, while the men proudly showed us the makeshift village they had constructed. They'd built the camp close to water, but not so close that heavy rain or a spring thaw would flood us out. Spring, I thought to myself. We surely won't still be here then. Still, it was Uncle Eustacchio who had mentioned the thaw and since he was a railroad man like Uncle Ercole, I had to take his words seriously. Not even seeing Uncle Ercole send him a stern look in response to the mention of a March thaw could lessen the import of his words. Those who worked on the railroad seemed to be our best source of information about what was happening in the towns below us, about what was happening all over Italy. Uncle Eustacchio, who was Uncle Ercole's brother, was married to my mother's sister Fiorina, so they were related in a couple of different ways. The Di Gregorio brothers had married step-sisters and, in the process, had become brothers-in-law! Although Eustacchio didn't have Uncle Ercole's natural warmth, I happily claimed them both as mine. They were two men who knew how to build things, how to fix what was broken. If anybody could get us through this, they could.

Logs—the larger ones split, the smaller ones not—were neatly piled and stacked in such a way as to stay mostly dry. Nothing had gone to waste when they had felled the trees to make the clearings and build our shelters. We followed a path downhill from the settlement. The men had dug latrine ditches a safe distance away. Shovels were jammed into the loose piles of dirt that surrounded the latrines.

The horse and mule that had carried our belongings here were tied under the pines. The low-hanging branches formed their own shelter. I was astonished to see more than just a horse and mule. In the days before the Germans had forced our evacuation, the men of Campo di Giove had driven a small collection of animals into makeshift stables under the pines. Thanks to the three goats my family had hidden, we'd have a supply of milk. The hope was that regular milking would keep them producing enough for at least the small children and anyone who might happen to fall sick. Others had brought sheep with an eye to butchering them should wild game prove scarce. The Capaldo and Di Gregorio families had each smuggled a mule against their largely correct fear that the Germans would not allow us to take much livestock with us. The men had brought not only animals, but also the hay with which they would feed them.

Uncle Eustacchio gestured toward the mountain above us. "We've hidden caches of dried corn and beans where they'll be safe from hungry wildlife," he grinned before continuing, "and other *animals*." Pasquale and I nudged each other. We knew he was talking about the Germans. "I just hope our sheep will be safe from those same wolves. Their usual winter pastures in the Roman country have been occupied by others." The men had thought of everything. Prior to moving us into our makeshift mountain bivouac, they'd hidden sheep in small clusters partway up the mountain. Tucked in between and hidden by rocky outcrops, these tiny mountain meadows could each support only a few sheep. The hope was that they would use their sturdy hooves to paw through and find sufficient dried grass to survive the winter. Uncle Ercole looked at the sky. "I suspect I'm not the only one praying for a mild winter."

Wanting to reassure my uncle, to erase the worried look from his face, I said, "You did a good job. We'll be okay here." I only wished I felt the confidence my words expressed.

CHAPTER THIRTEEN

Polenta and Prayers

We survived that winter on little more than polenta and prayers. Nothing came easily. Not even the prayers. How could we hope for German defeat when Umberto had been recruited into the SS? My grandmother Raffaela's cheeks were often streaked with tears as she worked her way through the rosary. Umberto's brother, my cousin Antonio, grew more and more silent as the months wore on. The easy laughter that he and my brother Giovanni had shared was gone. One day, I watched as they stood together just at the edge of our encampment. Even though their backs were to me, I could tell they weren't talking. Antonio's head was down and he just kept kicking and kicking at the snow that lined the path that led to the shelter where the horse and mule were tied. Finally Giovanni patted him on the shoulder and the kicking stopped. Watching the two of them, I couldn't help thinking back to the day in Fiera di Primiero when I first learned my cousins and brother were staying in the hotel just across the street from me. How long ago it all seemed. I'd been so envious of the closeness the three of them shared, but that envy had all disappeared when we sat together in the lobby of the Hotel Roma. How eager they had been for news of Campo di Giove. I wished I had news I could share with them now. I wished I could tell them about the farm in Garibaldi, could make them laugh with tales of little Ada, and could describe in great detail the bounty of the harvest our fathers had brought to fruition.

But I didn't know how things were in Garibaldi. None of us did. Had the war in Africa gone as badly as the war in Italy? I didn't even know if all my family members were still alive. And supposing someone had found a way to send us news, no letter would ever reach us hidden away here in the mountains. I was very tired. None of us was getting enough to eat. My uncle's claim to be an accomplished marksman proved to be correct, but there was not much game to be found that difficult winter. Once he managed to get a fox, a kind of double victory since the fox was after the same rabbits and pheasants we were. Small game belonged to the *capanna* of the lucky hunter. Anything as large as a boar was shared with the entire village. But successful hunts happened rarely, and as the months wore on, the portions the women dished out became increasingly smaller.

Our garments hung on thin frames. Being the youngest boy in my family, I'd always worn the clothes my brothers had outgrown. Now it occurred to me that if it could be done without leaving the little ones naked, it would make more sense to pass the clothing up the line instead of down. Only a piece of twine kept Giovanni's pants from slithering down past his knees. Except for the length, my things would have fit him better than his own.

None of us even bothered to ask anymore if the war was over. We didn't have to ask, we just had to look and listen. Increasing numbers of German and Allied planes flew over us. Echoes of German cannon fire bounced off the mountain in such a way as to make it difficult to tell where it came from. There were days when I thought we might be completely surrounded. I wondered if so many bombs would be dropped on Campo di Giove that there would be no town left to return to when the war ended. *When the war ended.* It was a phrase that no longer held much promise. We had more immediate concerns: staying warm, getting enough to eat. I sometimes tantalized myself with memories of those Sunday dinners with my godfather's family there in Fiera di Primiero. How simple my life had been back then when my belly was full, and I knew just what to believe and there was no question of whose side we were on. I also worried about Umberto and wondered how much of our dream he had still believed when he went away with the SS. Perhaps there was more to his enlistment than a desire to keep our grandmother safe. Was I the one who lacked courage, who had too easily given up on all that we'd been taught? But then I reminded myself that Umberto hadn't seen what I'd seen. He hadn't been there when we were turned out of our own homes at German gunpoint.

But mostly I was too busy scratching the lice that seemed just as hungry as we were to have much time for trying to figure out the complicated politics that had turned Italy upside down in that winter of 1943-44. It was cold. Everyone was dirty. Because the spring was reserved for drinking and cooking, bathing was limited to quick splashes of water from an almost-always-frozen mountain stream. We were busy waging a campaign on three fronts: hunger, cold, and lice. In many ways, the hunger was the easiest thing to bear. My stomach seemed to have forgotten what it felt like to eat. It had given up even growling. One meal a day was all we had, and we felt lucky to get that. Our animals were starving too. Milk was so scarce that even the amount set aside for the little ones was diluted with water.

At first, we kids had made a game of packing snow around any cracks in the walls of our cabins. "There," we said as we pounded this natural insulation in between the rough logs. "That ought to keep out the cold." But, of course, nothing did and our enthusiasm for the project dropped off with the thaws that sometimes happened between storms. As the winter wore on, blizzards producing drifts as high as six feet would blow the snow in against the buildings in a way that actually helped to create a kind of barrier to the drafts that were almost guaranteed to force their way through any tiny breach in the log walls.

Even the women seemed to grow resigned to futility of combing through each others' heads in search of lice each morning. They became too easy to find. No matter what we did, the population of lice seemed to be the only thing that thrived there on the mountain. Early on, I'd followed Pasquale's lead in darting away whenever one of the matrons approached us with a comb. Later the two of us would mutter to each other. "Let the lice eat all they want. At least something will have a full belly." Scratching while we spoke, we concluded by saying, "Besides it takes more energy to kill them than they can eat in a day."

It was a battle we continued to wage, even though it became increasingly difficult to win. Once a week, before going to bed, the kids gave the clothes they wore to the women so that they could boil them. The women's hands were so red and cracked from exposure that they bled. Our shirts and pants froze stiff as they dried. Not even boiling the clothes fully defeated our unwelcome invaders, but it helped. Since these were the only clothes we had, we had to shiver naked in the *capanna* until they were dry enough to put back on. We huddled together like litters of hairless mice as our grandmothers wrapped themselves around us to hold in what heat our little bodies managed to generate.

The arrival of spring also helped. Just the fact of our survival was a victory worth celebrating. Never had the warmth of the sun on our skin been more welcome. Birdsong did more than lift our spirits, it also reminded us that we would soon be able to supplement our meager diets with eggs stolen from their little nests. Boys are good at climbing trees and even better at searching out the first April mushrooms hidden under last fall's dried leaves. As the world around us came to life, the watery liquid that had passed for soup during the worst of the cold suddenly seemed to offer real nourishment. Bits of dandelion, sorrel, wild arugula, and nettles offered both flavor and real nutrition. However, when gathering the season's first greens, we had to be careful to stay hidden at the edge of the forest. There were rumors of informers who would gladly risk the lives of their own countrymen in exchange with the Germans for a wedge of cheese—cut from one of the wheels our own grandmothers had made and that had been stolen from us when we had been turned out of our homes!

The whole country seemed to be starving. Whenever Uncle Ercole and Uncle Eustacchio left the *capanna* on one of their trips to bring back provisions—either from a secret cache or stealthily recovered from the Germans—they also brought news of the outside world. "We are better off than those living in the cities," Uncle Ercole told us. "Only the very wealthy or the very corrupt can afford to buy food in the cities." He smiled with pride. "We at least know how to survive without money." When he laughed before finishing his statement, even I could hear the bitterness mixed with the pride. "Generations of poverty have taught us something."

In fact, he spoke the truth. Inflation was out of control all over Italy. Thin as we were, we were better off than many of our countrymen. The level of desperation was so great that anyone who looked well-fed was considered suspect.

By late May, my uncles didn't have to leave our *capanna* in order to get news of the outside world. It came floating to us down from the clouds. Rinaldo was the first to notice. "What's that?" He pointed to the bit of sky above our little clearing. We all squinted. Snow? It was too warm for snow, but there was definitely something white fluttering in the air not far from where a German plane had just passed overhead. We waited until we got a sense of which way the wind was going to blow the mysterious bits of what now looked to be paper. Then the four of us—Rinaldo, Domenico, Pasquale, and I—dashed off in what we thought was the proper direction. "I saw it first," Rinaldo cried. "I get to tell what it is."

Only a few scraps had made their way to the forest floor. The others remained stubbornly lodged in the pine trees. Given that paper was, in and of itself, valuable, Rinaldo, Domenico, and I scrambled up through the trees, grabbing the pitch-covered branches in close to the trunk. The jagged remains of dead twigs that had broken off years ago stabbed and scratched us. Leaning far out to reach pieces that were just beyond our reach, our movement sometimes dislodged them enough that they floated down to Pasquale who was busily gathering everything that had made it to ground level. Once back down, we compared notes. They were all the same. Knowing they were from the Germans added an extra bit of laughter to the jokes we made about using them in the latrine. Then it was back to share what we had found with the grown-ups.

Respecting Rinaldo's claim of first spotting rights, we let him be the one to hand a sample to Uncle Ercole. He read silently to himself before motioning the others in to hear what it was the Germans wanted to tell us.

"Whoever knows the place where a band of rebels is hiding and does not immediately inform the German Army will be shot. Whoever gives food or shelter to a band or to individual rebels will be shot. Every house in which rebels are found, or in which a rebel has stayed, will be blown up. So will any house from which anyone has fired on the German forces. In all such cases, all stores of food, wheat or straw will be burned; the cattle will be taken away; and the inhabitants will be shot."

I interrupted my uncle's reading. "Are we rebels?"

"I wouldn't worry, Vittorio. My sixteen-gauge wouldn't be much of a threat to the German Army." He gestured at what was left of the ragged population of Campo di Giove. "We don't look like a very dangerous bunch." Uncle Ercole raised his eyebrows and shook his head. "Besides, if I remember correctly, they've already taken our food, destroyed our homes. Not much left for them to do but shoot us, and I'm not sure it would serve them to waste bullets on the likes of us." He held the paper out in front of him and finished reading. "The German Army will proceed with justice, but inflexible hardness." He handed the paper back to Rinaldo. "We know all about the inflexible hardness part, but we're still waiting to experience the justice they promise." Looking angry, he gestured toward the latrine. "I think I overheard you boys describing how we can best put this information to use."

Only a week or so later, Allied planes had their own advice to give the people of Italy. This time the notes were found by the women when they were out gathering greens to add to the soup that had become our regular fare.

Once again, Uncle Ercole assumed the job of reading the leaflets to the rest of us. "At all costs refrain from reporting yourselves to the Army. Commit acts of sabotage on communication lines. Enter into contact with the foreigners in the German Army. Go on organizing groups. The moment for decisive action is near at hand." He handed the paper back to the woman who had given it to him. As she smoothed it out and carefully added it to her collection, Uncle Ercole summed up his view of the situation. "It sounds to me as if the war is not going well for the Germans. (The language on these flyers is taken from Iris Origo's, *War in Val D'Orcia, an Italian War Diary: 1943–1944*.)

Flowers bloom even in wartime. Birds sing joyfully through the air. Sunrises and sunsets gloriously hold to their expected rhythms. Spring moves toward summer. Pastures turn green. Sheep that have survived the cold graze without regard for politics. We had come through the worst of it.

However, the worst of the battle was still facing the Germans. By August, the truth of Uncle Ercole's assessment became obvious. Apparently Campo di Giove wasn't considered worth fighting for. Hidden at the edge of the woods, we watched while they loaded their trucks and got ready to move to where the combat was more intense. Even though the Germans did not surrender in Italy until May of 1945, by August of 1944, they had moved away from the towns and mountains surrounding the Abruzzo region in the Province of L'Aquila. "It's time for us to go home," Uncle Ercole said as the last of the German trucks disappeared from view.

CHAPTER FOURTEEN

Picking Up the Pieces

We packed up our few belongings and headed back toward our old homes. It's funny how we hesitated at the edge of the forest. I felt like a mouse afraid of running out into an open field where I might be seized by a hawk. But then Uncle Ercole assured us that he and a few of the other men had scouted the area, the Germans were gone, and it was safe for us to reclaim our town. Someone drove the few sheep that had survived their winter hiding places ahead of us. Our three goats were miraculously still alive, as were the D'Agostino's two horses, Rocco's mule, and one of the two draft animals the Capaldos had brought with them. It was August. The pastures at the lower elevations, ungrazed as they had been, had already gone to seed. One of the men gestured toward the waving grasses as we passed. "We should make hay, just in case the war isn't over and the flock has to remain up here through the winter months." The others nodded their agreement. "It will make better grazing once it's mowed and fresh growth gets a chance."

The flock. Were enough animals left to call it that? By concentrating on the fields, the easy part, the part that with just a bit of help could repair itself, the adults hid from the despair they felt on returning to homes that had been left the German way: destroyed. For some reason, maybe because it had been occupied by officers who'd come to feel it was their own, the railroad house had been spared the worst of the kinds of destruction that Grandmother Raffaela found waiting for her. Holes were punched in the walls, the windows were broken, the door kicked in. Aunt Cristina insisted that she and Antonio come stay with her and Uncle Ercole, but my grandmother would have none of it. "Antonio can fix it. Antonio can fix it," she repeated over and over. "The Germans destroy everything." She began to cry. "But Antonio can fix it."

Young as I was or maybe old as I was (eleven now), I understood the real reason for her tears and knew that not even my wonderful cousin Antonio could fix the thing, the person, my grandmother most feared had been destroyed. Sometimes we can't make ourselves give voice to that which most terrifies us. And, it may be true that by giving something a name, we give it a reality too brutal to even imagine.

And so, we set ourselves to the task of picking up the pieces. Men grabbed scythes hidden in some dark corner of the small sheds behind our houses and cut and raked the tall grasses. Once the sun had dried it, the hay was stored in anticipation of winter. Somehow it helped to be able to look at one place where order had neatly been restored. It helped to establish a rhythm, to believe that somehow the rest of our lives would fall into place. Slowly, hesitantly, the phrase, "When the war is over," began to creep back into our conversations.

Trying to remove the stain of the German occupation, the women grabbed brushes and scrubbed their homes until their knuckles bled. Borrowing material from houses that were truly uninhabitable, everyone worked together to repair those that could be saved. And so a life of sorts resumed. We were still hungry, but we had the fountain in the town square. The Germans had left in a hurry and had been unable to take everything with them. The women found the copper water jugs tossed here and there. We could resume bathing. Our neglected fields hadn't lain completely fallow while we were gone. Grain that had slipped away from us in last year's harvest had seeded itself, not in any sort of abundance, but we were able to forage enough that we nurtured what we found with a growing confidence in our survival skills. The roots of potatoes that had clung to the earth last year when we'd dug up those of a size big enough to eat had managed to send forth fresh plants. Their dark green leaves reminded us that life has its own force.

Anticipating the German invasion, the townspeople had buried some things close to home. Those secret caches were now located and treated like treasure. Any bit of food *was* treasure. The Germans may have been gone but the specter of hunger was not.

In those first months back in Campo di Giove, we worked to restore what had been lost to a year's worth of neglect. With very few resources other than our own sweat and ingenuity, we struggled to get ready for a winter that was all too fast approaching. And then something happened that made me believe in answered prayers, in miracles. One day in September of 1944, a lone figure showed up at my grandmother's door. He was in such bad shape that he had managed to stumble through the town square without anyone recognizing him. It even took my grandmother a few seconds to fully grasp who this person was, but then she threw her arms open wide. "Umberto," she cried. "I thought you were dead." Only when she saw the living, breathing person before her could she utter the words which had been locked like a thorn in her heart. "Umberto. Umberto. I thought you were dead."

He had been gone for a year. We'd all heard the whispered stories; when the Germans had no more use for the young Italians they had recruited to their cause, they shot them. Every one of us silently harbored the fears that had tortured my grandmother. Now Umberto was back. How had he done it? How had he escaped? How had he made his way over the mountain? What towns had sheltered him? It was difficult to get him to talk about it. His brother Antonio and Grandmother Raffaela didn't *want* him to talk about it. They shooed those who asked too many questions away. "Rest. He needs rest," Grandmother said. "Rest and quiet until he gets his strength back." He also needed food. How do you nurse someone back to health when there is no flour to bake the bread, no chickens, not even an egg? Grandmothers find a way. Warm sheep milk. Coffee made from barley or chicory. Soups that start as little more than water but that gradually are transformed by a clove of garlic, a bit of onion, a handful of grain, a potato, some dried herbs.

I remembered telling myself, back when we were still hiding in the *capanna*, that Umberto had been spared the sight of us being turned out of our homes at gunpoint, that he hadn't seen the things we had seen. Watching his hollow eyes dart around the room, I came to understand that he had seen horrors I could only begin to imagine, and that I was the one who had been spared.

A month passed and, except for occasional dizzy spells, Umberto seemed to be regaining some of his old strength. We told ourselves it was just the damp cold that triggered Umberto's attacks. When they grew more frequent, we all lamented the lack of a doctor. Anyone with medical expertise had been called into service on one side of the war or the other. Not even nearby towns had a physician we could consult. Grandmother tried brewing teas that were reputed to be good for headaches, but what Umberto suffered seemed very different from mere headaches. "The Majella Mountain is spinning," he would tell her. "I can see it going round and round."

Giovanni and I were staying with Uncle Ercole and Aunt Cristina in the railroad house, just as we had done since returning from Mussolini's *GIL* schools and from our mountain hideaway. Their sons Tonino and Luciano were still living there as well. The chilly rain that pelted against the windows that September seemed like nothing compared to what we had known in the *capanna*. Here at least we had a solid roof to keep out the weather. No more canvas tarps on the ground. Real beds. An indoor fireplace. I felt lucky. Things could be so much worse. And then, on the first day in October, they became much worse for all of us when Umberto suddenly refused to get out of bed. "The Majella is spinning," he would say over and over, even though, lying there in bed, he couldn't possibly see the actual mountain. "The Majella is spinning. I can't get up. There is no firm place to plant my feet." I was devastated. Thoughts of the Majella had been the one constant when so many other things in my world had changed and shifted. How could it be spinning?

Three weeks later, one morning when it was still dark and Aunt Cristina and Uncle Ercole were just beginning to stir, we were startled to hear someone pounding on the door. It was 5:00 a.m. Giovanni, my cousins and I stumbled from our beds, always alert to the potential for danger. Adelina Ciccone, a neighbor from Campo di Giove, had battled her way through pouring rain to fetch Uncle Ercole and Aunt Cristina. "You have to come help," she said, breathing hard. "Umberto is very sick. You must come quickly. Raffaela thinks he is dying."

Word spreads quickly in a community such as Campo di Giove. Those who had heard Umberto's brother Antonio calling outside Adelina's home had alerted their family members to the crisis going on in my grandmother's house. Those who had seen Adelina heading out in the downpour knew she was on her way to fetch Aunt Cristina and Uncle Ercole, and quickly concluded that there was some emergency. In the time it took us to pull on warm clothes, make our way through the rain, and rush up the steps to my grandmother's house, the room by the fireplace was filled with people.

Grandmother Raffaela looked at us, shook her head in disbelief, and then motioned us through the crowd of neighbors to come stand with the other family members by Umberto's bed. We kept watch by him throughout the day while Don Vergilio, the local priest, prayed over his frail body. Umberto wordlessly made eye contact first with Giovanni and then with me. He nodded when Don Vergilio asked him if he wanted to receive communion. Then, as the priest administered the last rites, silent tears streamed down Umberto's cheeks. He died just moments later. He was only eighteen. It was as if Umberto's last breath was a signal that released all the sorrow the people of Campo di Giove had been holding in check for over a year and a half. We wept in wordless communion with each other, as if we understood that ours was a grief so broad and deep that it could never be fully articulated.

In Campo di Giove, in Italy even today, we believe that the dead must be buried within twenty-four hours. It was October 26, 1944. No one had the money to buy a coffin or the wood to build one, but there was never any question that Umberto would have a proper burial. Chiara Pensa, my mother's cousin, said, "My family knows a man in Sulmona who makes caskets." Others nodded in agreement. They knew the man as well. "He would want Umberto to be buried in a real coffin."

One of the men broke in, "Once we have a harvest, once we are able to cut some firewood, we could see that we made it up to him."

"Sulmona is twenty miles from here." An older woman shook her head. "The path is so narrow. Mountain roads. Flooding from this storm. How could anyone travel there and make it back in time?"

It was understood that whoever made the trip would have to cover the distance on foot. No horse and wagon could possibly navigate those washed-out, twisted mountain passes.

"I'm strong," Chiara said. "I've walked to Sulmona many times."

"Not in the rain." The old woman refused to yield her point about the difficulty of the journey. "Not in weather like this."

"I'll go with you," Umberto's cousin Grazia Di Gregorio chimed in. "We'll go together. The men are needed here to prepare the ground." That part was true. It would be no small task to dig a deep enough hole with only the limited tools the Germans had left us. Adding to the difficulty, the Apennine Mountains are known for their rocky soil.

As I watched the two women head off into the storm, I wondered what they would find when they got to Sulmona. No one in Italy seemed to have anything of value. Even if this family friend were willing to give them a coffin in exchange for nothing more than their word and good faith, how could they be so certain that there were any coffins left? The war had claimed so many lives. In good weather, it took five hours at a brisk pace to walk to Sulmona. Chiara and Grazia would have to be back by four o'clock the next afternoon and, assuming they were successful in their quest, they would be burdened by a coffin on the return trip. I didn't know if I considered them brave or foolish.

The women wept. My grandmother hardest of all. She had never believed in this war, had never felt it could come to anything but grief. However, she had mostly kept her doubts to herself. Now she was unable to control her wailing cries. The other women tended to her as best they could, but sometimes the best way to tend to sorrow is just to let it happen.

Wanting to get away from the sound of loss, I joined the older boys as they helped move the sodden chunks of soil and stone back away from the graveside.

"The rain has let up," one of the men observed. "They're both young and strong. The sun will dry them." We all knew who he was talking about.

"They'll be chilled to the bone."

"Hard work warms us all," the first man said. He stopped to wipe a brow that gleamed with sweat even in the damp cold.

Another chimed in, "Just as firewood warms us twice—once when we cut it and then again when we stand in front of the hearth."

"Chiara and Grazia will be kept warm by the weight of…" He stopped, unable to name the thing they would be carrying. After a pause, he ended on a more optimistic note. "The sky is clearing. The moon will help them find their way in the dark."

Uncle Ercole and Aunt Cristina decided we would all spend the night in my grandmother's house while we waited for Chiara and Grazia to return. As I settled into my old bed, Giovanni beside me, I wanted to retreat back to that earlier time when we had all been so excited about the move to Libya. What had happened to those years? How had it all come to this? Poor Uncle Savino. "Sure, Roberto, sure," he had called to my father. "We'll go to Libya." And now his son Umberto, his middle boy, fourteen when his father had last seen him, was dead at eighteen and there was no way to even get the word to our family in Africa. I could hear my grandmother crying in the other room, and I suddenly understood all that she was crying for; not just for Umberto, but also for her daughter Raffaela, Umberto's mother, my mother's sister, lost and out of reach so far across the sea. How long would it be before Uncle Savino and Aunt Raffaela learned that the son for whom they still said prayers every night was no longer alive? No wonder Grandmother cried. It was not just her own sorrow at the loss of a much-loved grandson. She must also be weeping for the pain she knew her daughter Raffaela would feel when she finally learned what had happened to her middle son. *If she learned*. Who could tell if the members of my family would ever manage to find their way back to each other? As soon as Umberto died, my grandmother clothed herself completely in black. Once she had witnessed his burial, she refused to leave her house for any reason for the next three months.

I thought I would never be able to fall asleep the night after Umberto died, and when I finally did, my dreams were so filled with the voices of my family that it took me a moment to realize the talking I heard in the next room was real. I'd overslept, and Chiara and Grazia were back from Sulmona. The bright October light that happens after a rain had already filled the kitchen by the time I made my way from the bedroom. A plain pine coffin stained dark brown, as if to mimic some more majestic wood, stretched across two sawhorses beside the fireplace.

Chiara and Grazia had accomplished all they'd set out to do. They had fought against the gusting wind all the way to Sulmona, found a coffin, and made their way back to Campo di Giove before the twenty-four hours had passed. Grandmother was hugging them. "Bless you. Bless you."

Their faces were flushed red. Aunt Cristina fingered their wet clothing. "Stand over here by the fireplace until you dry out. Are you soaked to the skin?"

Chiara made light of the question. "It's nothing. We'll be fine."

"Come. Take your outer things off. Don't catch a chill," Aunt Cristina warned.

Uncle Ercole pulled a bench close to the fireplace. "Sit here. Sit down." He looked at the two tired women before him. "How…" He couldn't finish his question. We all knew the difficulties imposed by that steep mountain trail even in the best of weather.

"Was there flooding?" I asked from the doorway.

"The road was washed out in places."

"Was it heavy?" I inclined my head toward the coffin.

Shrugging off the question, Chiara gestured dismissively with her hands. "We carried it on our heads. We took turns, changing places every hour. Nothing compared to a jug of water."

"But Sulmona is twenty miles from here." In awe of what they had done, I pressed forward. "Over the mountain in heavy rain. How?"

"For Umberto. For Umberto." Grazia began to cry. "We had to make it right for Umberto."

CHAPTER FIFTEEN

Finding Our Way

Winter was over. *Two* difficult winters were behind us. April always seems to arrive in a rush. Trees are suddenly green with leaves. Life promises a fresh start, but old things have to be put behind us before the way forward seems clear. On April 27, 1945, Mussolini was caught by communist Italian partisans as he was trying to escape to Switzerland. He and the other Fascists with him were taken to Giulino and executed. Mobs of angry Italians mutilated their bodies and hung the disfigured remains from meat hooks on public display in Milan. On April 29, the last armies of the Fascist puppet state, the Italian Social Republic, surrendered.

On April 30, Hitler, learning of Mussolini's fate and hoping to avoid a similarly inglorious end, committed suicide in his bunker. By May 30, 1945, all German forces in Italy were ordered to unconditionally surrender to the Allies. For us the war was officially over. Once again, a few strokes of the pen had the power to silence armies, but, oh, the devastation that lay in the wake of those armies. How do the regular people who have been buffeted about by the winds of war begin putting shattered lives back together? In Campo di Giove we began as we had always begun, by plowing the fields and planting crops. The small flocks of sheep that had survived the war, the winters, and the Germans gave birth in their home pastures. We started over where we had always been, high up on the Majella Mountain. Used to making do with little, we made do with less. Familiar patterns and rhythms gave us a framework within which to move forward. We planted, we tended the fields, we milked the goats, we harvested what we had managed to grow.

As I said earlier, Gennaro, my oldest brother, had been captured by the Americans in 1943, while fighting for the Italian Army on the plains of Libya. He spent the last year and a half of the hostilities in a prisoner-of-war camp, Camp Stanley, in Taunton, Massachusetts. By September of 1945, he was sent to Pietro Grotta, a refugee camp in Naples. Gennaro was back in Italy, but he had no idea where the rest of his family was. Libya was a logical place to start looking; but, once again, those signing treaties were the ones making the rules, and Libya was a prize whose fate had not yet been decided. The English were opposed to simply allowing all the Italian settlers who'd been uprooted from their homes in Africa by war and politics to return there. War and politics were still too fresh in everyone's mind. Until the decision about what to do with Italy's colonial lands was settled, the Allies set up an interim policy that established a quota system for granting Libyan Italians a right of return. While waiting for a decision on what the quotas would be, interested Italians were required not only to register, but also to move to refugee camps until they were granted permission to travel to Libya.

These refugee camps, even Pietro Grotta where Gennaro was housed, were not like prisons. The people assigned to live there were free to leave during the day to conduct the details of the business regarding their status. The first thing on Gennaro's mind was locating his family. He'd no sooner landed in Italy than he began searching for word of his missing brothers and cousins. The last he'd seen Giovanni and me, we were heading for the battleship that was to take us from Libya back to Italy for enrollment in Mussolini's boarding schools for the children of the *Quarta Sponda,* the Fourth Shore. He had no idea what had happened to the children of those schools when Mussolini was overthrown. By late October 1945, he somehow managed to locate records that indicated that Giovanni, Umberto, Antonio, and I were safe and living with Aunt Cristina and Uncle Ercole in Campo di Giove.

Gennaro was eighteen when my family left Italy for Libya. I had just turned seven when we were separated the following July. I guess it's no surprise that I recognized him before he had a chance to understand that the twelve-year-old boy walking back from the fields our father had so carefully worked years earlier was actually his brother. At twenty-four, he looked much more worldly, but I knew him instantly. He carried the stamp of our father and grandfather even in the way he moved.

"Gennaro," I called as I ran toward him.

He hesitated just for a moment. After all, I was of the age Giovanni had been when we were last together as a family. I could see the quick calculations cross his face, but then he answered, at first with a question, "Vittorio?" And then, as he sprinted toward me, with an enthusiasm matching my own, "Vittorio!" As always in Campo di Giove, the news spread even as it was happening. So much to celebrate. So much to mourn. Where to begin? Words tumbled over each other. He'd expected to find Umberto here with us. He'd hoped our grandfather would still be alive. The town spent the next few days helping him fill in the missing pieces, but there was, of course, no way to occupy the space left by the missing people.

Gennaro had much to tell us about what had happened in the world away from the Abruzzo region. The best news for Giovanni and me was learning that our family in Libya was alive and that there was a way for us to be reunited with them. Antonio was equally glad to hear that his parents and brother and sister had survived the war, but everyone grew silent on learning the good news about his relatives. Antonio without Umberto. Who was going to have to break that sorrowful burden of news to his parents and siblings?

During his brief return to Campo di Giove, Gennaro stayed with Giovanni and me at the railroad house with Uncle Ercole, Aunt Cristina, Tonino, and Luciano. They'd been like parents to me for two years. Why does every reunion with one set of loved ones have to be accompanied by separation from another? By now, it was almost November. Here on the mountain, the leaves had already fallen from the beech trees. Frost had turned any remaining vegetation in the fields brown. "How long do you think the boys will have to stay in the refugee camp?" Aunt Cristina knew we wouldn't need warm clothes in Libya, but worried that we might be cold, even in Rome where Gennaro felt we'd be assigned to camps.

"There are three camps," he told her. "No one can give me a guarantee that the boys will be assigned to the same place."

"Yes," she nodded, indicating that she understood that part, "but for how long?"

"It's hard to get that kind of information." He walked over to the window and looked out on the little fountain that bubbled just across the track from the house. "Rumor is that they'll let only 500 return every six months. At that rate, it could take a year, maybe more. The youngest children will go first." He walked back and faced Aunt Cristina. "They have to get their names on the list. They have to register with the United Nations Relief and Rehabilitation Administration, the UNRRA. This is an organization whose main function is to oversee the relocation and unification of families separated by the war." He looked steadily at Aunt Cristina. "There are thousands who have already signed up. The sooner…" His voice trailed off.

"Just give me a few more days. Can you give me a few more days? There is something I need to do before they leave."

And that's how it happened that Giovanni and I headed off for Rome sheltered from the elements by my grandfather's old *mantella*, his woolen cape, the one with the missing buttons. Aunt Cristina took the cape, my brother, and me to a tailor in town and had him fit us for suits. There was enough fabric for us both to get almost identical jackets. Given that Giovanni was older, his suit came with knickers, mine with short pants. I was fascinated, even then, by the pattern-making process. I watched as the tailor made a jigsaw puzzle of pieces. Not only did he manage to get two suits out of the fabric in a single *mantella*, but he lined up the weave in such a way that all the seams came together as if new, as if there had never been another life in those yards of wool. No stranger would ever guess the history hidden in my suit, but I knew, and I wore it proudly, perhaps not really processing at the conscious level, but understanding in a deeper sense that my coat offered protection from more than mere cold.

Gennaro was a pied piper leading a group of four boys off to find a way to return to the land of milk and honey as promised by the UNRRA. Vittorio Del Mastro, Giovanni's friend, the boy Giovanni's age who with his family had first traveled from Campo di Giove to Libya with us back in 1939, was also seeking to be reunited with his parents and was part of the group Gennaro was taking to Rome. On this first day of November the narrow road to Sulmona was still free of snow. Aunt Cristina waved until we were out of sight, but Uncle Ercole had to turn from us even before we were through the town gate. It was hard for me too. I knew why he couldn't watch us leave.

Gennaro spoke to us as if we were all men in this together, as if he was just bringing us up to date on plans that affected us all equally. "Once we get as far as Sulmona, we'll be able to find someone with a horse and wagon to take us to Avezzano."

"There's a train station there," Giovanni said to no one in particular.

"Yes there is, Giovanni, yes there is." Gennaro was walking in confident strides that we all imitated. "In fact, there's more than a train station there." He laughed. "There's a whole town! Imagine that. Italy still has one town that hasn't been touched by German and Allied bombs." Gennaro knew these things because he had come this same way to find us. "We'll take the train to Rome." He looked thoughtful. "But first things first. Sulmona here we come."

Despite the heavy bombing it had suffered during the war, Sulmona still managed to claim some of the beauty common to mountain towns. The town center, the railway station, and the industrial area may have all been reduced to rubble by bombing from both sides, but nothing could flatten an entire alpine range. Of course, the fact that the German prisoner-of-war camp was built on a hill, meant that even the mountains surrounding the city had suffered some damage. Remember, the British soldiers that the Di Marzios saved had escaped from this camp. But winter has a way of transforming everything, and any bomb craters that might have been there were hidden by the snow covering the higher elevations. I focused on their jagged peaks as Gennaro headed for the old part of town. We followed him down a narrow twisted street until we came to the livery stable of a man who had been in the scrap iron business prior to the war. He was an older gentleman, and the negotiations between him and Gennaro were over so quickly that I sensed much of this had been decided before.

He talked quietly to his horse as he slipped the harness over its broad rump. With almost no urging, it backed in between the wagon shafts. Then he turned to us. "Okay, boys, climb on up there." The wagon had obviously been converted from its former use hauling metal. It was far sturdier than necessary had it been designed only for human transport. The owner had constructed benches that ran from side to side.

I slid close to Giovanni. The horse's hooves made a steady clomp, clomping noise as the wagon wheels creaked over cobblestones. "Beats walking, doesn't it?" Gennaro asked in a voice a bit too deliberately jovial. We nodded. I wanted to respond to all that my oldest brother had arranged with more enthusiasm, but we were, once again, moving from a familiar world and into one that held much uncertainty. I turned my head away when we passed by the hollow craters that seemed to have left their signatures all over Italy.

Once on the road that ran between Sulmona and Avezzano, I dozed off and didn't wake until I felt the wagon creak to a stop and heard the driver's, "Whoa, whoa." His gravelly voice vibrated in a way that made it sound almost like a horse's deep whinny. In any event, the directions he called to the gelding seemed almost more necessary to him than to the horse. It was a docile creature that appeared to understand exactly what was expected of it.

We were going to spend the night at a small hostelry within sight of the railway station at Avezzano. The station was a busy place, crowded with people as apparently dislocated by the war as we were. Family members urged each other to stay together. There seemed to be a general concern about securing passage. Gennaro saw me turn my head and study the size of the crowd. "Don't worry, Vittorio," he said, "I have our tickets. For tomorrow. First thing in the morning." And then he turned his attention to making sure we were all awake and in possession of our small bundles of personal items.

"You have a well-trained horse," I told the old man as he helped me down.

"He knows the way to the station." The driver paused, as if gathering words, but then simply shook his head and drew a deep breath. "Good luck" was all he could manage before turning his attention toward a cluster of people who were looking for a ride back to Sulmona.

The trains weren't running on time. By the time we got to Rome the following day, it was dark, and Gennaro herded his four sleepy charges through the streets until we came to the home of an old family friend. Since the UNRRA offices were already closed for the day, we would spend the night with people we knew.

"First in line," Gennaro whispered as he roused us from our beds the next morning. "We want to be first in line."

First in line for what? I thought to myself as we climbed the stairs to an official-looking building. A year in a refugee camp? That didn't seem like something worth waiting for. It wasn't until a slightly chubby, middle-aged woman sitting behind a desk motioned me to sit in the chair facing her that it dawned on me what this was really all about. The woman in the flowered dress was fluent in Italian, but her plump confidence quickly made me understand that she hadn't spent the war years in Italy. She'd been hired from somewhere else to help the rest of us find our way back home. She wanted to know my story: where my family lived, where I'd spent the time from 1940 until 1945, what town I called home. I almost answered *Campo di Giove* to this last question, but quickly caught myself. This was all about going back to my mother and father in Libya. I hesitated. "Garibaldi," I said softly.

The woman looked down at her papers. She had a way of thumbing through them with one finger that I found fascinating. At last she stopped at the page she'd been looking for. "Palumbo, right?"

I nodded.

"You *are* Vittorio Palumbo, son of Roberto and Angela, brother of Gennaro, Giovanna, Guerino, Giovanni, and Adalgisa?" She framed it as a question.

I hesitated, thinking of Uncle Savino and Aunt Raffaela. Feeling tears rush into my eyes, I wondered if perhaps this woman with all her official papers knew something I didn't.

Her voice softened. "Vittorio?"

I studied my lap.

"You *are* Vittorio Palumbo?"

I nodded again.

"And Roberto and Angela *are* your parents?" Her voice was very kind, which made me all the more afraid. "Your family is waiting for you in Libya." Again a pause. "It's simply that they no longer live in Garibaldi."

Of course. Gennaro had told me that. I'd just become frightened and confused when I'd almost told her my home was in Campo di Giove. "Giordani?" I said. "My family lives in Giordani?

"That's right." She smiled happily. "Now tell me about how you spent your years during the war."

The refugee camps were overseen by the British government. There were three of them: Cento Celli, Santa Croce, and Cinecittà. When we walked out into the street and compared assignments, Gennaro could tell that something was bothering me. I hung back while Giovanni, Antonio, and Vittorio Del Mastro excitedly chattered about the information on the documents.

"It's okay, Vittorio. It will be okay. You're all in the same camp." He patted me on the back. I looked up at him. How quickly he was beginning to feel like a father. I didn't want to tell him that whether we were in the same camp or even the same pavilion wasn't the real issue. It was clear that the three older boys were bonded in a way that excluded me. I felt lonely in a way that was difficult to describe. Gennaro must have sensed something of what was making me sad, because he offered reassurance. "You'll see. You're the lucky one. Youngest first." He smiled. "You'll be the first to go back home."

Home? I had almost forgotten the name of the town where my family lived. I'd never been there. How could this be home? I thought of my mother and father. I'd carried a longing for them in my heart all these years. Drawing a deep breath, I tried to muster a smile.

Gennaro laughed. "There. That's the spirit." He glanced over the documents in his hands. "Besides, think of this. Did you ever want to be in pictures?"

I remembered the time Brisolin, la Morgia, Airo, and I had gone to see *The Wizard of Oz*. How long ago that all seemed. Nevertheless, the memory made my smile real.

Encouraged by my tentative look of joy, Gennaro continued. "You're assigned to Cinecittà. It's where they make the movies, Vittorio." He started to walk more quickly. "The British have taken over the section of Rome where the film industry was located." Giovanni and my cousins moved in closer to hear all that Gennaro was telling me. "Just like Hollywood. You'll be staying in the pavilion where they used to make the movies."

CHAPTER SIXTEEN

My Life in Pictures

There were maybe fifteen pavilions in Campo Cinecittà. We were assigned to #66. Before Gennaro left to go back to Pietro Grotta, the refugee camp where he was housed, he waited to make sure everything was okay with us. The director of the camp, Mr. Balestieri, was an American who lived in Rome and spoke fluent Italian. Hundreds of people were lining up waiting to receive the supplies they would need for life in the movie colony of post-war Italy. As Mr. Balestieri handed me my things, he identified each item and checked it off on the list in front of him. "One mattress." I folded the burlap sack filled with straw over my arm and could feel the chaff scratching me through the rough weave of the cloth. "One pillow." In matched fabric and stuffing, I thought to myself, piling it on top of the mattress. "Two blankets." Speaking rapidly, the director just as rapidly handed me my aluminum eating utensils. "One dish. One spoon, one fork, one knife, one cup." Struggling to gather my things without dropping them, I nonetheless waved Gennaro off when he reached in to help me carry something. Sensitive about my size and age, I didn't wish to be seen as a child. I saw Mr. Balestieri glance at Gennaro with just the flicker of a smile. "Watch your things carefully," he glanced down to remind himself of my name before continuing. "Watch your things carefully, Vittorio," he repeated. "If one of your items comes up missing, just take someone else's. If we start accusing each other of stealing, fights will break out. Living so closely under one roof requires cooperation and patience." Pulling a little number-covered card from a pile bundled together with a rubber band, he handed it to me with a deliberate firmness that suggested its importance. "This is your meal ticket. It will be punched three times a day when you go to pick up your food." Three meals a day! He may have spoken the words in Italian, but it all sounded very American to me.

The building itself was about a half-mile long and divided into two sections by a six-foot wall running the full length. At either end, large doors, wide enough to admit all manner of film-making equipment, opened out. Since the pavilion was unheated, anyone exiting or entering also admitted cold blasts of air. Not knowing this, the four of us picked a spot close to the end to claim as our own. There were 300 men living in this one pavilion. We ranged in age from twelve to eighty. As always, I was the youngest, but once I got over the sense of having been rejected by the other three boys, I could see that there was some advantage in being seen as a boy among men. Successive years of malnutrition had left me small for my age, and it's possible that our neighbors thought I was even younger than I claimed.

The three gentlemen who established themselves in the spot right next to us became my friends and seemed to go out of their way to make sure I was taken care of. Mr. Cilurzi and Mr. Muoio were both Italian. Mr. O'Brian was Irish, but somewhere along the way he had picked up enough Italian to help me understand the various functions of this former film-works. Of course, by now my exposure to boys from all over Italy was such that I had developed a skill in translating dialects that enabled me to grasp what Mr. O'Brian was trying to tell me. What we lacked in words, we made up for in gestures. He was as fascinated as I was by the prior use of our new home. Pointing to the high ceilings, he convincingly mimed a camera on wheels making its way around the narrow balcony that circled above us. Before falling asleep that first night, I tried to imagine all the movies that might have been made here; then I pictured a camera bringing me into focus lying there on my straw mattress, and I wondered what kind of an ending the director would write for my story.

The lavatory facilities were in their own building and were very similar to those used in military camps. Long sinks with faucets every couple of feet stretched along one wall. The latrines were nothing more than holes in the ground, but at least they were inside and sheltered from the elements. It would take more than latrines such as these to discourage a boy who had spent nine months hiding in a *capanna* in the mountains. However, not even in the refugee camp was there a place to take a bath, so we managed as best we could by scrubbing up in front of the sinks. One area where the camp was clearly superior to our hideout on the Majella was in the approach to lice. Once a month, we took our blankets to a special building within the camp for disinfecting. There, they were swirled around in a large tank for several minutes. It was some sort of dry-cleaning process, because there wasn't a trace of dampness to them when they emerged from the machine.

We were in charge of washing our own clothes in fountains just outside the pavilion. These fountains were divided into two parts: one side was reserved for washing dishes, the other side was equipped with little washboards on which we scrubbed our clothes. Once our garments were washed, we draped them over bushes to dry. Giovanni, who found this task irksome, came up with a system that he tried hard to get the rest of us to adopt. "You waste so much time," he told us, pulling his shirt off over his head. "Look." He demonstrated how he was able to pass the shirt off as clean simply by turning it inside out. Pulling it back on and completely oblivious to the exposed seams, he turned around to show us. "Not a spot in sight. It's clean as far as anyone can tell." I couldn't bring myself to walk around with my shirt inside out and backwards. Not that it would have made any difference in how we looked. We were given used clothing without much regard for size. Other than the suits Aunt Cristina had made for us, everything we had was ill-fitting. Only one person among us affected a sense of style, and that was Mr. Pio Cappelletti.

The Cappelletti family and the Mazzoni family each consisted of two brothers; and these four people, all of them from Libya, had claimed a spot in the pavilion just across from us. I remember Bruno and Pio Cappelletti best, perhaps because Pio made himself memorable by the paisley silk scarf he wore, ascot-style, wrapped around his neck. I couldn't help admiring it and wondering how he ever came to possess a thing of such beauty, especially since no one else seemed to own a single item of value. He obviously treasured it as well, for he was never seen without it. Perhaps fearful that someone would steal it—it clearly was worth much more than an aluminum plate—Pio wore his scarf even to bed.

Were there arguments over missing pieces of flatware? We must have all taken Mr. Balestieri's warnings to heart, because except for occasional outbursts unrelated to accusations of theft, we managed to live fairly peacefully. That is not to say there weren't moments of drama. The bizarre behavior of an old man from Tunisia kept us entertained. Sanna, as we called him, was never seen without his hashish pipe. At the time, I had no idea what hashish was, but that was the explanation given whenever I asked, "What is wrong with Sanna?"

"Too much hashish," Mr. O'Brian told me. "Stay away from hashish, Vittorio."

Sanna owned a pickax, a possession of which he was as proud as Pio Cappelletti was of his paisley silk scarf. His crazy swaggering and muttering while waving the pick around his head made me glad he lived on the other side of the wooden barrier dividing the pavilion. One night, Sanna's neighbors shouted at him to shut up and go to sleep. The more they yelled at him, the angrier he got. Finally, I heard one man threaten to take Sanna's pick if he didn't quiet down.

"You want this pick, do you?" Sanna cried. "I'll give you my pick!" And with that, he threw it with such force that it crashed through the flimsy wooden barrier, just missing Pio Cappelletti's head by inches. Those on our side screamed and shook Pio to make sure he was alright.

"What's the matter? Let me sleep," he said angrily. "Why are you waking me up in the middle of the night like this?" Pio had slept through the entire argument and had no idea how close he had come to having the sharp end of a pick driven into his brain! After that incident, Sanna and his pick were separated, but no one seemed to figure a way to separate him from his hashish. The deranged muttering continued, but he was less threatening when unarmed.

The kitchen area was outside the buildings under a tin roof supported by four large poles. We would line up with our plates and meal tickets to get our food. Three times a day, someone ran a steel rod around the inside of a large metal triangle. This was our call to meals, but the initial promise of breakfast, lunch, and dinner proved disappointing in execution. However, even knowing what waited, we seized on this break from the monotony of camp life and eagerly rushed to get in line. Our morning fare never varied: one scoop of milk reconstituted from powder, a small bun, and a little spoonful of sugar. We were expected to sweeten our milk with the sugar, but as nothing could disguise the insult of the former, we saved the latter until we had a large enough store to sell in the market in Rome. The warm sheep milk my grandmother had ladled over a chunk of her homemade bread, however stale, seemed grand by comparison to the thin chalky liquid that passed for milk in the camp. Still, we were hungry. And not only did I always finish my breakfast, but I also walked away dreaming of what that precious sugar could buy in an Italy still starved for sugar.

I can't say the same for lunch. Nothing worth saving there. And, according to my stomach, there was hardly anything worth eating. It was always soup, a watery grey mix that seemed more broth than substance. The beans that floated randomly through it were often riddled with holes. One look and I knew that worms had gotten to those beans before I had. It was enough to make me want to push my plate away. I'd sit there tentatively stirring my spoon through the offering, unable to bring it to my mouth.

"Eat, Vittorio, eat," Giovanni yelled at me. "You have to eat if you're going to keep up your strength." He shook his head. Once he was truly certain I wasn't going to finish my lunch, he reached for my leftovers. "How can you be so picky? You weren't this picky when we were hiding from the Germans."

He never had a problem with the food and would gobble down anything put in front of him. My appetite was affected by not knowing where the food had been before it reached my plate. Giovanni was right. I hadn't been that picky back in Campo di Giove, but when we were living in a *capanna*, I had watched as my grandmother and the other women from our village stirred and tasted. A liquid seasoned with love is always delicious no matter how thin.

Because I ate so little between breakfast and dinner, I was always hungrier by the evening meal. Except for Sundays, the menu varied very little. Boiled potatoes, maybe string beans or carrots. "Nothing wrong with potatoes," Mr. O'Brian always said as he set his plate down in front of him. "Until the blight, the noble potato fed an entire race of Irishmen." It's funny how the predictability of little things like that make life bearable. Part of *my* ritual was to keep my eyes glued on Giovanni, Antonio, and Vittorio Del Mastro who always waited for Mr. O'Brian's pronouncement, almost like waiting for someone to say grace, before picking up their forks, exchanging an amused smile, and starting to eat. I wished I could think of something equally profound to say about the pasta and sauce we were served on Sundays, but could never quite come up with anything.

Just across the way from us was another camp filled with refugees from all over the world. It was its own little League of Nations. Therefore, we called it *Campo Straniero*, which means foreigners. Walking past that camp and hearing all the different languages spoken at once, I couldn't help but wonder how they had ended up in Italy. Were they, like my brother Gennaro, former prisoners of war? I sensed a million stories buried in that jumble of words and somehow felt less alone. Were we all nothing but wanderers, trying hard to get back to a place where we belonged? How strange that a war that had set nations against each other now brought the people from so many different countries together in one spot in Rome. In Campo Cinecittà we were mostly from Italy, Libya, and Albania. Of course we had a few others like Mr. O'Brian and crazy Sanna from Tunisia thrown in, but behind the barbed wire in Campo Straniero men from Russia, Germany, Hungary, Bulgaria—men from all over—were crowded into that one place.

Home. What makes a home? Filled with longing for the childhood I had left behind in Libya, I never stopped thinking of my parents. When would it be my turn to leave? From time to time, Mr. Balestieri would come to read the names of those who had been cleared to return to Africa. In the beginning, I crowded eagerly to the front, certain I would hear my own name called. I remembered Gennaro's words. "You'll see. You're the lucky one. Youngest first. You'll be the first to go back home." But months passed. More than a year passed, and still my name was not called. I began to understand that Gennaro had meant I would be the first of our little gang of four, not that I would be the first to leave the camp. So many others had gotten their names on the list ahead of us. Unable to continue trying to hide my disappointment, I no longer crowded to the head of the assembled group when Mr. Balestieri showed up to read the names. I hung back, expecting disappointment.

In the meantime, I was building my family where I found it. As I said earlier, Mr. Muoio, Mr. Cilurzi, and Mr. O'Brian—the three gentlemen who occupied the spot next to ours in Campo Cinecittà—made a point of watching out for me. On Sundays they often invited me to go with them when they headed into Rome to do their errands. There was an amusement park in the Piazza San Giovanni. "Here, Vittorio," they would say, slipping a small amount of money into my hand. "Go enjoy yourself. We'll be back in an hour or two." So many places had been bombed in Rome, but somehow there was enough of the amusement park standing to keep a boy happy.

Vittorio Del Mastro, Antonio D'Agostino, and my brother Giovanni, did at least include me in the little scheme of saving up sugar. I guess they could see how important my contribution was in that area. For once I felt equal, maybe more than equal, because in my fierce desire to be part of their group, I never once cheated and allowed a secret longing for sweets to drive me to sample a small bit before pouring my share into the communal store. At the end of each month, I always had contributed either thirty or thirty-one very full spoonfuls to the cause. Being the oldest, my cousin Antonio was in charge of assembling the sugar into one sack. Then the four of us would head off to Piazza Vittorio, the market in Rome. Antonio had a confident way of negotiating with the different vendors. He knew just when to shake his head and walk off. Sometimes one would call after us, and then Antonio would go back and settle up; but if we got no call, we would just proceed until we found someone who dealt fairly with us. In time, we learned which vendors we could rely on and the job of finding a buyer became more efficient. Then the four of us would head to a flight of marble stairs rising up from the market. We gathered around, watching carefully while Vittorio Del Mastro divided the money into four piles. Hungry though we were, there was no point trying to buy something to eat with our newfound wealth. Inflation had driven the cost of food to over 600 percent of what it had been. So, this rise in prices was our friend when it came to selling the sugar, but not when it came to filling our bellies. We used the money for soap, transportation, and only occasionally for a piece of fruit so tempting that we felt compelled to splurge. Then, after much precision measurement and cutting, we shared it among us. I also saved what I could from my small store of cash, so that I might be able to help Giovanni finance his visits to see his girlfriend.

We all worked in order to help contribute to the cost of running the camps. I sensed that Mr. Balestieri had taken a special liking to the four boys, formerly from Campo di Giove, who had settled close to the wide doors of the movie studio. Looking back, I wonder if he might not have detected some special fire in the youngest of those boys, but at the time, I was so busy trying to be like the other three that I had lost all sense of myself as an individual. I don't remember the job Vittorio Del Mastro took. He never settled into the camp routine and always seemed to be looking outward, trying to think of a way to be somewhere else. I suspect the director saw that quality in him as well and gave him work that didn't demand a serious commitment, maybe even shifting him from one job to another.

When he asked Giovanni what he wanted to do, my brother just shrugged his shoulders. "Come on, young man, isn't your father a farmer in Libya?" Giovanni just shook his head as if he didn't know. "I thought you came from people who work the fields."

Perhaps seeing where all this was leading and not being particularly fond of plowing, Giovanni said, "Sheep. We herd sheep."

"Well, we have no sheep in Campo Cinecittà, but we do have grass that needs cutting, some landscaping. And there is a farmer who wants help with his tomatoes." He smiled like Giovanni himself had suggested the idea. "Fine. Good. Well, that's settled then. I'll make the arrangements."

I'm sure he came to regret the enthusiasm with which he assigned Giovanni to the tomato farm. On his first day on the job, Giovanni was given a hoe and told to make sure the soil around the base of the plant was loose and weed-free. He and the other boys decided to have a contest to see which one could work his way to the end of the row first. They slashed their hoes into the earth vigorously, making a great show of knocking weeds to the ground. "I won," Giovanni crowed, as he turned to survey the row behind him. Not only were the weeds gone, but the tomato plants were also beginning to wilt and tip over. The boys who had finished not far behind Giovanni noticed the same problem with their rows. In their race to the finish, they'd cut through the roots of the tomato plants themselves. It was Giovanni's first and last day on the job. The irate farmer informed Mr. Balestieri that, in the future, he should send him older, more experienced workers. From then on Giovanni toiled, minus a hoe, pulling weeds by hand from around the landscaping in the camp.

In 1946, Antonio got a job that benefited us all. He worked in the camp kitchen. Seeing how thin we four boys were after two difficult winters in Campo di Giove, Mr. Balestieri quietly allowed Antonio to scrape a few leftovers into an empty tomato sauce tin and bring them back to us at the end of the day. This little bit of extra food helped us survive those years in the refugee camp. Years. Yes, years. When Gennaro told Aunt Cristina that we might be in the camps a year or more, we had heard only the "year," but we should have paid greater attention to the "or more."

Working helped pass the time, and strange as it may seem, it was in the refugee camp that I came closest to being encouraged to pursue my dream of becoming a tailor. When the director asked me what job I would be interested in doing, I answered with honest longing. "*Sarto*, I want to be a tailor," I told him.

"*Sarto,*" Mr. Balestieri said, smiling broadly. "*Sarto!*" This is a profession held in high esteem in Italy, and at first I worried that his smile might mean he was amused by the grandness of my dreams, much as I might smile today if a child told me he wanted to be President of the United States. However, his smile quickly softened into kindness, and he looked at me with respect and nodded slowly. "Yes, yes. There is someone who might be able to help you with that."

This postcard ("Roman Countryside – To the pasture") depicts my grandfather Gennaro Palumbo's life as a shepherd in a pasture outside Rome, circa 1930.

With my maternal grandmother Raffaela (Angelucci) Pensa, paternal grandfather Gennaro Palumbo (second marriage for both of them), and my older brother Giovanni, in Campo di Giove, July 1942.

Our arrival in Garibaldi (now Al Dafniyah, Libya), June 21, 1940 — BACK ROW: brother Guerino, sister Giovanna, brother Gennaro, brother Giovanni; MIDDLE ROW: mother Angela and father Roberto; FRONT ROW: sister Ada and me.

Aunt Cristina and Uncle Ercole Di Gregorio with their son Tonino (center), 1947.

Uncle Domenico Palumbo, circa 1930; and my father Roberto in his Army uniform of Bersaglieri, in Caserta, Naples, 1937.

Uncle Ercole Di Gregorio (brother of Eustacchio Di Gregorio), Aunt Cristina, and their son Luciano, in Campo di Giove, 1948. I planted the pear tree behind them in 1944.

Uncle Antonio Palumbo and family, 1920— STANDING: cousins Salvatore, Bruno, Jane, Luisa, Rose; SEATED: Aunt Filomena Antonetti and Uncle Tony, my father's brother.

LEFT: Cousin Umberto D'Agostino, with a military supervisor and cousin Antonio D'Agostino, all in Mussolini's school uniforms, 1942.

BELOW: Cousin Umberto D'Agostino (Uncle Savino and Aunt Raffaela's son), in the uniform of Vanguardista—Mussolini's school, in Fiera di Primiero, 1942.

Uncle Savino and Aunt Raffaela D'Agostino (my mother's sister), taken in Giordani (now Annasiria), Libya, before they returned home to Italy, circa 1954.

The women who carried Umberto's casket from Sulmona to Campo di Giove on October 27, 1944 – Chiara Pensa (my mother's cousin, married to Pietro Zavarelli) and Grazia Recchione (wife of my cousin, Rocco Di Gregorio).

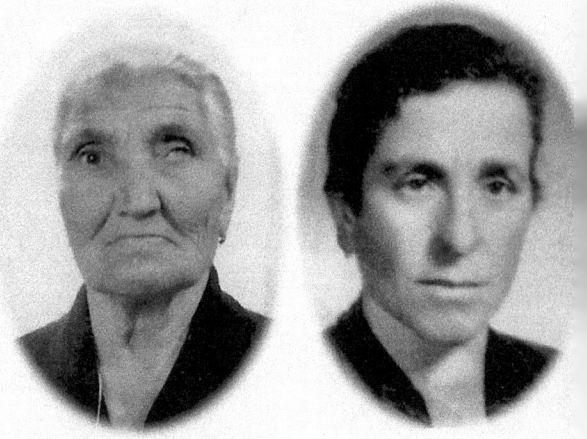

Hotel Orsingher — My first residence and school in Fiera di Primiero, 1941.

4TH AND 5TH FROM LEFT: Miss Rossi and Mrs. Bevelo, the supervisors for younger boys, 6TH AND 7TH FROM LEFT: two male supervisors for older boys, at school in Fiera di Primiero, 1941. The arrow shows my cousin Umberto D'Agostino.

Raising the flag at school in the morning. We formed the letter "M" for Mussolini, 1941.

Scenes from Fiera di Primiero, 1941

Our dining hall at school in the Hotel Orsingher. I am seated in the second row from the left, third boy from the front.

Working in fields.

Training in the courtyard of the Hotel Orsingher.

Learning the shoemaking trade.

Me (circled) at my First Communion and Confirmation in Fiera di Primiero with Bishop Vittorio Facchinetti from Tripoli, Libya, September 20, 1941.

The Palumbo and Del Mastro families in Giordani (now Annasiria), Libya, 1944—Valerino Del Mastro, my mother Angela, my brother-in-law Salvatore, my sister Giovanna, Mrs. Antonia Del Mastro, my father Roberto, and my sister Ada in the foreground.

IMAGES FROM GIORDANI (NOW ANNASIRIA), LIBYA

My teacher from 1948 to 1949, Mr. Ottavio Balsamo, circa 1952. He was the one who encouraged me to go to America.

My school, 1948 to 1949.

My brother-in-law Salvatore Del Mastro; my sister Giovanna; their children Rosanna and Antonietta; on their farm, #126, March 26, 1951.

ABOVE LEFT: My brother Gennaro as a prisoner of war, in clothing provided by the U.S. government, in Camp Stanley, Taunton, Massachusetts, circa 1944.

ABOVE: The Palumbo brothers: me, Guerino, Gennaro in Giordani (now Annasiria), Libya, 1949.

LEFT: Neighbor Mr. Fontanella and Mr. Valerino Del Mastro in his peanut fields, on farm #139 in Giordani (now Annasiria), Libya, circa 1952.

At the Cinecittà refugee camp, 1946 —
BACK ROW, FROM LEFT: my brother Giovanni, Mr. Di Leonardo, Domenico Muoio, unknown, Bruno Cappelletti, FRONT: Mr. Fabro Renzi, Mr. Di Nicola.

Me at age 13, with my brother Giovanni, in the Cinecittà refugee camp, 1946.

Ada, me, my mother and father in corn fields on our farm in Giordani (now Annasiria), Libya, 1951.

My mother and father in Sabrata, Libya, 1950. This picture was taken after the competition between all the farms. We won three blue ribbons for the town—for the wheat (V. Del Mastro), for the horses (the Palumbo), and for the school (Mr. Balsamo).

Aunt Fiorina, my mother's sister, and Uncle Eustacchio Di Gregorio (Ercole Di Gregorio's brother), circa 1940.

IMAGES OF GIORDANI (NOW ANNASIRIA), LIBYA

LEFT: My father in a sweet-potato field on our farm, 1951.

ABOVE: On farm #100 harvesting peanuts, 1951 — Ashuir; Mohammed, Ashuir's cousin; me; Tumia (Mr. Marani's wife); Ada; Tumia's son Saad's two wives; and my father.

BELOW: Ashuir's mother, Tumia, my father with his concertina, Ada, me, 1951.

An Arab family coming to help with the harvest, near my family's farm, #100. The tent is a *zeribba*. You no longer see these tents, except in museums.

The procession before our wedding ceremony in Campo di Giove, August 28, 1960 — FRONT TO BACK: Giovanni's children, Roberto and Angela; Rosalba and her brother Erberto; Rosalba's sister-in-law, Anna, and me; Gennaro's wife, Ilde, and my father.

After the wedding ceremony, with our guests and the Majella Mountain in the background.

LEFT TO RIGHT: My mother Angela, Gemma Vella, Filomena Di Gregorio (Marietta's mother), August 1960.

IN BACK: Rosalba's Aunt Adela Sciuba, FRONT ROW: my mother, Gemma Vella, Leonilda Villani, in Campo di Giove, August 1960.

Family friend, Giovanna Vella, with me in Campo di Giove during the wheat harvest, August 1960.

On my way to America aboard the *Cristoforo Colombo*, May 4, 1955.

A portrait taken in Milford MA, in 1956.

My godparents, Gino and Gemma Simion, in Fiera di Primiero, circa 1970.

Uncle Pasquale Villani and family — STANDING: cousins Benny, John, Alba, Danny, Susie, Rose; SEATED: Pasquale, Auntie Angela Palumbo (my father's sister), 1954. Missing from photo is cousin Guerino.

Cristina (age 11) and Steven (age 4), 1979; at Cristina's wedding, September 15, 1996.

CRISTINA'S FAMILY — with Paul Hurley on their wedding day; daughters Olivia and Caroline (ages 4 and 6 in the center, ages 3 and 5 at right).

U.S. Marine Corps General James L. Jones, me, and Sergeant Major Alford L. McMichael, July 19, 2002. (Official Marine Corps Headquarters photo by Sgt. Marshall Paull)

Marine Corps Lieutenant Colonel Gabriel Patricio (Retired) presenting USMC award for my civilian service at the retirement ceremony for Rosalba and me, December 7, 2005.

After fifty-eight years, I am reunited with my childhood friend, Hadi Forga, in Giordani (now Annasiria), Libya, October 26, 2010.

My family's first farm, #32, from 1939–1944, in Garibaldi (now Al Dafniyah), Libya. This photo was taken exactly seventy-one years to the day after my family arrived in Libya, on November 1, 1939.

Rosalba and me at the Roman ruins in Sobrata, Libya, November 2010, recreating the photo taken of my parents in 1950.

CHAPTER SEVENTEEN

So, You Want to Be a *Sarto*?

The barbed wire around Campo Straniero made me hesitate before following the social worker inside. She was the person Mr. Balestieri had told me might be able to help me fulfill my dream. She smiled encouragement at me. "It's okay, Vittorio. There's nothing to be afraid of here, but there is work you might find interesting."

Not wanting her to know she had read my hesitation correctly, I pretended to be busy scratching the back of my leg. Then I trotted after her. The grown men who lived and worked here watched me follow the social worker down a long aisle. I heard the soft treadle action of the sewing machines before I saw them. Once we turned the corner, I found myself staring at twenty sewing machines, all of them occupied by men hunched over while busily tracking the lines of their stitching. I watched in fascination as their fingers lightly guided the cloth into the proper position. I longed to feel my own feet rocking back and forth on the treadle, my own fingertips easing the fabric toward the up-and-down action of the needle.

The tailor shop was run by two German gentlemen and Matilda Farmungari, a woman from Hungary. These three would be my mentors and would teach me almost everything I know about constructing a shirt. Matilda smiled at me with a warmth that accurately predicted her disposition. My heart raced with joy as I listened to the social worker make her introductions. "This is Vittorio, the young man I was telling you about. He wants to be a tailor."

Matilda smiled broadly. "Good. Yes. We can use him here."

Next, the two Germans walked over and shook my hand with a firmness that made me feel already a part of the team.

"Have you ever used a sewing machine before?" Matilda asked.

So afraid that my honest answer might cause everyone to change their minds about me, I waited just a few seconds before sadly shaking my head to indicate that I had not.

"Don't worry about that," Matilda reassured me. She gestured at the men working away. "None of these gentlemen had ever operated a sewing machine before either." She walked over to one man who had just flipped up the little lever that raised the presser foot so he could remove the piece he was working on and start another. She tapped him on the shoulder. "Would you mind letting Vittorio sit down at your machine for just a minute?"

He gladly got up, and I slid into place. Matilda pointed to the brass label that identified the maker. "Singer. All our machines are made in America. The UNRRA has supplied us with them."

I glanced over my shoulder to see what the social worker thought of my progress and realized that she must have slipped out once all the introductions were completed. I understood at that moment that I had a job. It was settled. I was going to learn to be a *sarto*.

In the beginning, I was given jobs away from the machines: sorting piles of fabric, carrying the assembled pieces to the table where the two Germans inspected them for potential flaws, sweeping scraps from the floor. No matter how menial the task, I took pride in it and in my place here. Unlike the work my brother did, I was actually paid a small stipend. It wasn't a lot of money, but it served to elevate my status in Giovanni's eyes. He had a girlfriend back in Campo di Giove, and his primary obsession was to find a way to see Marietta. As I've said, we were allowed to leave the camp, but not for more than a week at a time. Travel cost money, and I felt very important as I granted Giovanni the fare he would need in order to visit the young woman who had claimed his heart. Of course, he told the director he was going to see our grandmother. Since he stayed with her, there was truth in that, but the real strength of his devotion was to someone of the opposite sex who was much closer to his own age!

When I showed up for work one morning, Matilda was waiting for me. There was an unoccupied sewing machine in the second row. "Constantine has been transferred out of camp," she told me, gesturing toward the quiet Singer.

I glanced up at her wanting to be certain I had heard correctly. Did she really intend for me to learn to sew?

She nodded in answer to my unasked question. "You are ready, Vittorio." Her two German helpers, who stood just behind her, were trying to suppress grins as they waited for my reaction.

I squeezed my eyes shut and tightly closed my lips against the explosion of joy that threatened to burst from me. I heard the Germans laughing out loud. "You pay close attention to every detail," one of them said, as if reinforcing Matilda's opinion of me.

"A good worker. Natural talent," the other agreed.

"Really?" was all I could manage when I finally allowed myself to open my eyes so that the truth could sink in.

"Really. You are going to make a fine topstitcher," Matilda said. "Here, let me show you how to operate the machine."

I held up my hand, signaling for her to wait until I had a chance to demonstrate what I had taught myself by observation. They all nodded. And by showing them that I already knew how to thread the machine and rewind bobbins, already understood when to lift the presser foot and when to put it down, already had mastered the back and forth rhythm of the treadle, I happily proved that their faith in me was not misplaced.

And, so it was that my dream of becoming a *sarto* was given wings. In the process of learning to fashion a man's shirt, I also developed a deep friendship with my three mentors, especially Matilda. Once I was assigned my own machine, it was so difficult to separate me from it that I often ignored the call to lunch. Given how unimpressed I was by the noonday offerings, one might assume that wormy beans influenced my ability to ignore the metal triangle's signal, but that assumption would be incorrect; I simply got lost in the joy of my work and hardly knew what was going on around me. Aware of my commitment to the crisp white shirts springing to life under my direction and worried that I was too thin, Matilda sometimes brought me a sandwich from her own home. And even Matilda would have to tap me on the shoulder in order to get my attention. "Just a minute," I would tell her. "I don't want to stop until I'm done with this piece."

Once it became clear to everyone that providing a clean finish to collars, cuffs, and front plaits was more important to me than food, Antonio also took it upon himself to put together a lunch that could be carried from one camp to the other and bring it over to me. "Eat, Vittorio, eat." He repeated what had become a familiar refrain. "You have to eat if you want to keep up your strength." I don't know how to explain it, but sewing seemed to provide more nourishment than any amount of eating could do. To this day, all that I learned in Campo Straniero has stayed with me. My favorite process remains topstitching a shirt. There is such precision in the work. Done right, the collar, the front plait, the cuffs all indicate the overall quality and speak to the skill of the tailor. There. Finished. Everything fashioned smoothly into place.

I wish I could remember the social worker's name. Why do some memories vanish, while others, of much less importance, stick fast? She was a wonderful woman who always took a special interest in me. Every time I ran into her, she remarked on what a fine job she'd heard I was doing. And, once we'd established this relationship, she took me home with her on those occasions when holidays emptied the camp of everyone who had relatives living nearby. Her brother had two boys about my age, and the three of us had a grand time playing with their toys. I lived in Campo Cinecittà from November, 1945 until July of 1948. In all that time, the social worker's two nephews were the only children my own age I got to play with.

Toward the end of 1946, I heard a familiar voice call out to me by a name that only one person ever used. "*Baccetto.*" I whirled around. I hadn't heard wrong. It was indeed Gennaro! "*Baccetto. Baccetto.*" Little one. He had started calling me that before Ada was born. It was my name from so long ago, from back when I had been the youngest, from back when we were all together as a family, from back when I was still a child.

"Oh, Gennaro," I cried. "It is *good* to see you." And it was. And it was good to hear myself called by a name that signaled so much that no one else could understand, so much that I hardly understood myself. Why then did I offer correction? "Vittorio," I told him, wanting to take the words back as soon as I had uttered them. Why had I done that? Because I was trying so hard to become a man, to be seen as a man, but mostly because the name triggered such longing for all that had vanished that I feared indulging myself in it would rob me of the strength that had carried me to this point.

Gennaro did not take offence. He nodded in understanding. Although he was my brother, twenty-five years old to my thirteen, he was in many ways like a father to me. In fact, if a person could pick the traits one would want in a father, Gennaro had them all. And, on this day, Gennaro had good news for me. He had been transferred out of Pietro Grotta in Naples and had been reassigned to our camp in Rome. My brother was back. Three of the Palumbo boys—Gennaro, Giovanni, and myself—were once more joined as a family.

We had so much news to share. Gennaro listened in amazement as I described the steps involved in topstitching a shirt.

"Vittorio, do you remember a *sarto* by the name of Giacchino?"

Did I remember Giacchino? Of course I remembered Giacchino. Everyone knew who Giacchino was. Whenever we saw someone who was especially well-dressed, who cut a figure of natural elegance, we quietly would say to each other, "Dressed by Giacchino." This was a shorthand phrase that paid tribute to someone's fashion sense. It's funny because the real name of this *sarto* was Lucci Berardino. I knew his wife's name too. Annina Capaldo. Our family had a special connection to Lucci Berardino, because he had lived for a time in Campo di Giove.

Lucci Berardino was known to most Italians simply as Giacchino. The name alone conjured up the image of expertly tailored suits. He was a professional in every sense of the word; his skill being of the level that caused Italians to say the word *sarto* with special reverence, like a *mastro*, a teacher. A fine Italian hand. Giacchino was blessed with a fine Italian hand.

"Vittorio," Gennaro said. "What do you do with yourself when you are finished sewing at Campo Straniero?"

I turned my hands palms-up. "Nothing. Not much."

"Do you know that Giacchino's shop is in Quadraro?"

I hadn't known that, but I knew Quadraro was in a section of Rome not far from Campo Cinecittà. It was a short tram ride away. Studying Gennaro carefully, I could feel my hopes rising. What was he about to suggest?

"I think we should go talk to him. Your skills are of a level that perhaps he could use you after you are finished sewing here."

"I'm not of that level yet." I was afraid that in telling Gennaro of my work, I had made myself sound more grand than I knew myself to be.

"No. Of course not." He smiled at me. "But it wouldn't hurt to go talk to him. It would be a way for you to learn more. Perhaps he would take you on as an apprentice."

Italian Days, Arabian Nights

*

That's how it came to be that I studied under Giacchino. Gennaro introduced us. Suddenly Giovanni was not the only one using my earnings for transit. The money I received for topstitching shirts enabled me to pay for the tram that carried me to Giacchino and a whole new level of understanding. If letting the word *sarto* slide off my tongue filled me with joy, imagine how I felt on the day when I first walked into Giacchino's shop and addressed him as *Mastro*. He was my teacher. Under his kind but demanding instruction, I learned how to construct men's suits and topcoats. First I watched him, and later I helped him fashion coats, vests, and trousers, all from scratch.

When his customers came in to be measured, they brought the fabric they wanted along with them. Giacchino taught me that tailoring a suit involves many steps and, no matter how minor each one may appear to be, carelessness at any stage could ruin the final product. Measuring is a case in point. It seems a simple enough thing, but there is much that can go wrong, starting with not checking to make certain the client has assumed a natural posture. Then one has to position the tape properly and accurately read and record what is there. Failure to do so would result in disaster. "Dressed by Giacchino" meant only one thing: perfection and pride from start to finish.

Most of the suits Giacchino tailored were of wool. I learned to smooth the fabric out so that the weave was not pulled in such a way as to later distort the relaxed drape once the customer slipped into the finished garment. Only when the wool was properly aligned did we wrap and roll it between wet sheets, where it would remain for exactly one day and one night.

Making the pattern is another crucial step. Only the *mastro* himself translated the careful rows of measurements into the cut of a finished suit. I learned to do this from Giacchino. It's a skill I relied on, right up until 2005 when I retired from fashioning prototypes for military uniforms. I sometimes smiled to myself as I worked. "Dressed by Giacchino." Soldiers take pride in their uniforms. I wondered what they would think if they knew all that had gone into the design of the clothes they wore. I remembered to honor every detail. Giacchino taught me that.

Just as in Campo Straniero, I learned by watching exactly how things were done. Ah, the ease with which my Mastro used his scissors to create the pattern. The sound of the shears, the way the fabric fell away and already hinted at what it would become. By the time I was allowed to cut my first bit of cloth, I had imagined many times over exactly how it would feel when the resistance of the wool met the insistence of the sharpened blade. A clean cut. A confident cut. It's a knowledge that is carried in the wrist, in the hand, more than it is carried in the brain.

Once we were considered sufficiently advanced, the other apprentices and I were given these pieces to stitch and put together. At some point in the construction of a suit, the customer would return for another fitting. This was done before the suit was finished, before the sleeves had been attached. If there were adjustments that needed to be made, this was the time to make them. And then, finally, the suit would be completed. I loved the moment when Giacchino helped its new owner into the jacket, smoothed a hand across his shoulders, and indicating in the mirror, said, "There. See. What do you think?" We all knew the question wasn't asked without our Mastro knowing full well what the customer's reaction would be. A slowly spreading smile, almost of disbelief, and then a nod of happy confidence followed by a slow turn in front of his reflection. Who would have known that a man could look this good?

CHAPTER EIGHTEEN

Of Bread and Cigarettes

Days stitching in Campo Straniero; evenings learning from Giacchino; and free time on Sundays spent with Gennaro, my brother, my surrogate father, my friend. We didn't talk much about feelings, but I could read love in his gaze when I would glance up and realize he'd been studying me. Everyone was worried about how thin I was.

There was a bakery in Quadraro that made very fine bread. It wasn't too far from Giacchino's shop. One day Gennaro gave me a bit of money and a net bag made of string. "Vittorio," he said, "before you come back tonight, stop by the bakery and get us a loaf of bread." He raised his eyebrows in anticipation. "I've heard it's very good. We'll have a private feast when you return."

Before hopping on the tram that evening, I found my way to the bakery. I could feel my mouth water as I waited to be served. If one could believe the promise held out by the aromas filling the area, the bread was going to more than live up to Gennaro's expectations. The apron-clad woman behind the counter smiled as she put my purchase into the net bag.

Once I got to the station, climbed on the train, found a seat, and was on my way back to Campo Cinecittà, I positioned the bread on my lap in such a way that I could admire the shiny beauty of its crust. Stroking it with one finger, I discovered it was every bit as smooth as it looked. In one place the netting was ripped just enough to allow a fairly large piece of the bread to poke through. I decided it would look better if I evened that spot out. I tore it off and popped it in my mouth. Sooo delicious.

Gennaro was really going to love this! Hmm, but now when I looked at the bread, the unevenness of the place where I'd broken the chunk off bothered my eye. Some balance was upset. So I tore a matching piece from the other end. Equally delicious. However, the site of my original sample suddenly lacked symmetry. Before I knew it, there was so much of the loaf missing that its reduced size was an uncomfortable reminder of my guilt. I had no choice but to finish it all off.

When I walked into Campo Cinecittà with the empty bag dangling uselessly from my hand, Gennaro said, "What happened to the bread?"

"I got hungry."

Gennaro just shook his head and smiled. He seemed unable to get angry at me for any reason.

*

I was now thirteen years old and had never had a new pair of shoes. Being the youngest boy in the family, I'd always made do with hand-me-downs from my brothers. Then, of course, the war came, and nobody had new shoes. Sometimes I would catch Gennaro staring at my feet. No matter how ill-fitting or shabby the rest of my clothing, it was always my shoes that concerned him most. "Someday, Vittorio," he would tell me, "someday when I find a job that pays a bit of money, I'm going to buy you a pair of hiking boots."

His words brought to mind the hiking boots worn by my godfather and his brother back in Fiera di Primiero. Those had been fine boots, magnificent in all they seemed to indicate about a man. A readiness for adventure. The ability to face any challenge. I had loved those boots and fiercely dreamed of a pair of my own. How long ago that all seemed, another lifetime really. I remembered the boy I had been and sighed. I envied the innocence with which he had embraced those moments of simple joy.

Gennaro was true to his word. One day he said to me, "Okay, today is the day."

I looked up puzzled. "What day?"

"The day I take you to the Piazza Vittorio to buy a proper pair of shoes."

The Piazza Vittorio. What an appropriate name for the place where my brother gave me a gift I will never forget. It was in the Piazza Vittorio that Gennaro satisfied a longing he couldn't even have known I had. He had never met my godfather. He had never been to Fiera di Primiero, but his generosity restored some bit of the boy who had believed a pair of boots could change a man's life. There's truth in that. In some way his gift did change me. I'll never forget that day and my brother's generosity. I'll never forget those boots. I can still remember how it felt to stroll out of the shop with them on my feet, the ease with which they carried me over the cobblestones.

*

Early in 1947, I felt so ill that I found it difficult to get up from my straw mattress. Not even the desire to head over to Campo Straniero and the sewing machine could help me to my feet. When I failed to show up, everyone knew something was wrong. The social worker was alerted and came right to me. Placing her palm against my forehead to determine whether or not I had a fever, she murmured, "You must try to stand, so that I can help you to the camp hospital."

Located within the borders of the camp, this hospital was staffed by American and Italian doctors. They shook their heads and consulted with one another. "He's badly undernourished for a boy heading into puberty." Since they could find nothing wrong other than severe malnutrition, they decided that a course of calcium shots might supply some missing nutrients and stimulate my appetite. My failure to have much interest in food only compounded the damage already done by insufficient calories for a growing boy. I dutifully submitted to the shots and dragged myself back for daily weight checks. However, it quickly became apparent to everyone that the calcium shots weren't working. "We're going to have to have him checked out at the Policlinico here in Rome."

Gennaro, having already lost a cousin to some unidentified disorder, was beside himself with worry. He was afraid I might be the next to die. Tuberculosis was prevalent in Rome at the time. So much hunger. So many former strangers crowded together. The chill dampness that penetrated every corner of the camps. All my brother had to do was hear the words,

"Policlinico," and he took it upon himself to take me there. He paced the corridors anxiously while I had blood drawn and X-rays taken. I was so tired. All I wanted to do was lie down, but there was no place for me to do so. Gennaro and I sat on hard wooden chairs in a crowded waiting room for the better part of a day. By the time they finally called my name, it was difficult to gather the strength to stand and follow the nurse. And if mere sitting made me tired, walking turned my legs to jelly. When we reached the doctor's office, I wanted to do nothing more than stretch out across the floor and just sleep.

My X-rays were pinned in front of a panel that illuminated the gauze-like filaments of my lungs. The doctor tapped his pointer against the negatives. "We don't see any sign of TB yet. However..." He turned his attention from the X-rays and picked up a sheet of paper with the results of my blood work. Holding this in front of Gennaro, he said, "His immune system appears to be collapsing. You have to get him out of Rome. We're seeing too much disease here. His resistance is just too low."

Gennaro held his chin in his hand and shut his eyes against the news.

"Have you anywhere else you can take him? If he's going to recover, it should be somewhere outside the city."

"Yes. Campo di Giove. Mountain air. Vittorio's aunt is like a mother to him." Gennaro looked at the doctor. "But how long...how long do you think it will be before he is better?"

The physician looked confused. "I can't make those predictions. I only know what I fear will happen if he remains in Rome."

"Yes, yes. I understand. It's just that the camp...Vittorio has been waiting there since November of 1945 for clearance to return to Libya. If he stays away too long, he'll lose his place in the queue." Gennaro looked as if all his efforts to reunite our family were slipping from him as he watched.

For the first time, the doctor managed a small smile. "*That* I can take care of." He reached for an official-looking pad of paper and scribbled something on it. "Give this to the director, to Mr. Balestieri." He smiled more broadly. "I know him. There won't be a problem. Vittorio is to stay with his aunt until he is fully recovered. His place on the list will advance uninterrupted while he is gone."

I wish I could remember feeling joy on hearing the news that I would get to go back to Campo di Giove, but all I remember is wondering how I would ever find the strength to make the trip. Gennaro accompanied me, of course, at times carrying me from one place to another. I was so exhausted by the time we got to the railroad house that I don't even recall the reunion with Aunt Cristina and Uncle Ercole. For almost six weeks I remained in bed. As long as I lay still I would think I was getting better, but the slightest bit of exertion—even something as simple as trying to walk across the room—would leave me sweating and weak.

Aunt Cristina's neighbor kept a small flock of chickens. In those difficult times, living chickens were testimony to a person's ability to endure immediate hunger based on nothing more than faith in a chicken's potential to keep one supplied with eggs against hunger that might occur in the future. Eggs, the payment made for past denial, were truly precious. Aunt Cristina gave her neighbor a generous enough portion of the grain she and Uncle Ercole had stored that I was guaranteed three eggs a day. Certain these should be eaten raw if I was to derive the full benefit of their nutrition, Aunt Cristina had me suck them directly from the shell. Two every morning, one every evening.

In addition to the daily offering of eggs, I knew I was remembered in Aunt Cristina's frequent prayers. It was common for her to attend church twice a day. During the period of my convalescence, she found time for a midday visit to the priest as well.

I could see the worry in Aunt Cristina's eyes as she ministered to me and felt sad that I was causing her pain. However, memories of those times also fill my heart with love. No one had ever cared for me with such tenderness. Gennaro had told the doctor she was like a mother to me. Since my own mother and I had been separated for so long, Aunt Cristina was actually more than a mother to me. There aren't words to explain my gratitude, the depth of the affection between us. I named my daughter after her. I can't think of a higher tribute.

Determined not to lose another grandson, my grandmother also prayed for my recovery and made frequent visits to my bedside. Since her every touch carried a memory of Umberto with it, I felt her sorrow as deeply as I felt her love. While recuperating, I spent a total of three months in Campo di Giove. Leaving at the end of that time was even more difficult than the earlier separations had been. This time I knew what was waiting for me back at Campo Cinecittà. And despite the promise the doctor had made to Gennaro, I was beginning to despair of ever finding my way back to my parents in Libya. So my farewell to my relatives and boyhood friends was weighted with sorrow, a sorrow that would have been all the heavier had I realized that I would never again see some of these people alive.

Gennaro and I talked quietly on the return trip to the camps. "You ought to know that Vittorio Del Mastro is no longer at Campo Cinecittà."

"Was his name called?" My voice was tinged with envy as I asked the question. I was the youngest of our little group. I was supposed to be the first to return.

"No, no. That's not what happened. He's in Campo Forte Aurelio now." Gennaro patted my shoulder. "It's good the doctor got permission for you to stay at home until you were well again." Although his words were intended to offer comfort, he looked sad. "Your friend stayed too long with his sister, Rosina. He didn't have permission. He's had to reapply to the quotas system. He's starting all over in another camp."

I was silent. I couldn't imagine how that would feel. To have put so much time into waiting only to lose one's place in line. I drew a deep breath. "Thanks, Gennaro, for making sure that didn't happen to me."

"And there's something else, Vittorio."

His words frightened me. I didn't feel up to more bad news. I wanted to change the subject but sensed that Gennaro was waiting for some signal from me that it was okay to go on. Dutifully I asked, "What?"

"Antonio is gone."

"What do you mean gone? Gone where?"

Sensing that I might have misconstrued his words, Gennaro hurried to elaborate. "Disappeared. He's probably okay, but we just don't know where he is." He reached protectively toward me. "Don't worry. He told Giovanni he had heard about a Sicilian fishing vessel that was headed for Libya. We think he must have asked if they could give him passage."

"But why?"

"He was angry about what happened to Vittorio Del Mastro, about him staying away too long and losing his place, being sent to the back of the list in another camp."

I nodded. "Yeah, Antonio and Vittorio were really close." I looked at my older brother. "He didn't have papers?" I asked.

"No, but I think he'll be okay. You know how good he is at negotiating things."

I smiled. I did know. I remembered Antonio's skill at finding a buyer for our sugar. He would somehow figure out a way to get back to Libya, papers or no papers. I pictured him talking his way onto that Sicilian fishing boat. Still, so much had changed that I was almost afraid to inquire about anyone else. Gennaro spared me having to ask.

"Giovanni is fine. He's waiting for you in your old spot near the Mazzoni brothers."

Not long after my return to Campo Cinecittà, Mr. Balestieri came to our compound to read the names of those who had been granted approval to return. Sensing a change in my luck, I allowed myself to move to the front of the group. By now, I was one of the established members of the camp. It was the summer of 1947. I'd been assigned to the refugee camp for almost two years. I knew practically all the names he read off. By the time he announced the inclusion of both Mazzoni brothers, I was certain my name would be next. We'd arrived not too long after they had. Their quarters were just across the aisle from where my brother Giovanni, cousin Antonio, Vittorio Del Mastro, and I had plopped down our own straw mattresses. However, after mentioning only two other names after the Mazzonis, Mr. Balestieri folded up the paper he'd held in his hands and tucked it into his pocket. The cheers of those who had been selected mixed with murmurs of disappointment from the rest of us.

I put my head down and made my way back to my spot by the wide doors. The Mazzoni brothers were already gathering up the things they intended to take with them. Seeing my long face, one brother came over to me. "Psst," he whispered. "I have something to show you." With his hand, he motioned for me to follow him to their side of the aisle. Looking around to make sure no one else was watching, he reached behind his mattress and pulled out a little metal machine.

The other brother had now joined us. He tapped the gadget in his sibling's hand. "Do you know what this is, Vittorio?"

I had an idea, but not wanting to look foolish and not quite understanding what all the secrecy was about, I shook my head *no*.

He smiled and leaned close to me. "It's a gold mine."

Nodding vigorously, the first brother confirmed the statement. "A little gold mine." He looked at me. "Have you ever rolled a cigarette?"

"No."

"That's okay. You're a smart boy. You'll learn." The two of them then fumbled through other hiding places and produced a bag of loose tobacco and a stack of thin white papers. "We'll teach you. We've decided you're the best one to take over our business now that we're leaving."

And that's how I became a black-market dealer in cigarettes. Since the government was the only one licensed to sell this product, the Mazzoni brothers explained the importance of keeping a low profile as I conducted my illegal activity. They showed me the ropes, introduced me to their regular customers, explained the need to retain some of my earnings to purchase fresh supplies. One of the purposes of these refugee camps was to provide vocational training. I'm not sure this crash course in small business management was quite what the U.N. had in mind when it set up the camps, but my instructors were correct. Their machine was a little gold mine.

Once again, I had become the family wage earner. I was good at earning money; Giovanni was good at spending it on Marietta. I think the UNRRA would have been pleased with one lesson I took away from this unauthorized bit of schooling: seeing how desperate my customers were for the product I offered and puzzled by their willingness to spend scarce cash on cigarettes instead of more useful items, I promised myself I would never become a smoker. It's a promise I have kept.

*

Life went on in the way I had begun to understand that life does: punctuated by death. During my months of recuperation in Campo di Giove, Aunt Cristina was burdened by a sorrow unrelated to my illness. Her son Tonino had somehow found the courage to break from his mother's dream that he become a priest. She had failed in her attempts to persuade him to follow the vocation to which she was certain he was ideally suited. Instead, Tonino chose to become a lawyer and had only recently passed the bar exam. Whenever something bad happened, such as my getting so sick, Aunt Cristina would say, "Madonna. Maybe God is punishing me because Tonino didn't become a priest."

So, in October of 1947 when a telegram addressed to Gennaro arrived at Campo Cinecittà, he hesitated before opening it. Why would Uncle

Ercole have such an urgent need to get in touch with Gennaro that he would turn to a telegram? Giovanni and I waited anxiously as Gennaro read silently to himself. I could tell the news was bad by the stricken look on his face.

"Aunt Cristina...?"

He shook his head, almost unable to speak. "Tonino."

Tonino? Hadn't he recently passed the bar? I knew Aunt Cristina wasn't happy with this turn of events, but was her grief so strong that Uncle Ercole felt compelled to send us a telegram? I started to say something more, but Gennaro cut me off.

"He's dead. Tonino has suffered a stroke and died."

None of us could believe it. He was only twenty-five years old. If Aunt Cristina blamed herself for my *illness*, how would she ever be able to survive the *death* of her much-cherished son? Surely she would conclude that God was punishing her further for failing to give this son of hers to the Church. "Oh, no. Oh, no," I said over and over again. Tears filled my eyes. Would the Majella Mountain never stop its spinning? My sympathy for my favorite aunt was so strong that Gennaro and Giovanni decided that Aunt Cristina and I would only drive each other deeper into sorrow. Much as I protested, at some level I was relieved when my older brothers ruled that I must stay behind in the refugee camp while they traveled back to Campo di Giove for another funeral.

CHAPTER NINETEEN

Reunion in Libya

I'd waited so long for my name to be called that when it finally happened, I was too stunned to have much of a reaction. As other names were announced, people cheered. Someone threw his cap in the air, but I just stood there wondering how I would ever manage to leave without my brothers.

I was going to need new clothes. Gennaro and Giovanni insisted that I had to be presentable. My parents hadn't seen me in over eight years. Mussolini had taken a child; I wanted to return as a young man they could embrace with pride. It was important that their "first" impression did honor to all of us.

Gennaro clapped his hands together. "Back to Piazza Vittorio we go." He and Giovanni exchanged smiles. They were truly happy for me. "I know just the place. You'll leave here looking as if you'd been dressed by Giacchino."

At that we all laughed. No one had a budget for a tailored kind of elegance, but my brothers made sure I was dressed in clean new clothes that fit me well when I headed off on the first leg of my journey. I returned the favor by granting Giovanni custody of the cigarette-making machine. "A family dynasty of petty crime," Gennaro remarked, trying hard not to smile when he overheard my whispered instructions. He was well aware that almost everyone with any authority in camp had turned a blind eye whenever I had wandered around with contraband cigarettes hidden between my upper arm and my body.

All those who'd been selected for this round traveled together. The first destination on our itinerary was Santo Alesio, a convent just outside of

Rome. We were there for three nights. At the time I was puzzled by, but not totally unappreciative of, the delay. In hindsight, I suspect it was what we all needed—a kind of necessary decompression, a pause between life in the camps and life in the real world. While there, we were brought up-to-date about current events and the conditions we could expect to find in Libya. This was the first time I had stopped to consider that I was not the only one in my family who might have changed. Garibaldi was gone. My family lived in Giordani. Yes, yes, I knew that; Gennaro had told me, but it wasn't until those few days at the Santo Alesio convent that I sensed what that might actually mean for the relatives I had left behind.

After three nights and four days of rest and instruction, we climbed on the bus for a return trip to Rome. However, we weren't going back to Campo Cinecittà; we were headed for the train station where we would begin our one and a half day journey to Siracusa, a port city on the coast of Sicily. We were returning to Libya in baby steps. How different it all seemed from the journey that had first carried me from Italy with my parents and, then, only ten months later, the one that had too quickly snatched me from my childhood and enrolled me in boarding schools designed to transfer my loyalties from father and mother to Mussolini. I shook my head. Was I being subjected to a reverse form of brainwashing? I didn't think so. It wasn't going to happen. Uncle Ercole's words in answer to the question I'd asked him about loyalties when we were in the *capanna* returned to me. "Whose side are we on?" he'd asked, repeating my question before answering, "Our own. We watch out for each other now." Uncle Ercole was right. I knew where my loyalties lay. With my family.

A small boat, the *Campidoglio*, was waiting for us in Siracusa, a city which had been heavily bombed by both German and Allied planes. As we pulled away from the dock, I squinted my eyes to hide the recent damage and concentrated on the way the morning sun splashed burnished gold over the old stone lining the harbor, a shade that matched that of the houses. Much beauty still remained in Siracusa. It all depended on where I decided to direct my gaze.

Feeling a bit like a tourist instead of someone in a hurry to be reunited with his family, I was happy when I learned we would be stopping in Malta, where we would be given a tour of Valletta, a city known for the abundance of its churches—275 in all—half of them Roman Catholic, half Greek Orthodox. As we disembarked, we were directed to an elevator large enough to accommodate a car. Since Malta is essentially built on an enormous rock jutting high above the ocean, this elevator would be the only way to get from the port up to Valletta. I'd exchanged bits of conversation with a man about five years older than I was. He had a clear memory of being carried from Libya on the battleship *Giulio Cesare*, the very same ship, the very same journey that I had made on my return to Italy. "This isn't our first stop in Malta," he reminded me. "Only there was no sightseeing back in July of 1940. We had to remain on the ship while active mines filling the water were detonated all around us." He looked at me expectantly. "Don't you remember all those explosions?"

Embarrassed that I did not, I mumbled something about being very young. "Oh, boy," he said. "We were all a lot younger then. Kaboom! Splash! They had to wait until every mine was blown up before we got clearance to move ahead." The elevator doors opened. As we walked out behind a tour guide, my new friend remarked, "Churches instead of fireworks. This time around, the British government is providing a different form of entertainment."

*

When the *Campidoglio* maneuvered its way next to the dock in Tripoli early the next morning, I couldn't stop memories of my earlier arrival in Tripoli from flooding my mind. It wasn't just that I'd been younger; that first ship had been much larger. We'd been far, far above the dock then; however, the deck of the *Campidoglio*, the ship that guided my return, was only a storey or so above the crowd below. In 1939, everything had been gleaming and new. But the Tripoli waiting for me in 1948 still bore the scars of a port that armies from two sides had fought to control. I was on a journey to reclaim what I had left behind and, instead, found myself once again entering a new world. As I made my way down the gangplank, I scanned the crush of people for my parents. Surely they would not have changed so much that I would be unable to recognize them. My moment of panic intensified when I realized that, once on the dock, it was difficult to see over the heads of those milling about. Was no one here to meet me? Would I have to find a way to Giordani all by myself? My rising sense of abandonment was cut short by a gentleman wandering through the crowd loudly calling my name, "Vittorio Palumbo. Vittorio Palumbo."

Since the man obviously did not recognize me and since I had no idea who he was, I could only conclude that my mother and father had sent a stranger to escort me back to them. I hesitantly walked toward him. Patting my chest with my fingertips, I said, "Yes. That's me. I am Vittorio Palumbo."

We stood taking the measure of each other. I could tell he was as puzzled as I was. "Vittorio? Vittorio Palumbo?"

"Yes." A headache that had plagued me since Malta was now pounding with such intensity that it distorted the features of my courier. Who was this handsome blond man? Should I know him? I swallowed hard, wanting to explain that I had a headache but my mounting confusion and nervousness prevented me from saying anything.

"Vittorio Palumbo?"

"Yes," I was finally able to say. "Yes. Who are you?"

"Salvatore," he said smiling broadly. "I am Salvatore Del Mastro." He laughed. "Don't you remember me? Well, we have a lot of catching up to do. I'm your brother-in-law now."

Unable to respond to him in any coherent way, I finally had the courage to press my hand against my forehead. "Excuse me. It's hard for me to understand. I have a terrible headache."

"The heat. Of course. I'm not thinking. You are unaccustomed to the heat."

It was 130 degrees there on the dock, and anxiety caused my heart to pound with the strength of a horse. Every beat seemed to move directly from my chest up into my head. I mumbled something. "Did you really say you are my brother-in-law?"

Salvatore reached for the small bag I was carrying. "I have lots of news for you, but, forgive me for not understanding, this isn't the place to do it." He looked at me with concern and, apparently deciding I was up to walking, motioned for me to follow him. "I spent the night in a nearby hotel. I've arranged for us to stay there until it cools off enough to travel back to Giordani."

Once we reached the hotel room, Salvatore motioned for me to lie down on the bed. Finding it such a relief to be able to shut my eyes against the heat and the confusion, I didn't argue. Not wanting him to think I was ignoring him, I said, "Tell me now. Tell me everything. I'm not sleeping." Once again, I touched my temple. "My headache will stop if I can just block out the light for a bit."

It was easier to listen with my eyes closed and Salvatore started where he had left off. "I am your brother-in-law. I married your sister Giovanna."

Suddenly I found myself able to smile. Someone from my family had been there to meet me after all. I actually opened my eyes. "Really?"

"Yes, really." Encouraged by my interest he continued. "And you're an uncle. We have a three-year-old daughter, Antonietta."

I leaned back against the pillow. Everything was going to be all right. I was on my way home. In the cool darkness of the room, my headache finally eased and Salvatore filled me in on much that had happened while I was gone. The Del Mastros still lived in the same Giordani farmhouse they had occupied ever since 1939. At the time we received our first assignments, the distance between Garibaldi and Giordani seemed so vast that it was almost as if the Del Mastros had been banished from our lives. But now, I realized it was that very distance that had given my family a place to go when forced to retreat from Garibaldi.

Salvatore told me much about the destruction of Garibaldi at the hands of both Allied and Italian armies, but his story was the kind of factual accounting that comes from many retellings. In other words, it was one from which most of the emotion had been scrubbed. Only later would my sister Giovanna fill me in on the real story of what had happened to my family as they fled the first farm they'd established in Libya.

"So, your family came to us, two German soldiers brought them to our farm at #139." He looked at me proudly. "They stayed there three months, long enough for me to decide I wanted to marry Giovanna."

I was feeling much better and sat on the edge of the bed while we talked. "Where are they now? Where did my parents go when they left you?"

"Just about the time Ada's hand began to heal, they learned of another farm that was for sale," he paused, realizing I would have had no way to learn about Ada's injury. "Ada's finger had been badly cut by flying shrapnel."

Just that short explanation hinted at a larger story, but I was having enough trouble absorbing all this information, so I didn't press him for details but just listened to him tell the part he had experienced directly. I nodded and he continued.

"Ada's whole arm was swollen. Your parents arranged to travel by horse and buggy to a doctor near the San Sabastiano Church." He rubbed his own finger as he told the story. "A male nurse who worked there gave your mother a homemade poultice she could use to draw out the infection. Ada hated her treatments, so much so that she would begin to cry the moment she saw San Sabastiano's steeple coming into sight. She knew it meant they were almost at the doctor's. She required treatment every four days for a couple of months, until everyone was certain the blood poisoning was under control."

I still pictured Ada as a baby and found it hard to imagine her being able to understand the connection between the steeple and the painful changing of bandages. Wanting to draw the conversation back to one where I had information, I asked if he had known that his brother Vittorio had been assigned to a different refugee camp and would be delayed in his return. It suddenly occurred to me that Salvatore might have been expecting Vittorio to arrive with me.

He nodded. "Gennaro sent a telegram."

"Then you know..." I fumbled for words. "I guess he also told you about Umberto."

"Yes, the D'Agostinos told us as soon as Gennaro sent word." He looked as sad as I felt.

"And Antonio...?"

He let out a great sigh of relief. "He beat you here. Some Sicilian fishermen gave him passage in exchange for help with the nets." Salvatore shook his head and laughed. "Antonio D'Agostino always finds a way."

After hearing the next part of Salvatore's update, I decided that Roberto Palumbo was also good at knowing how to find a way. My father had managed to save enough money working the farm in Garibaldi that when he learned that farm #100 in Giordani was going to become available, he arranged to buy it. Just four months after the destruction of all he had worked so hard to create, he once again was managing a prosperous farm. I smiled when Salvatore told me all these things. I remembered my father's skill, had fond memories of going with him and his horse and mule when he had worked the neighbors' fields back in Campo di Giove. Roberto Palumbo had a talent for rising to the top.

"His new farm," Salvatore corrected himself, "*your* new farm." He looked at me to make sure I was taking all this in. "After Giovanna and I got married, we were able to purchase farm #126. That's where we now live with our daughter Antonietta. We're close enough to your farm that we are able to help with some things." He laughed. "For a while, farm #100 was a very busy place. When your Aunt Raffaela and Uncle Savino needed a place after *their* farm in Garibaldi was destroyed, they lived there with your cousins, Filippo and Caterina. Caterina is married now and she brought her son Bruno with her." Almost as an aside, Salvatore added, "Caterina's husband Attilio was still a prisoner of war in England."

I was having trouble taking it all in and sighed loudly. So much had changed. My sister married. Caterina married. And babies. I had a niece. What was her name? I could feel my headache starting to return.

Perhaps sensing that all this news was too much for me, Salvatore quickly summarized, "The D'Agostinos were with your parents for close to a year, and then they bought farm #6. It's only ten miles away."

"And do we still live close to your family, the Del Mastros?"

"We go see them about once a month, and by the time we travel back and forth and spend some time visiting, it takes a full day. Your new farm is a lot closer to the D'Agostinos." Salvatore tapped the face of his watch. "It's almost time for us to catch the bus." He stood up. "So, you have lots of family waiting to see you, Vittorio. Everyone is settled in Giordani."

We climbed on the bus at three in the afternoon. Since the late-July sun was still blazing down, I shut my eyes, hoping my headache wouldn't return. Jamming myself into the corner of the seat, I slept off and on. Whenever we hit a bump, I'd wake up startled, unsure of where I was. It always took me a few seconds to recognize the blond man sitting next to me. Salvatore Del Mastro, my brother-in-law. Brother-in-law! As soon as I managed to get my bearings, I would think of another unanswered question. I had lots of new relatives, but what about my old ones? My brother Guerino? I tapped Salvatore's arm. "Gennaro told me Guerino was back, but he didn't know where he'd spent the war years."

"Of course, you'd have no way of finding out all the details. Telegrams are expensive." He rubbed his chin. "We should have had Guerino figure out a way to tap the news to you." He chuckled at his own little joke. "That's what he did, you know. He was stationed somewhere in the mountains near Sudan, maybe Nigeria. He was a telegraph operator for the Italian Army, but now he's helping with our cheese business."

How easily the word *our* slid off Salvatore's tongue. I envied him. I'd spent so many years figuring out how to survive on my own, I wasn't sure what it would be like to be able to say *our* with such confidence. "Does Guerino know how to make cheese?"

"Yes, he and your father work together. Your father never learned to operate a motor vehicle, you know. He leaves that side of things to the younger generation." Salvatore cracked his knuckles. "Guerino and Filippo drive the delivery truck." He examined his hand. "Let's just hope they manage to keep all their fingers." Salvatore laughed. "It's quite something to watch them crank the engine to get it going. You know how Guerino is. He hurries through everything. We all tell him he'd better pay attention, or he'll lose a hand. He's a wild man when he turns that crank."

Even though it was almost seven in the evening when the bus pulled in, it was still daylight. Like the one I had left behind in Garibaldi, this village center had been constructed in anticipation of the great influx of Italian settlers. However, in ten years time, enough of the newness had worn off that Giordani had the gentle beauty that comes with evidence of use. The sun captured all the human touches, making it clear that this was an established community. Ten marble steps the width of the central portion of the small white church led up to doors that closed into a transverse arch. The flat-roofed steeple boasted a clock in the center and three little bells were housed just below the cross that crowned the whole affair. Like so much Italian-inspired Libyan architecture, the church had dark green shutters. Porticos extended from either side, one of them leading to what was obviously the rectory.

"It's just a short walk," Salvatore said, interrupting my reverie.

The look of Giordani had a familiar feel, and I wasn't in a hurry to abandon the comfort that just standing there offered. I wordlessly signaled for him to give me another minute. The church and the buildings surrounding it connected in such a way as to form a central square. Each of the various establishments featured arched entryways. There was a small hotel, a police station, a butcher, a grocery, a candy shop, a fabric store, a grist mill, and restaurants. People worked and shopped here. My people. This was a more vibrant version of what I had left.

Turning to Salvatore, I nodded my head to let him know I was ready to resume our journey. However, the further we got from the town center, the more I dragged my feet. I reminded myself I would soon be home. All the years of anticipation were over. Why then was I walking so slowly? Because although I could place myself somewhere among the storefronts, I had no memories of what waited just down the road. Salvatore looked over his shoulder and stood quietly until I caught up. I tried to explain some of what I was feeling. "When I left our old farm, it was all sand and desert." I gestured at the farms we were walking past. Enormous eucalyptus plants marked the borders between each farm. "Was Garibaldi like this when…" I drew a deep breath and began again. "Did our farm in Garibaldi look like this? Orange groves and everything?"

"Well, of course it did. Your father knows better than anyone how to make the desert flourish."

I stood still for a moment so that I could sort it all out. How long does it take an orange tree until it is ready to bear fruit? Could all this have happened in less than a decade? Salvatore waited beside me while I studied the farms, and then I finally indicated that I was ready to continue. We walked past just a few more properties, all of them laid out just as our old homestead had been. Four houses facing toward the small plot in the middle of each estate. Each farm carefully measured into two square miles. Still not quite ready, I was startled by Salvatore's proud announcement. "There it is. Farm #100. You're finally home, Vittorio."

A man was waiting with a young girl by the door. My father? Yes, of course, he was so like his father, my grandfather, that I would have known him anywhere. Had he been there, I would have recognized him on the dock. Moving awkwardly forward, I hesitantly spoke his name, "Papá."

He walked briskly toward me and extended his hand. "Welcome back." His grip was firm, but his smile, although genuine, reflected the confusion we both felt. What does a father say to a fifteen-year-old son he hasn't seen in almost nine years? Neither one of us apparently wanting to be the first to disengage, we shook hands a bit too long. Finally, he pulled away in order to gesture to the eight- or nine-year-old girl who was watching us curiously. "You remember Ada? Your sister?"

Remember? How could I possibly remember or even recognize this shy girl as the baby sister I had left behind? I simply nodded and repeated her name. "Ada. Of course, Ada." I remembered her name and, as that was really all I had to hold me in this place, I said it again. "Ada."

Salvatore walked toward the door. "Giovanna has been counting the days."

It felt odd to be welcomed into my family home by a brother-in-law I hadn't known I had until that morning, but we all seemed glad to follow his lead. My mother had been watching us from the window. When I came through the door, she extended both hands and said, "Vittorio."

"Ma." Her skin was very dark from the sun and she had more wrinkles than I remembered. She was by this time, of course, fifty years old. However, just seeing her face again stirred something very young in me. Overcome with emotion and confusion, I gestured to a pregnant woman who was chasing a small child across the kitchen. "Who are these people?" I whispered.

Apparently I didn't whisper softly enough, for my brother Guerino laughed and strode confidently toward me. "Don't you recognize your own sister, Vittorio?"

In a near panic, I looked at Salvatore for confirmation. Understanding my sense of dislocation better than the others, he nodded and said almost in apology, "I didn't have time to tell you we were expecting another baby." He pulled me into the room. "That's our daughter, the niece I was telling you about, that's Antonietta."

Giovanna now moved to greet me. She gave Guerino a dirty look. "Of course he knows me. I'm his sister." She indicated her belly and smiled. "Salvatore should have warned you."

I nodded and returned her smile, seeking refuge behind the excuse she had so readily offered. It dawned on me that I was going to have to learn to pretend to know a lot more, to remember a lot more, than I actually did. After all the years of longing for these people, for this place, I realized it was no longer home for me. Giordani had *never* been my home. Why hadn't I thought about how it would feel to leave one settlement and be returned to another? How could the social workers from the UNRRA have left that part out when they were instructing us at the Santo Alesio Convent? I tried my best to hide my disappointment behind a pleasant face, but I knew beyond any doubt that I was a stranger among strange people living in a strange land.

CHAPTER TWENTY

Tailoring a New Life

As long as you water it three times a week, you can grow anything in Libya. Before I'd left for Mussolini's schools, my family had planted wheat so that my mother would have flour for bread. In the beginning, we grew potatoes, corn, and white and red kidney beans. I remembered watching as my parents and brothers had staked out the first grape vines. How excited we'd been at the thought that we lived in a climate warm enough that we could plan to make wine.

Not in my wildest dreams would I have been able to envision the Eden that waited for me on my return. My father had established a business selling fresh vegetables, at first to the military. But once he'd earned a reputation for superior produce, he supplied wholesalers, some of whom even exported his crops. My mother managed the actual farming. Lettuce, tomatoes, spinach, cabbage, celery, radishes, ruga, artichokes, parsley, peppers, eggplant, peanuts, asparagus, watermelon, and peas. They weren't, of course, all in season that late July when I returned, but my mother explained the rotation of this abundance as she gave me a quick tour of the farm on my first morning back.

She gestured to groves of fruit and almond trees, then turned to me proudly. "But of course the product for which we're best known is cheese." Pointing to a small outbuilding in the fenced courtyard just behind our house, she said, "That's the *casificio*." A small cheese factory. My family seemed to have businesses that reached in all directions. "Provolone is our specialty."

Cheese. Oranges. Peaches. Pears. Apples. Whatever else my family had suffered during the war, the threat of starvation must not have been part of it. I felt my mother waiting for some response and knowing that reference to hunger was somehow impolite, I quickly asked a question. "How do you do it all?"

"Hard work. Farming is hard work, Vittorio." She looked at me slowly, as if trying to figure if I would be up to the task. She shrugged and gestured to a series of exotic-looking tents positioned at the border of the property. "I oversee the Arabs who help us. Your father runs the business side of things." At the mention of my father, we both looked back toward the house. He had announced that he was going to take me into town to buy some clothes suitable for the jobs I would be doing. "It's a family operation. Your Uncle Savino is partners with us in the cheese business. Guerino and Uncle Savino's boy, Filippo, manage the deliveries. We have a number of buyers in Tripoli."

Deliveries sounded like something that I might like to do, but I held my tongue until I understood just what my family had in mind for me. I was a bit awed by the transformation in my mother. Despite the fact that she still wore the long skirts and sleeves typical of the Abruzzo region, I was having trouble reconciling the confident woman beside me with my memories of my mother. She claimed that my father ran the business side of things, but she seemed completely in charge and knowledgeable about everything that went on. Who was this merchant of cheese and produce? I'd never imagined that she might have this strength. Sure, the wives had always worked beside their husbands in Campo di Giove—some of them even helping to drive the sheep into the Roman country—but the woman striding beside me seemed very comfortable talking about buying and selling.

I thought of my grandmother knitting the lace stockings that brides wore on their wedding day and needed for their dowries. They ordered twelve pairs at a time. Using a very fine cotton known as *perlĕ*, my grandmother's fingers flew over the needles. Soon a dozen pairs of stockings in a variety of muted shades—off-white, grey, blue, tan, and black—were waiting for the excited bride. Everyone in town came to her when it was time to get married, but no money ever changed hands. They'd bring her eggs, a bit of lard, perhaps some wheat. What would she think to hear her daughter talking so comfortably about buyers in Tripoli?

I was surprised to find Guerino waiting to walk with me and my father into Giordani to purchase the fabric for my new clothes. A little disappointed at losing this chance to explain that I was used to earning my own living, handling my own money, and taking care of myself, I mostly remained silent while the two of them talked about purchasing another flock of sheep. I quickly gathered that my father was in the habit of buying young animals and then hiring Arabs to graze and look after them on their own lands until they were mature enough to slaughter or to turn to the production of wool and milk.

Hesitantly I broke in with a question. "Sheep? You raise mainly sheep?"

Guerino answered for my father. "No. Cows too. Horses. Racehorses. The Arabs understand horseracing. We buy and sell the animals. Some they raise for us and then we split the sale price."

"I didn't see any cows."

Guerino looked at me with what I thought was the impatience of one explaining the obvious to an idiot. "Cows require too much land for grazing. We're most interested in the milk. The other farmers sell their milk to us. And we also make arrangements with the Arabs to help with the purchase of the necessary animals, and then they supply us with the additional milk we need." He looked bemused. "Where did you think we could keep enough livestock for all the milk we need for our production of butter and cheese?" He shook his head. "We have arrangements with the Arabs." Then almost as an afterthought, he added, "Beef cattle too. We do some business with beef."

I didn't think I'd imagined his look of contempt and resolved not to ask any more questions. I'd learn by watching. Besides, my growing discomfort with the ease with which everyone except me used the words "our" and "we" had a way of sealing my lips.

I'd noticed the fabric shop in the town square when Salvatore and I had gotten off the bus the night before. Guerino might know a lot about farming, but I was fairly certain I had more expertise when it came to tailoring. However, before I'd even had an opportunity to run the selvage edge of the cloth between my thumb and forefinger, my father had placed the order for enough yardage to make me a couple pairs of trousers and two shirts. "We'll get you measured for the trousers in Micca." He turned, sizing me up with his eyes. "Antonietta San Antonio, a seamstress here in Giordani, can make your shirts."

Mustering my courage, I said softly, "I know how to do topstitching. They taught me to make shirts in Campo Cinecittà."

My father raised his eyebrows and smiled. "Really? I thought only women made shirts."

I nodded. That *was* the tradition, but not willing to yield my end of the conversation this easily, I continued. "Do you remember Giacchino? Dressed by Giacchino?"

"You'll not be dressed by Giacchino for working in the fields," Guerino interrupted me.

"That's not what I meant. I know I need work clothes. It's just that Gennaro…" The mention of my older brother's name caused my father to turn to me with a bit more interest. "Gennaro arranged for me to apprentice with Giacchino. I want to be a *sarto*."

Guerino laughed. "Fine. But first you're going to have to learn to be a farmer." He walked beside my father as if they were equals. "Sandals, don't you think? He'll need two pairs of sandals. Until he gets used to how we do things now, he should start in the fields." He turned to me to explain his reasoning. "You may have forgotten how hot it gets in Libya. Open shoes work best."

*

The first explanation for my lack of appetite was that I was just having difficulty adjusting to the heat. "Give him a little time," Giovanna said, as she tried to tempt me with a bit of soup. She was so kind that I did my best to eat it. Of all my relatives, Giovanna seemed the one who was most truly glad to have me home. "You can't expect him to come directly from Italy and go to spending hours in the fields."

Guerino spoke as if I wasn't there. "He's been back for almost two months. That should be time enough to get used to the heat."

I knew Guerino thought I was just faking. And in my heart of hearts, I wished it *were* something as simple as needing time away from the farm work, but I'd been sick before and sensed this was something more serious. Vittorio Del Mastro had finally been granted passage back to Libya. For all the fuss about him losing his place in line, he'd arrived in Tripoli just a week behind me. When we got word that he was also sick, my mother said, "Perhaps they caught something in the camps. I think we need to take Vittorio in to see the visiting doctor. And if he can't do anything for him, I have a lot of faith in Augusto."

She started to explain that he was the one who had saved Ada from blood poisoning, but at the mention of a trip to see Augusto, Ada interrupted her to lean in close to me. "Don't go, Vittorio," Ada told me. "It really hurts."

I held out my arms for her to examine. I was very quickly growing quite fond of this younger sister. For her part, she seemed fascinated to have suddenly gained a brother. "Don't worry, Ada," I told her. "I'm not going to let him touch my hands or my arms."

"Promise?"

"Promise."

With that promise, we gained Ada's approval, and my mother made an appointment for me to be examined by the doctor. He wasted no time in arranging to have me admitted to the hospital in Tripoli. Salvatore packed me up for the journey to the hospital.

I protested. "Salvatore, it hasn't been that long since you brought me here. You're going to wear out the road between Giordani and Tripoli." I thought I might be able to manage traveling on my own by bus.

"Don't be silly, Vittorio. Just think of it as a trial run. By the time I get back, I may have to turn right around to take Giovanna to the maternity ward." He smiled warmly at my sister who was due later that month.

My mother, who was busy adding up columns of figures, had, up until this point, appeared to be unaware of the conversation around her. However, at the mention of maternity wards, she cleared her throat impatiently. "Whoever heard of having a baby in the hospital? All my children were born at home." She never lifted her head from her work. It was almost as if she were talking to herself. "Even Ada. She was born in Libya, and I managed just fine at home."

Salvatore and Giovanna exchanged silent glances in a way that informed me that, despite the fact that this was a subject that must have been endlessly debated, nothing was going to change my sister and brother-in-law's mind.

As we walked out the door, my mother did look up from her work. Her face was sad. "Get well, Vittorio." She stared at me and her eyes clouded for a moment, but she said no more.

Weak though I was feeling, I found the trip back to Tripoli easier than the one to the new farm had been. At least this time I didn't have a pounding headache that forced my eyes shut. Knowing that Tripoli had been the site of some brutal battles, I was surprised that the hospital seemed untouched by the ravages of war. The up-to-date medical facility had been built by the Italians in a beautiful section of town in the late 1920s and consisted of five separate buildings surrounded by landscaped gardens. How restful it all seemed. Salvatore pointed out the different compounds. "Giovanna will have our baby over there in the maternity facility." He gestured as we drove through an elaborate wrought-iron gate. Oleander bushes and palm trees surrounded each of the rectangular structures. "You'll be in the medical section." We circled toward a parking area. "The lab work and research is conducted over there." As we moved slowly past the surgical division, I stared down the driveway at some people on crutches walking around one of the smaller buildings. "That's rehabilitation," Salvatore told me. "Now come on, the Vittorio Emanuele Hospital is waiting for one of its namesakes to keep his appointment."

I was assigned a place in a long ward on the second floor of the medical building. There were three rows of beds, one on each side, and one down the middle, with no walls separating them. I'd been there only two days when Salvatore showed up with his brother Vittorio Del Mastro. "I told you you'd wear out the roads between here and Giordani," I told him with a weak smile.

While they were settling his brother at the other end of the ward, Salvatore stood by my bed. "Are you feeling any better?"

I nodded. "A little," I said, because that seemed to be what was expected of me, and I didn't want to disappoint. "They've drawn lots of blood and have done a series of tests."

"Any word on why it's so hard for you to eat?"

I shook my head and changed the subject. "The nuns are very nice." We were attended by a Dominican order. "They'll take good care of Vittorio."

"And of you, I hope. Perhaps you'll both be well enough to return when it's time for me to bring Giovanna back home after she's had the baby."

"Your brother will be better by then too?"

"I hope so. My brother too." He looked thoughtful and just stood there quietly for a while. "You've both gone through so much." He cleared his throat. "Vittorio has told me things I didn't know." He walked away from my bed and looked out one of the windows. When he came back, he quickly squeezed my hand. "Nobody can change the past. And sometimes people who love you don't want to hear about things that they can't change." He looked at me sadly. "It's too hard for them." Then he excused himself to go say goodbye to his brother.

I knew that he had been talking about my parents and Guerino. I was beginning to understand that much of my story was going to have to remain locked inside me. Maybe all I needed was a little time and my nightmares and the knot in my stomach would go away on their own.

One good thing about my stay in the hospital is that I finally met a boy my own age. True to form, Bardella and I called each other only by our last names. He was from the nearby town of Bianchi and worked in the village store in Giordani. It was comforting to know that a friendship I formed here in the sick bay would continue after we were both released from the hospital. The time spent with him was even more valuable than the few days the UNRRA had arranged at the convent outside Rome. Bardella gradually filled me in on what life in Giordani was like. I could take it in a bit at a time and ask questions without giving anyone in my family the impression that I was stupid. Because he worked in a store, he knew a lot of people. He even knew my father. "Your father always looks sharp. He wears nice suits when he's out on business." I confessed my lack of aptitude for farming to Bardella and he smiled at me. "Maybe you and your father share some gifts. Perhaps you'll end up more businessman than farmer too." I knew he was trying to make me feel better and I just smiled and held my tongue. If anyone was going to take over the business end of the farm, I knew it would be Guerino. It felt a little strange to learn about my father's reputation as a well-dressed livestock dealer from someone I had just met, but everything Bardella shared with me gave me confidence I would return to the farm more self-assured than I had been at first.

Even though Vittorio Del Mastro was five years older than my new friend and I were, as soon as he had permission to leave his bed, he wandered down and took part in the informal tutoring on life in Libya that Bardella offered. I think the conversations between the three of us did as much to restore my health as the medicine the doctors prescribed to settle my stomach. Vittorio Del Mastro knew what life in Mussolini's boarding schools had been like. He'd been there when the Germans had turned us out of our homes at gunpoint and had suffered through that cold winter in the *capanna*. We'd both spent almost three years in refugee camps. Somehow Bardella, with Vittorio Del Mastro sitting beside him on the bed, served as the link between the past and present and enabled me to make a coherent story of my life so far.

Given the scarcity of vehicles and the difficulty arranging transportation, it made sense that Salvatore was the only member of my family who was able to visit me during my hospital stay. In some ways it gave me a needed break, a little time to reconcile the distance between the way I had thought I'd feel on being reunited with my parents and the way it had actually turned out. Besides I had two friends with me: Vittorio Del Mastro from my old home in Italy and Bardella from my new one. Suddenly I was able to envision myself living here. There were people who understood me, after all.

In the process of walking back and forth in the ward to visit with them, I met a man, Mr. Battaglia, who was obviously seriously ill. He seemed so alone that I ached for him and would sometimes stop and chat for a few minutes. Nothing of any consequence. An exchange of names. *Good morning* or *Good afternoon.* Nothing more familiar than that. Because he was so sick, I had trouble lingering too long beside his bed. It was difficult to watch the nuns inserting tubes into his stomach. They needed a bucket in order to hold all the dark green bile they drained from him. I knew he was dying.

Mr. Battaglia still lingers on my conscience. I can't think of him without a haunting sense of guilt that I let him down in his hour of need. One day the nuns gathered around his bed in a great flurry of activity. One asked, "When did you last receive communion?" I couldn't hear his answer, but whatever it was he said caused a great emotional outcry. I wanted to make them stop scolding him and, gathering my courage, moved close enough to his bed that he could see me.

He reached out to me. "Vittorio, oh Vittorio, please hold my hand."

I couldn't. I couldn't do it. He had no way of knowing that all I could see was Umberto dying. He had no way of knowing that my image of death was not of a near stranger reaching out to me. I had watched Umberto die with tears streaming down his cheeks. I had seen Don Vergilio administer the last rites. I had heard my grandmother wailing in pain as the family pressed in around Umberto's bed. Because I couldn't be all those people to Mr. Battaglia, I backed away from him, and he died alone, with no one to offer comfort.

I curled up in my own bed, crying. When Vittorio Del Mastro wanted to know what was wrong, I explained my anguish and the feeling that I had deserted a dying man.

"Nonsense," Vittorio told me, "you have seen too much. A perfect stranger had no right to ask that of you. He should have asked the nuns."

I nodded, but I have never lost a feeling of sadness over Mr. Battaglia's death. How can there be perfect strangers when we will all one day die?

Giovanna gave birth to a little girl, Rosanna, on September 26, 1948. Just as he had predicted he would, Salvatore took all of us—Giovanna, their new baby, Vittorio Del Mastro, and me—home at the same time one week later. On the ride back, I reached my finger out to Rosanna, and she curled her own little hand around it. I was already getting to know my newest niece. I was no more foreign to her than anyone else in the family would be.

*

In early October, my father explained that since the law required that I finish my education, I would need some new clothes. "You're fifteen," he said. "You can't head off to school in short pants. Not to church either. It's time for your first pair of trousers." He had some business to conduct in Tripoli. "We'll take the bus."

Since he didn't drive, the mention of the bus gave me hope that Guerino would stay behind this time. "Just the two of us?"

"Just the two of us. I'll show you the sights. Tripoli is a beautiful city."

There's something about sitting alone together in a bus that makes it easier to talk. We both looked straight ahead or out the window. The hum of the motor carried on a conversation of its own, and so there was no awkwardness to the silent spaces. I don't remember exactly what we said to each other. Nothing important, but I do remember feeling close to my father on that trip to Tripoli.

He hadn't been wrong in his promise of beauty. One edge of the city followed the coastline. A marble railing separated the street from the ocean. The shore was lined with palm trees and the oleander bushes that blossomed in a riot of hot pink regardless of the season. Tripoli seemed to hold out the offer of perpetual summer. A wonderful castle anchored a part of the city that must have survived the series of invasions that periodically had swept through Tripoli. The hot sun, the ocean, the Moorish architecture, the street noises, the mosques with the sound of communal prayer spilling out and becoming part of the heartbeat of the city—I took it all in and fell a little bit in love with Tripoli. In the Sulco Turco section of the city, a series of boutiques offered clothing and gold and silver jewelry. My father seemed so at home here. I was impressed with the ease with which he made his way.

I followed him to a store that sold both fabric and ready-made clothing. "Arbib," he said to the gentleman who owned the store. "I'd like you to meet my son, Vittorio." The two of them greeted each other like old friends.

My father and Arbib made their decisions without consulting me until after the deal had been struck, but I was pleased to be included in this world of men and nodded happily as Arbib fitted me for brown pinstriped trousers. He had me slip into a burgundy-colored cardigan sweater. The burgundy and brown looked so handsome against each other, that I understood the pride with which Giacchino's customers had turned and admired themselves in the mirror.

"We'll need some fabric for his shirts," my father said as I stepped away from the mirror.

I wandered over to where the bolts of Egyptian cotton were displayed and lovingly ran the edge of the cloth between my thumb and forefinger.

Arbib moved to my side. "You have a gentleman's taste," he remarked, looking toward my father.

To my amazement, my father nodded. "Yes, we'll take enough to make a shirt from that white pinstripe." And then he consulted me for the first time. "What do you think? Blue with a pinstripe for the second shirt?" He turned back to Arbib. "Antonietta San Antonio back in Giordani will make them up for him."

I knew better than to mention my skill with topstitching. Only the final purchase, shoes, brought me back to more familiar turf. I reached to examine a pair of tasseled loafers. My father took them from my hand and returned them to the display area. He pointed toward a gleaming pair of leather wingtips, which even I knew were much too mature a style for a fifteen-year-old. Arbib was enthusiastic. "Our finest leather. The most elegant pair of shoes in my shop."

"Try them on," my father said as Arbib set the box down in front of me. He must have misread my hesitation, because he continued in an expansive manner. "Don't worry about the cost. They're well made and will last you for a long time. It's important to buy high-quality shoes."

On the ride back to the farm, I was annoyed with myself for letting the business with the shoes mar my joy in what was an otherwise perfect day. I made a silent promise that when I was grown and in a position to purchase my own shoes, I would buy tasseled loafers. To this day that is the style I prefer.

CHAPTER TWENTY-ONE

School Days

Since the war had interrupted my education, I never completed fifth grade as was mandated by the Italian laws instituted under Mussolini. His concern for education was one legacy that, although not credited to him, continued to shape the structure of life for Italian citizens. Therefore in October in 1948, I began instruction under Mr. Ottavio Balsamo, who on government assignment had come to Giordani to help those of us who needed to meet the requirements for a fifth-grade diploma.

Here in America, there would be jokes about a fifteen-year-old who was just entering the fifth grade; but in the Libya of the time, I had lots of company. A whole cohort of us had come back to Africa, nearly grown but with limited formal education. I liked school. No matter what province of Italy had originally been our homes, all the students in Mr. Balsamo's class spoke the same language in terms of our experiences of the world. Not everyone had been sent to Mussolini's schools, but the war had interrupted all our lives with traumas of one sort or another.

For the first time, I was attending a school that also included girls. There were five grades. The four lower sections were taught by nuns dressed entirely in white—habits, robes, shoes, even the headdresses—everything was completely white. Those of us in the fifth grade were blessed to have Mr. Balsamo. Even the girls, maybe especially the girls, were taken with him. My class quickly formed a bond around our friendships with each other and with him. I was able to walk to school, but many of the students arrived by horse and buggy. There were only three or four motorized vehicles in our entire village, and those risked getting ticketed by the police if they parked for more than a few minutes. I liked to get there early. The Rifatto and Toson brothers and I made a game of seeing who could be the first to strike up a conversation with Loretta Zamariolo and her two sisters. Suddenly my life had space for laughter. After school let out, boys and girls separated into groups and pretended not to notice each other; but there were sly looks and lots of giggling as Solidea, Fernanda, and Antonietta Guzzon whispered to Italia and Lina San Antonio and the Zamariolo sisters. The boys didn't giggle, but we practiced the art of the sidelong glance, and exchanged good-natured punches on the upper arms when our attentions to the fair sex appeared to be noticed and appreciated.

The names of my former friends and classmates sometimes roll through my mind as easily as they used to roll off my tongue, and I can see those faces before me, just as they were back in 1948. Where does that come from? What triggers that almost instant journey back to another time? Fiorino Frezzato. Tony Galantini. Aurelio Iezzi. Marino Paglia and his sister Luisa. And the Spreggiaro sisters: Pierina, Tersesa, Mirella, and Giustina. I wonder then, do they ever think of me? Are our memories still entwined? Where are they now? How widely have my classmates scattered around the globe? And how many of us are still alive to tell our stories?

The children of the Italian settlers who'd been older—like my brother Giovanni, my cousin Antonio, and Vittorio Del Mastro—had already finished fifth grade in Mussolini's boarding schools by the time the Germans marched through Italy, destroying landscapes, people, and dreams, and causing the population to turn against both Mussolini and those of us who'd been enrolled in the *GIL*. I'd completed fourth grade in Italy and had only a year to go in Giordani. By the time I graduated in July of 1949, I'd done more than earn my diploma; I had finished all the formal education I would ever receive.

So many things happen in life that later influence the direction one takes. So it was with Mr. Balsamo. An almost immediate bond formed between us, one that went far beyond that of student and teacher. He was both a father figure and schoolmaster to those of us who were newly returned to our families. Mr. Balsamo paid attention to me in a way that instantly reminded me of all those who had come before him and had made it possible for me to feel connected to other human beings even in the midst of difficult times. Signorina Turra. Espedito Simion. Uncle Ercole and

Aunt Cristina. My brother Gennaro. Even Mr. O'Brian, Pio and Bruno Cappelletti, and the Mazzoni brothers from Campo Cinecittà. I'll always be grateful to the social worker who took me to her home on holidays and introduced me to Matilda Farmungari, the woman from Hungary who taught me topstitching and would sometimes share her sandwich at lunch. And of course, Giacchino ("Dressed by Giacchino"), the man who helped me hold to the dream of one day becoming a *sarto*.

I talked to my new teacher, Mr. Balsamo, about my hopes, fears, and goals, and he had a way of listening that made it easy to describe the distance between what my father wanted for me and what I wanted for myself. I think it was because he always saw both sides and never took anyone's part. Knowing that he wasn't making judgments, just helping solve problems, made it easy to open my heart to him without feeling I was betraying my family. He introduced me to the art of letter writing and suggested I keep in touch with some of those people who had been so important to me. Now that the war was over, it was once again possible to send mail back to Italy. I was thrilled when the first letter I wrote was answered almost by return post and contained incredible good news. My godfather, Mr. Espedito Simion, had married Signorina Dellazzeri, the lovely young woman who'd been so often by his side around the time of my Confirmation. Gemma, her name was Gemma, and she was now his wife. Mr. Balsamo helped me understand that it was the constraints imposed by the war that had caused the gap between me and the family I'd left behind in Libya. If we'd been able to write to each other, to send a snapshot, we would have followed the changes and developments in each other's lives and the reunion wouldn't have been such a shock. He smiled when I showed him my godfather's letter. "I told you. It's possible to keep old friends even when you live apart." He tapped his finger on the sheet filled with Espedito's careful handwriting. "Married! See, there is even a way to acquire new ones."

While I progressed with my schoolwork, my brother Guerino continued his involvement with the farm. One morning in November of 1948, it was so cold, so very uncharacteristically cold, that I was not even out of sight of the house when I turned around to go back and get my sweater. My classroom had no source of heat, and the day was filled with the kind of damp chill that I thought happened only in Italy. Dark grey clouds lowered overhead, blocking the sun and pressing down in a way that made me apprehensive. I was not the only one who appeared worried. Mr. Balsamo and the nuns stood in front of the school instructing the parents of the students to turn their horses and buggies around and take the children back home. "Snow," one of the nuns said. "They're saying we could get snow." Just hearing the words spoken out loud filled the small cluster of white-robed women with nervous agitation that reminded me of the way my grandmother had reacted to the fighter planes roaring overhead back in Campo di Giove.

I looked to Mr. Balsamo for reassurance and he provided it as he urged the nuns back inside. "It's not the end of the world. Even if snow does fall, it won't last long in Libya." He held the door to the schoolhouse open. "Almost everyone has been sent home already. I'll wait here and inform the stragglers."

"Can I do something?" I asked.

"No, go home. Your family may need you to help reassure the Arabs working for you. They've never seen snow and could panic."

I got to the farm just in time to see Guerino struggling with the horses. He was trying to get them hitched to the wagon so that he could go collect the milk from those who produced for us. By now the snow was starting to fall in large wet flakes, and it blew against the horses with a cold force that caused them to buck and prance nervously. I moved forward to give my brother a hand, but he warned me off. "Stand back. They don't know you, you'll only make it worse."

I didn't see how it could be much worse than it was, but I respected his wishes. I knew I didn't have a natural way with livestock. Guerino was probably right. Once inside, I watched from the window. The horses were almost completely out of control. One reared up on his hind legs, shaking his head and fighting the bridle in such a way that it looked as if he would break loose from my brother altogether. Once Guerino had managed to ease him into a stand with all four hooves skittering on the ground, he was finally able to turn both horses so they couldn't see the wagon, only the door to their shed. With that action, they calmed enough that he was able to lead them back to their stalls.

He and my mother hurried in from outside just moments apart. "I can't get the horses hitched," he told her.

"No matter. I can't even find most of the Arabs. Nobody will be milking today." She looked around as if I might be hiding someone in the kitchen.

"Have you seen Mr. Marani?" Mr. Marani and his family were our most responsible workers. It was their tents and those of the others my mother employed that lined the edge of our property. "I checked in their *zeribbé.*" My mother used the Arab word for these cloth dwellings as easily as Mr. Marani's sons communicated with my mother in her own Italian dialect. "Only a few people are still in there and those who remain have wound their *barracanos* so tightly around themselves it is as if they were already mummies." Knowing that the three yards of fabric with which the Arabs clothed themselves were woven of wool, I thought that they might be better able to stay warm than I had been during that awful winter I'd spent in the mountains, but I didn't say anything. I suspected, perhaps correctly, that I was a bit jealous of the ease with which my mother communicated with young men about my own age who were totally unrelated to her. And hearing the Arab words roll off her tongue reminded me anew of the distance between us.

"I'll look in the woodshed," I told her, truly wanting to be helpful.

This was a small hut-like structure adjoining the outdoor oven where my mother baked the family bread. Since I kept my rabbits in there, I was in and out more often than the others and knew Mr. Marani was also aware that the heat from the oven served to dry the *ginestra,* a desert bush used in the place of firewood. My mother followed behind me, and sure enough, that's where we found him huddled in a corner trying hard to stay warm.

"Come," my mother said in her firm manager's voice. "Into the kitchen. I'll brew you some hot tea. I've told your wife to come with us until this blows over, but she'll do nothing without your say-so." Now she turned to me and, using the same tone, said, "Vittorio. Go tell la Azusa Marani we've found her husband and that she is to join him in our kitchen."

Mr. Marani and his wife waited out the storm drinking warm tea in my mother's house. Even though the snow lasted for only a day, not all the Arabs in the area were lucky enough to find sufficient shelter and many died in that freak snowstorm. Mr. Marani was unable to abandon his conviction that the Arabian people were being punished by God for some awful transgression. In all the years I knew him, he never gave up trying to figure out what it was.

Vittorio Palumbo

*

Now that I had proper clothes to wear, I was eager to accompany my family to church every Sunday. The D'Agostinos lived not too far from us in Giordani, and we attended the same church. Remember, Aunt Raffaela was my mother's sister, and it was Uncle Savino who had so readily agreed to follow my family to Libya. Salvatore had told me Antonio had made his way back to Libya with Sicilian fishermen, but even though I had heard he was all right, I needed to see him with my own eyes.

Aunt Raffaela, like my mother, still dressed in the long skirts of the Abruzzo fashion; but, of course, given Umberto's death, her garments were now entirely black. I hesitated just briefly, looking from her to Uncle Savino to judge how they were doing; but then Antonio walked toward me grinning, and any sorrow was quickly replaced with joy at our reunion. I laughed. "So, did you manage to catch a lot of fish? Are you now a fisherman instead of a farmer?"

He showed me his roughened palms. "Mostly I mended nets. So, maybe I'm neither a fisherman nor a farmer, but a *sarto* like you."

At the mention of the word *sarto*, I turned to quickly check my father's reaction, but he was busy talking to Uncle Savino and hadn't noticed.

Seeing Antonio again was like finding a missing piece of myself, and I knew there was much to be thankful for as we walked in together to attend morning Mass. In the stillness of the church I wished my brothers Giovanni and Gennaro could also be sitting among us, a wish that became a prayer even though I understood that when it happened, Antonio would drift back into his friendship with Giovanni and the strong connection Antonio and I had experienced that morning in front of the church would weaken.

I was beginning to feel at home in Libya. Although our new house was not as luxurious as the one I remembered in Garibaldi, there was much about its design and the way it related to the other three farms in the estate that made it familiar. Everything, even the courtyard wall, was constructed of white stucco trimmed with what was generally known as colonists' green. When I'd come to Libya as a six-year-old, I had simply admired the striking contrast between the white walls and the dark green shutters without realizing the political significance. Green was the color of the conquering country and was a subtle reminder of the power imbalance between the indigenous people and, in this case, the Italians. However, the lives of the Arabs and the settlers were so intertwined that, upon my return, I was mostly aware of the strength of the connections that bound the two groups.

With the clear vision afforded by hindsight, I can see that a friendship between people as equals occurred mostly within the community of Italian settlers. We visited back and forth in each other's homes, even when we had little in common besides our country of origin. For example, whenever Mr. and Mrs. Palladino formerly of Avellino, Italy, would stop by, the conversation that most fascinated us consisted of Mrs. Palladino's directions to her husband. To listen to the steady stream of guidance Mrs. Palladino offered him, you would think the poor man didn't have a brain in his head. "You can go in," she would say to him as soon as my mother opened the door in welcome. "You can take off your hat," she'd tell him. "You can sit down." There was no action too insignificant for her attention. And he dutifully waited for word from his wife before doing anything more complicated than drawing a breath. "The coffee's cool enough now. You can drink."

Poor Mr. Palladino. Poor Mrs. Palladino! She has no idea that more than sixty years later, she is still part of the vocabulary of my life. Whenever Rosalba tells me to do something that is rather obvious, I say to her, "And who are you? Mrs. Palladino?"

However, not all the interactions between and within the Italian families gave rise to laughter. I suspect that some sort of trouble relating to each other was typical among those of us who'd come back as near strangers to our families after years apart. This may have been true in each of the four farms in our estate. Our property faced the Milano compound (#50). The Marangone's (#98) were opposite the Michelone's (#99). My mother and Beatrice Milano were close friends, helping each other with sewing and the kinds of back-and-forth advice that women seem good at sharing. Beatrice's husband, like my brother Gennaro, had been taken as a prisoner of war while serving in the Italian Army. He still had not returned and Beatrice lived with her son Franco, who was somewhere in age between me and Ada and played with us. Beatrice's father-in-law, Primo Milano, was the head of a household that also included his daughter, Fernanda. Given how often Beatrice came to talk with my mother, I sensed that living without her husband in her father-in-law's household wasn't always easy.

The Michelone's were a quiet family with five daughters. Despite the fact that I had briefly met three of those girls while in the refugee camps, the family kept mostly to themselves in a way that seemed sad. Our only real exchanges occurred when Mrs. Michelone walked over every morning to deliver the pails of milk that my family used to make the balls of provolone. As we did with all our suppliers, someone in my family would mark Mrs. Michelone's *la tessera*, or ticket, to record how much milk she brought us. Every other Saturday, my father would tally up the totals and pay everyone an agreed-upon amount per gallon.

Other families also cracked under the strain of reunification in ways that were new to us. We got to know the Pomettos (#101) in the same way that we were connected to many of the families in our area: through the purchase of milk they brought to us. Mrs. Pometto was a widow with three sons. I'm not certain how her husband died, but the eldest of their three boys, Guerino, was forty years old and assumed many of the responsibilities associated with their farm. For example, he was the one who made the daily trip with the milk. Silvestro, in his twenties, was the youngest. In 1950, Mrs. Pometto surprised everyone by taking the middle son, Valeriano, with her and headed back to Italy. Just the two of them. People shook their heads in shocked disbelief. What would make a woman take one son while leaving the others behind? We never saw either Mrs. Pometto or Valeriano again.

Because of what it may indicate about the difficulties involved in reuniting families who had been apart for eight or nine years, the most memorable incident regarding the Marangone family is also the most troubling. They had a son and a daughter. Like so many of the children who returned after the war, the kids seemed to have a hard time reconnecting with their parents. Perhaps it was this kind of loneliness that drove the attachment between their only daughter and one of the Arab workers. In 1949, she ran away with a young Muslim who was her age. Those sorts of things were just not done back then. Because of the influence the family was able to exert under normal circumstances, it was unheard of for different religions to marry. But, of course, these were not normal circumstances and no matter how conventional our families might have appeared to an outsider looking in, the magnet that had once held the center together now pushed a daughter away from her parents and into the arms of someone very different. It was a heartbreak for the Marangones, and their sense of embarrassment and failure was so profound that they stayed away from church for years and only returned when time had softened the scandal.

My mother had her own opinions as to what was happening. "They've been living too close to the Arabs and forget the ways of their own country." Since Mr. Marani Ben Maiuf and his wife Tumia lived with their grown sons and their wives in the *zeribbé* that occupied the land along our property line, my mother knew firsthand about Arabian marriage customs. We were all fond of this family, using the father's first name when we addressed him but always prefacing it with Mr. as a sign of respect. We called Tumia "la Azusa," as a way to indicate that she was the oldest female, or the matriarch, of the family. Two of their sons—Ali and Saad—had their own tents near the parents. Mambruk had not yet reached the age when he would be expected to take a wife and still lived with his parents. Saad and Ali were both married. Ali had only one wife. I say *only* because Saad had two, which was accepted within their religion. But it was through knowing those two wives that my mother decided that the ways of her own country were preferable to Arab traditions.

Saad's two wives did not get along, perhaps because one was astonishingly beautiful and the other was rather average in appearance. There was bound to be jealousy between them. Complicating matters was the fact that, although each of the two women had blessed Saad with a son, the contrast between the boys was as great as the contrast between the mothers: one was both smart and handsome and the other was mentally challenged. However, in an unexpected twist, the boy with difficulties was born to the beautiful wife and the handsome one to the plain-faced woman. The two wives often got into explosive arguments that no one except my mother seemed able to break up. We lost track of the number of times that Saad ran to our house pleading with my mother to come and make peace in his troubled *zeribbé*.

Ending a marriage was a rather simple affair in Libya. All that had to happen was for the wife to leave on her own and return to her father. If the wife was the one who broke the marriage vows, the husband was not required to provide any kind of support as in the Western tradition of alimony. She was even free to remarry, but the dowry that any potential second husband had to pay her father was substantially smaller. Now, given the amount of conflict in Saad's tent, we would not have been surprised if one of his wives had decided to go back to her family of origin. However, the runaway wife in this story was Ali's. One day she simply packed up and was gone.

CHAPTER TWENTY-TWO

Together Again

Giovanni came home to Libya in March or April of 1949, and it was obvious that he was going through some of the same kinds of adjustments that I'd found difficult. One day it dawned on me that Giovanni, born in 1928 and returned to Libya in 1949, had spent almost half his lifetime away from his parents. Stunned by that insight, I quickly did the calculations and realized I'd spent almost two-thirds of my life away from my mother and father and only the first third of it with them. No wonder we all felt like strangers. We were strangers. My parents had spent more time with their Arab workers than they had spent with me.

The awful snowstorm we'd had the winter before Giovanni returned marked a period of unusual weather also characterized by severe droughts. Our farm was protected from the effects of the droughts by an electric pump that made it possible to irrigate our crops every third day. We used this water not only to irrigate, but also to supply running water to the kitchen and outdoor bathroom. After our years in the refugee camps, the convenience of a toilet that flushed from an overhead tank and an outdoor shower with water naturally warmed by the Libyan sun was a real treat for both Giovanni and me. Standing under the stream of water while looking out across our fields from head-high portals was a far cry from trying to keep clean in front of the sinks in Campo Cinecittà, and an ever farther cry from the ice-cold water from the stream that winter we spent in the *capanna*.

Electricity was delivered to us only on the days that we were authorized to draw water up from the communal well and into a storage tank that kept us supplied by way of gravity feed on the days when we had no power. When a light flashed in the kitchen, it was my job to go into the bedroom shared by Guerino and Giovanni and flip the switch on the box that controlled the flow of electricity. I was explaining the importance of the system to Giovanni when Guerino happened by. Since there was a little short in the wiring, there was no predicting when I might get a shock. Therefore, I'd devised a system whereby I used a long stick to push the on/off button. Guerino stood in the doorway shaking his head as he watched me demonstrate how I did it. "Giovanni," he said, "you'd be better off learning farming from me than from him. He's useless."

Accustomed to Guerino putting me down, I just sighed. Giovanni didn't challenge this brother with whom he'd been so close, but he did offer a bit of comfort after Guerino walked away. "He doesn't understand what it's like to come back and find it hard to fit in."

Wanting to find a reason to keep Giovanni there with me even though I was finished explaining how the electric switch worked, I told him about the snow storm in which so many Arabs had perished. "When the drought I was telling you about came right on the heels of the snow, many people of Libyan descent then died of starvation. Our family has a good relationship with the Arab workers, and Papá brought back an enormous bale of dates from one of his trips into Tripoli. He went around to every Arab family who supplied us with milk and cut off huge chunks of dates to help them get through." Giovanni and I stared quietly at each other. The memory of what it felt like to be hungry was still very fresh in Giovanni's mind. I knew that once it faded and he became accustomed to the abundance here in Giordani, he would naturally gravitate back toward his old connection with Guerino, who was, after all, closer to him in age. But as long as he was still getting used to things in Libya, we had a bond forged by our recent past.

Neither one of us was really cut out for farming. Given that everything was already running very well without us, it was hard to feel useful. Oh, I was given a series of jobs but I didn't feel I was trusted with anything of importance. Once a month when we and the D'Agostinos were scheduled to make the long trip and spend the day with the Del Mastros, it was my job to polish the buggy and take the leather harness down from the hooks in the tack room and shine it until the leather gleamed. This was a task that satisfied both my pride and my father's, but I knew the fate of the farm did not depend on the impression our harness made on those trips to visit with family and friends.

In contrast to the jobs that Giovanni and I were assigned, the responsibilities that fell to Guerino and Mr. Marani's sons were much more central to the actual production of the farm. Mambruk and Guerino didn't even need to be asked. When it was time to plant, they simply took the horse and plowed the field. Saad helped Giovanna with her chores at her farm. Ali and Mambruk both took directions from my mother and worked side by side with her. My parents had complete faith in them. In describing our Arab workers, I'd often heard my mother tell people, "They are absolutely trustworthy. They care as much about doing the job right as I do."

I know her words weren't intended to wound Giovanni and me, but it was hard not to compare them with a phrase she occasionally used when talking about the two of us to our father. Given how smoothly the farm operated without us, Giovanni and I did not always respond quickly when our mother asked us to do something. She got angry at our dawdling and would later tell our father, "You know, Roberto, these aren't our kids anymore. They belong to Mussolini." The sorrow in her voice hurt me almost more than the actual words.

It has taken me a long time to understand that it wasn't Giovanni and I who caused our mother's disappointment; it was the situation. After all, it was equally true that Mussolini had stolen *our* family *from us*. It's funny how the passage of time has helped me feel how much my mother loved me. Once I had children of my own, I understood the force of a parent's devotion and realized that it was something too powerful for even Mussolini to have destroyed. My mother loved me. Of course she did. I know it now, but it was hard to realize as a teenage boy who was struggling with so much.

Things got a bit better when Gennaro returned toward the end of 1949. Now our family was truly reunited. Not only that, but also Gennaro slipped easily back into his role as my defender and surrogate father.

One of my jobs was to plant and tend the flowers that surrounded our house and the courtyard. There was a certain peace associated with planting and weeding, with picking off the dead blossoms before they had a chance to go to seed, so that the cycle of bloom would continue. I was proud of how the colors in the oleander, pervinga, coleus, and geraniums brightened our home. Miseria vines climbed around the wooden gate and stucco walls. Shortly after Gennaro returned, Giovanni was keeping me company while I was trimming back the vines. The two of us were laughing about how Giovanni had lasted only one day at the tomato farm near Campo Cinecittà, before being assigned to weed pulling near the pavilion. "So," I asked him, "how is it that I'm in charge of the grounds here, when you're the one experienced in this kind of work?" My back was to the road, and I didn't see Guerino and Gennaro walking toward us. "I think you should ask Guerino to put a hoe in your hands so you can demonstrate your skill with chopping off tomato plants."

Because we were both chuckling at the thought of Giovanni arranging races to see if he could beat Mambruk and Ali to the end of a row of corn, it was only when Guerino was already close enough to address Giovanni that I realized he had heard everything we'd been saying. "Giovanni, don't listen to him. He's good for nothing. He doesn't want to do any real work on the farm. If you don't know how to work, you shouldn't eat." Guerino was pulling on Giovanni's arm to get him to come away from me. Gennaro stepped between them and Guerino softened his voice, but continued his criticism. "If he starves, I won't cry."

At that point, Gennaro's voice filled with emotion and he reached out and pushed Guerino toward the house. "Leave him alone," he said, referring to me. He was clearly angry. "Just leave him alone. You don't know what this kid has been through."

*

Because Gennaro was four years older than Guerino, he had been the first one eligible to join the army. So Guerino enlisted last and returned first, coming back to the farm almost as soon as the war was over. Unlike his older brother, Guerino had never been captured and sent to a prisoner-of-war camp. He'd never had to return to Italy for a couple of years in refugee camps before being allowed reentry to Libya. Given all the years Gennaro had been away, it is quite understandable that when it came to authority on the farm, his younger brother Guerino outranked him. Guerino had worked hard to help my parents make the farm prosper. Not even during the war had he left Africa. Having spent most of his life on the continent, he was at home there.

It took Gennaro's return to help me find my place. He brought a sense of fun back into our lives. Salvatore's brother, Enrico Del Mastro, owned a dance hall in Giordani. We loved to gather there on the weekends. Even those who weren't skilled dancers liked to stand on the sidelines—talking, laughing, and drinking—while we watched the others whirl around the floor. I mostly hung out with the friends I'd met in school, kids my age. Giovanni and Guerino had their own crowd, but one night I noticed Giovanni looking very sad as he watched the dancers. He caught me looking at him and wandered over to where I was standing. "Oh, Vittorio, seeing all these pretty girls just makes me miss Marietta." Marietta was his old girlfriend back in Campo di Giove. I was touched that he chose to share this with me rather than with Guerino. But, after thinking about it for a few minutes, I saw the logic in his confession. After all, it was my skill with topstitching and contraband cigarettes that had financed the trips from Campo Cinecittà so he could keep his romance alive.

There was a cinema about twenty miles away in the village of Bianchi. Very few adults attended, but some Saturday nights a bunch of us boys and girls would pool our money and rent a bus to take us there. The trip to and from the movies was even more entertaining than the actual film. A guy named Bevilacqua used to stand up in the front of the bus and lead us in song. Oh, could that guy sing! I have often wondered if he went on to become a professional performer. When singing along with Bevilacqua, we all felt more talented than we were. Caught up in the camaraderie born of music and shared space, I suspect I wasn't the only one who was disappointed when the bus pulled into our stop. Magic happened on those nights when Bevilacqua sang.

With my voice lifted in song, I was able to forget for a moment that the allowance my father gave us before we headed out for our Saturday night's entertainment was not equally divided. At the time, I thought the disparity was an indication of our worth to him; but viewed in hindsight, I realize that if that were the case, Guerino would have been the most highly paid. The truth is, the amount we got probably had more to do with our ages than with our value on the farm. Gennaro got twenty *mail,* Guerino and Giovanni fifteen, and I received only five. However, even in retrospect, I think I should have gotten at least ten!

It was strange not to be able to earn my own spending money. Although I never heard Gennaro complain, it must have been even more difficult for him. He was twenty-eight years old when he returned to us; had fought in the war; been captured; imprisoned in the United States; and then, when the war ended, had been released to Italy where he initiated the paperwork that made it possible for all of us to be cleared for a return to Libya. And even after all of that, my father still treated him like a child who had to stand in line to receive his allowance. I don't think kids today understand the absolute authority a father had back then. Just as *my* father had had to yield to *his* father's decision about who he should marry, so did our father rule my generation with an iron hand.

It was difficult to challenge him, but Gennaro was able to do it on my behalf even though he wouldn't argue for himself. Shortly after Gennaro returned, my stomach began acting up again. Certain I was faking, my father was furious. "We've been through this before," he said. "There's nothing wrong with him. He's just looking for a way to get out of work."

Gennaro stood his ground. "No," he told our father. "He is really sick. He has been damaged by malnutrition. He needs to see a doctor."

Our father shook his head in anger, refusing to yield.

"You don't know what he has been through," Gennaro told him. "The doctors in Italy knew because they had seen other cases like his." I watched Gennaro as he glanced out at fields overflowing with food and sensed what he wanted to say. However, after a period of silence, he spoke more softly. "There are errands I can run for you in Tripoli." When my father didn't challenge this and appeared to be listening, Gennaro continued. "I don't think they'll want to keep him, but he does need more medicine for his stomach pains. I'll ask to see Professor Tripoti. He's the head of the hospital and will be able to find out what they gave Vittorio when he was there before."

Gennaro was correct. The doctors didn't keep me, but they did agree that I needed to continue taking the medicine that had helped me get better the last time. Encouraged by Gennaro's victory, as soon as I was feeling well enough to get back to work, I decided I would find a way to approach my father about my dream of becoming a *sarto*. It was a dream that just wouldn't go away. Even little things kept the passion alive in me.

Before Giovanna got married she had been very involved in helping my parents run our farm, and now she and Salvatore had established their own residence on a farm (#126), walking distance from where we lived. It was fairly common practice to open your home to others who temporarily needed a place to stay. This was a tradition that we carried with us from Campo di Giove. Families were used to sharing their space. My parents had lived with their parents. After Mussolini's schools were dismantled, it seemed natural that Umberto and Antonio live with our grandmother, while I moved in with Aunt Cristina and Uncle Ercole. Therefore, it was routine when Giovanna and Salvatore had his sister Aquilina live with them for a few months. My clearest pre-war memories of Aquilina were of her as a ten-year-old waiting with us for the train that would begin our adventures in Libya. And here we were, friends again, only there was no longer anything childlike about her. She was a gracious young woman of twenty-one who was intent on learning the dressmaker's trade.

She had to walk right by our house on her way to and from Vilma Cinque's establishment. Vilma was a professional dressmaker who was pleased to pass the secrets of her craft on to Aquilina. On her way back from her lesson, Aquilina would often stop and visit with my mother. There was an ease between them that I envied. How could my mother be so enthusiastic about Aquilina's studies and so resistant to my own longing? I blamed my father for not seeing the value in anything unless it related to profits for the farm. Still, although those visits with Aquilina did serve to keep my own goal in mind, I remember them mostly for the good times we enjoyed when she was there. *Croccanti* is a candy similar to what Americans call peanut brittle. Discontent had a way of fading when my mother and Aquilina made *croccanti* together: stirring the sugar and butter until they reached a certain temperature, adding the nuts, pouring the mixture out on a marble slab to cool, and then whacking it into chunks to be eaten on the spot. This sweet can be made with any nut, but as peanuts were one of our major crops, we had an entire grain silo (a *magazino*) full and wouldn't have thought of using anything else. Ada and I were probably the most eager to sample the final product. Because I had grown so fond of this younger sister, I wanted to look after her in the same way Gennaro looked after me, and I assigned myself the job of seeing that she didn't blister her tongue in her eagerness to be the first to sample the candy. Making a game of it, we entertained everyone with our antics. The smell of burnt sugar still calls up pieces of laughter from those evenings in Giordani.

The proximity of my sister and brother-in-law's house contributed to another of my Libyan adventures. Vittorio Del Mastro rode over to our house one day on his brother Salvatore's horse. Not wanting to take the time to saddle her up, he had simply thrown a blanket over her back. Although I lacked confidence in my skill with large animals, seeing Vittorio so comfortable and in command up there made me want to see what it was like to ride a horse. It didn't look so hard.

"Can I try?" I asked. "I just want to see what it feels like to walk her around the courtyard."

"Sure." He slipped off and landed gracefully beside the chestnut mare. She never moved a muscle. This looked easy. Once down, Vittorio locked his hands together to form a kind of human stirrup into which I could slip my foot and hoist myself up onto her back. I could feel her muscles ripple under my weight.

"Grip her sides with your knees."

I did as I was told and the horse just stood there. "How do I make her go?"

"Just nudge her a little bit with your heels."

I hesitated, afraid any movement might dislodge me.

"You won't fall off. Hold onto her mane for balance." He nodded encouragement. "Go on, just do it."

I did as I was told, and all was going fine until she turned at the end of the courtyard and saw a space wide enough to slip through. Before I knew what was happening, she was off to the races. The two of us went flying down the road. Terrified I was going to fall off, I dug my heels ever tighter into her sides. The action just served to spur her to even greater speed. The eucalyptus trees that lined the road blurred into a continuous wall of green. Around the corner past the Pometto family farm we flew. I leaned down over her, pressing my chest and belly into her back. Not wanting to fall off, I tried to make her body and my body one animal. My eyes screwed tightly shut, I wrapped my arms around her neck and waited for my heart to burst in an explosion even louder than the sound of her galloping hooves. And then, just as suddenly as my wild ride had begun, it stopped. She went from full speed ahead to a complete halt, and I went sailing off over her and onto the ground. Thud. I don't know how long it had taken us to cover the six miles between my house and my sister's, but it had felt like a lifetime to me. However, the one witness to my exploit, Mr. Guerino Pometto, was certain that we'd needed only seconds to go the distance.

He'd been on his way to deliver milk to my father when the mare and I had rounded the corner near his property. I certainly hadn't seen him. He was just a part of the blur of eucalyptus and terror that had characterized my introduction to horseback riding. But Mr. Pometto couldn't wait to tell my father about my skill as a jockey. Certain that it had been either Giovanni or Guerino on the horse, my father had refused to believe him. However, when Giovanni poked his head into the milk-house to see what all the excitement was about, my father realized it must actually have been me on a runaway horse and told my brother to quickly grab our gelding and find a way to rescue me.

By the time Giovanni got to Salvatore's farm, my sister had already picked me up, dusted me off, and brought me inside for a drink of cool water. Only the fact that I was still white as a sheet gave Giovanni any sense of how terrifying the whole experience had been. From then on, whenever Mr. Pometto saw me, he would start talking about the day I broke all records. "I tell you, Vittorio, you're a natural on a horse. Really something. I've never seen anyone ride like that." I was unable to convince him of the truth of my version of the story. It was as if he couldn't hear anything that contradicted what he knew he had seen. "You belong down at the Busetta race track in Tripoli. You're really something. A natural born jockey." If my father happened to be present when Mr. Pometto got started, he would just roll his eyes and shake his head. He knew there was no point in trying to convince Mr. Pometto otherwise.

*

We all sensed an uncomfortable shift in the political climate in Libya. Sometimes I overheard my father talking with the other men about what Italy's future in the country would be. "The Jews and the Arabs used to get along. Friends." He sounded bewildered. "But now it's as if everyone is just trying to grab all they can. The Arabs don't want the Jews owning anything."

Some of the Jewish Libyans were making plans to leave for the new nation state of Israel. Those who remained behind were increasingly subject to threats of violence. A number of Jewish shops in Tripoli had been vandalized.

My father looked thoughtful. "The Arabs seem to resent the taking of land for Israel. I wonder if it would be different if the Arab people had been allowed to remain…" His voice trailed off and he tried starting again, "In Libya, we all…" He seemed unsure of how to finish the sentence and finally summed things up with the air of authority which was more familiar to me. "It's the uncertainty. Nobody can be sure what will happen if Libya gains independence." He slapped his palms against his thighs before standing up to signal the end of the discussion. "We have to start making plans in case our situation here changes."

He saw a role for me in one of the plans he was considering. Although it was generally agreed that I had no skill with livestock, I was the only one of the Palumbo brothers who was able to slaughter an animal without fainting at the sight of blood. That somewhat dubious talent fed my father's dream that there was a future for me as a butcher. I was horrified. Just because I could kill an animal without fainting, didn't mean that it was something I enjoyed. Quite the contrary; I hated it.

Overhearing talk of my future as a butcher made me decide it was time to really marshal all the help I could get in planning for my career as a *sarto*. Gennaro had been very supportive of me in the past, but talking directly with my father was as difficult for him as it was for me. I thought perhaps there was some way that Gennaro's friendship with our local priest could serve as the link to answered prayers. The Del Mastros, D'Agostinos, and Palumbos all attended the same church in Giordani. Father Achille had served this church for many years, and after he retired, Padre Valerio took his place. Since the new priest and Gennaro were the same age, they became very close. Padre Valerio visited his far-flung parishioners by means of a Guzzi, a wonderful Italian motorcycle that drew a crowd of admirers wherever he went. When Gennaro needed a ride into the village of Bianchi or Micca, Padre Valerio would take him.

The Del Mastro, D'Agostino, and Palumbo families decided that—as a way of demonstrating our relationship with and affection for the church— we would request a permit to have a statue made in honor of St. Joseph. On the day that it was delivered, one of the men carrying it into the church slipped, and the statue crashed onto the marble steps and shattered into thousands of pieces. The custom was that when a statue broke in this way, all the tiny shards must be gathered up and buried. Everyone in our family was upset, but having been convinced that our connection with this patron saint might ease a career path for me, I took it particularly hard.

Luckily Padre Valerio turned a circumstance that could have made me deeply morose into a funny story. One Sunday after church, Gennaro invited his friend and our priest to join us for dinner. In the period of conversation following the meal, my mother brought up the misfortune with the likeness of St. Joseph. "Why do they make statues of a material that is so easily broken?" She was still upset over the accident. "Maybe the way things were done in the old days was better." Although I was used to my mother's complaints about modern times, I was a little embarrassed when she continued speaking so frankly to our priest. "In the town I come from, the statues were made of wood, and we didn't have that kind of problem."

"In Milano, where I come from," Padre Valerio shot back, "they are made of rubber. That way, when someone drops them, they bounce right back up and into place!"

Not too long after this all happened, I received a package from my Aunt Angela in America. I shook it to try to figure what might be inside and could feel the soft, weighted thump of fabric against the side of the box. Unable to endure the suspense, I tore off the brown paper wrapping. It was a blue pinstripe suit! I held it up and immediately sensed that it was going to be a bit too big. However, rather than being disappointed by this observation, I immediately recognized the opportunity presented by a garment that would require some alteration. In the village of Bianchi, three deaf-mute brothers worked together as professional *sartos*. I thought my new suit might provide a pathway to the tailors of Bianchi.

"What a shame that it doesn't fit quite right." My mother reached behind me and pulled some fabric from the jacket into her hand. "We'll have to get someone to take it in."

I held my tongue and my breath while Gennaro made a suggestion. "If we gave him bus fare, he could take it to Bianchi and have those three brothers work on it."

And that's how it was decided. I was so used to talking with my hands in Campo Cinecittà that I had no trouble communicating with three deaf tailors. They quickly understood that I had some experience in the profession and were only too happy to let me take the suit apart and help tailor it to my proportions. I hadn't felt so fully myself in a long time.

On the bus ride back to Giordani, I came up with a plan. Once home, I tried the suit on for my family. Only after everyone had expressed delight in how well it now fit me, did I confess that I had helped with the tailoring.

"Well," my father said, "since you did some of the work, I hope they charged you less."

"No," I told him, "but I think they would allow me to work with them as an apprentice."

"Bus fare is expensive. We can't be paying for you to ride the bus back and forth to Bianchi every day."

"I could ride a bike."

"You don't have a bike." My father was obviously growing impatient with the direction the conversation was taking. "Bikes cost even more than bus fare." With that, he turned and left the room.

Later, when Gennaro and I were alone in the fading Libyan light, I asked him a question. "Do bikes cost more than a cow?"

"No. Cows cost a lot more than bicycles."

"How about a pig? Does a bike cost more than a pig?"

Gennaro was quiet for a long time before answering my question. At last he said, "It doesn't matter how much a pig costs." He looked at me sadly. "I can tell you won't be getting a bicycle."

CHAPTER TWENTY-THREE

A Few Tales Short of a Thousand and One

Pigs had a way of complicating things in Libya. Once during my early days back in the country, in the year of the drought, a lone Arab had wandered in from the desert on his camel in search of water. The memory of hunger very fresh in my own mind, I could tell just by looking at him that he was starving. After I had offered him some of the sweet water we pumped up through the sands, he quietly asked if he could have something to eat. I found my mother in the kitchen and explained the situation to her. Although she wouldn't let us enter the *zeribba* to eat with Mr. Marani and his family, she often invited them to sit with us under the eucalyptus trees in the courtyard and share in a meal of leftovers.

"I have some pasta and sauce you can give him," my mother said.

When I brought it out to the gentleman, he looked at me and addressed me with the Arab word for friend, "Rafiq, does it contain pork?"

Knowing what it felt like to starve, and wanting to make it easy for him to eat what I offered, I lied. "No," I told him, "it has no pork."

He took one bite and looked at me steadily as he set the bowl down. "Thank you. Although I am very hungry, this food won't go down my throat."

"Why not?"

"It must contain some pork." He nodded his appreciation for my efforts and turned and left the farm. I never saw him again.

Vittorio Palumbo

*

We sold our fattened livestock to Mr. Pelosi, a butcher in Tripoli. He would bring his truck to the farm and we would load it with whatever he was purchasing to supply his customers for the week. Uncomfortable with the way he negotiated with my father—always pointing out some supposed flaw, a scar on the skin, an imagined limp—I formed an initial dislike of this man. Or maybe it was just that I had heard my name linked with his profession a bit too often. As things would have it, on a day when my brothers weren't there to help, a large boar decided to lead his fellow pigs in a rebellion. What normally would have been a simple task of guiding the animals onto the truck became a nightmare of rampaging pigs. The boar went trumpeting around the courtyard, his cousins squealing and clattering their little cloven hooves after him. The ringleader dodged every one of our attempts to herd, corner, or catch him. Mr. Pelosi may have had a way with a pork chop, but he was useless in dealing with a live, angry pig. Boars can be mean, and when this one lowered his head and came charging out of a tight space, we all jumped back. I have to admit, I wasn't much more help than Mr. Pelosi. And because Mambruk's religion considered pigs unclean, my father's usual right hand could do nothing but stand by, shut his eyes, and cover his ears against the chaos unfolding before him.

Not used to being disobeyed, even by a pig—perhaps especially by a pig—my father's famously short fuse exploded in a violent tirade against everyone involved in the whole wild circus. He swore he was going to shoot us all: the pigs, me, and Mambruk. Perhaps because Mr. Pelosi was shielded by the thickness of his wallet, his name did not appear in the list of those scheduled for assassination. Mr. Marani had come running to see what all the commotion was about and, upon hearing his son threatened with a bullet through the brain, made some rapid accommodations with his religion. He quickly grabbed one of the large cloth bags used to transport grain and pulled it down over his son's head, completely covering him. Face, body, arms, hands, legs, feet, not a bit of Mambruk was exposed. Showing the ghost in burlap far more respect than the rest of us had been able to command, the pigs surprised us all by calming down immediately and trotting docilely onto the truck. At that point, they may have felt it to be their only safe haven. Given that it could have been reasonably argued that the panting swine had run off a bit of their body weight, it was even more astonishing when Mr. Pelosi, without a word of protest, paid my father the formerly agreed-upon price. He'd hardly pulled his truck off the property, when my father, true to the quicksilver nature of his temper, collapsed laughing against the courtyard wall. We were all only too happy to join him.

*

Mambruk was reaching the age when it was time for him to take a wife. Since Arabian tradition charged a young man's father's with the responsibility of finding an appropriate bride and providing the young couple with a dowry, Mr. Marani traveled with Ramadam, the local imam (or Islamic equivalent of a priest) to visit with the father of the prospective bride. Once accord was reached on the appropriate number of sheep, cattle, and horses to be included in the bride price, a contract was signed. As soon as this agreement was in place, Mambruk's family began construction of a new *zeribba* to shelter him and his new wife. At this point Mambruk could no longer stay with his parents, but had to leave the family tent and go live for a while with other young males close to him in age.

Mambruk made invaluable contributions to the operation of the farm, and my parents were glad that, by the time the prospective bridegroom had to temporarily leave our property, the widow of Mr. Marani's brother had come with her three sons to live in a *zeribba* next to his own. Although one corner of our acreage was beginning to resemble a small Arab village, the farm was prospering and additional workers were welcome. The widow's oldest son, Mohammed, was twenty-one and quickly fell in alongside his cousins. Ali, age thirteen, and ten-year-old Ashuir were still too young to work.

As Mambruk's wedding day approached, excitement built to the accompaniment of beating drums. Each of the neighboring Arab tribes had its own trademark rhythm, a way of communicating across the desert as they followed their nomadic way of life. Date, time, and place were all conveyed in the signature tempo that announced the upcoming nuptials. Mambruk's *zeribba* stood decorated with corded rope and tassels and billowing, fully appointed and ready to welcome him and his betrothed. On the day of the ceremony, the fathers of both the bride and the groom decorated one camel with an elaborately festooned saddle and colorfully ornamented harness, specially chosen to mark the significance of the day. Since the young maiden had to remain completely concealed behind the curtains of what we Italians called a *baldacchino,* her camel was characterized by a kind of a throne carried high on its back.

As representatives from the scattered tribes traveled in from the desert by camel, Mambruk's bride arrived and slipped from the *baldacchino* and into the new *zeribba* to wait for her intended's arrival at sundown. He still had not seen her. Just as it was getting dark, Mambruk's friends, all traveling by foot, escorted the young groom to the ceremonial location. As you can imagine, there was much good-natured laughter and teasing from the other young men. The feasting and celebration went on for hours. The guests didn't leave until Mambruk indicated that it was time for him to join his bride. He hesitated in front of the new *zeribba* for just a moment, then pushed the fabric aside, and stepped across the threshold. The curtain fell shut behind him as he moved to start his life as a married man. When he emerged from the tent the next morning, he indicated that all was as it should be, and he was well pleased. His bride remained concealed in the *zeribba* for the next three or four days. When she finally emerged, her face was fully covered, only her eyes now visible to the rest of the world. After a period of time, she joined Mambruk in working for my family.

*

Salvatore was known as a great prankster. He drove his horse and buggy when he needed to go to town and often stopped to visit with us on his way past our farm. On this particular day, one of our youngest workers, Mambruk's cousin Ramadam, was harvesting peanuts close to the house. Salvatore noticed that he was sampling the product as he worked and walked over to him. "Ramadam, you have to come with me to be weighed." Before the inexperienced Arab fully understood what was happening, Salvatore had tied a rope around his waist and hoisted him up onto the meat hook we used to take the measure of a side of beef. He made a great show of making note of Ramadam's weight. "Okay," Salvatore said as he lifted him down, "I'll weigh you again this evening." Shaking his head, he continued, "I'm going to have to charge you for every kilo you gain while harvesting." Poor Ramadam took him seriously and didn't eat another peanut all day.

Salvatore and Mr. Marani's grown son, Ali, were quite fond of each other, but that affection did little to protect Ali from Salvatore's teasing. In some ways, it just made it worse. Ali was very tall, 6' 4", and could run like a gazelle. Perhaps because he was impressed with how fast Ali could make it into Giordani and back, Salvatore often sent him on errands. One day he had a letter that he wanted sent to Italy and asked that Ali take it to Mrs. Vilma, the postmistress, for him. When Ali got back, he asked Salvatore to explain how the letter could possibly travel from Libya to Italy. "That's easy," Salvatore told him, "they just put it in a tube that travels under the ocean, and it goes all the way to Italy."

Ali tapped himself on the head, and in the mix of languages that he used when speaking to us said, *"Per dio, ras ghibir,* how smart the Italians are!"

Although we all laughed at his willingness to believe, we had enough respect for how *ras ghibir* (head smart) Ali and the other Arabs were that we knew there was always a chance Ali was just pretending to accept Salvatore's explanation in order to be in on the fun.

Another time, Salvatore needed razors. Since he wanted a witness to the feat he was about to ask Ali to perform, Salvatore called me over to listen as he put him to the test.

"I need some razors." He handed a bit of money to Ali. "I want you to run to Giordani, make the purchase, and then sprint back as fast as you can." He paused, giving his instructions a moment to sink in. "Now, I'm going to spit on the ground. That's your signal to start running. If you're not back by the time my spit dries, I will have you put to death."

With an abrupt nod to indicate he accepted the challenge, Ali was off and running. Given how quickly Ali covered the miles between us and Giordani, I don't know how he had time to make the purchase; but in what felt like only a matter of minutes, we saw him flying back over the hill, razors in hand. At the first sight of him passing the Milano farm, Salvatore quickly spit on the ground again, so that Ali could take full credit for having successfully accomplished the feat.

Ali's very eagerness to learn the Italian language left him open to some of the same confusion of words that often entertained even Italians who were trying to communicate with each other in the dialects peculiar to their home regions—like the time my family thought Mr. Garavello was asking to be struck by lightning when all he wanted was a match for his cigarette.

Prior to 1939, Ali had served with the Italian Army in Libya in the *Ascari*, one of the mixed units composed of both Arabic and Italian soldiers. Knowing this, my mother assumed that he'd once had a more muscular physique than he now possessed. One September, during the peanut harvest, he and his family were sitting under the eucalyptus trees with my family, relaxing after a hard day in the fields. "Ali," my mother said, as she studied his slender frame, "surely you weren't this thin when you served in the Army?"

He tried to explain in my mother's Italian dialect that he had been heavier but had lost most of that bulk because of all the guns or cannons he'd had to carry on his shoulders. Acknowledging that the war had taken its toll he said, "It's because of the weight of the *coglione* I had to carry."

"Don't ever use that word!" My mother reacted in horror. "There are children here. Don't ever use that word in front of women and children!"

Since all the Italian men present laughed robustly at his statement, it was difficult to make Ali understand that he had confused our word for testicles, *coglione,* with the word for cannon, *cannone.* Perhaps because the men found the mix-up so entertaining, it took a while before Ali mastered the difference between the two words. However, he was eventually able to respect my mother's wishes.

There was an innocent openness to Ali, a kind of reckless joy in life, an ability to surrender himself to the fun of the moment that got him in trouble with my mother on another occasion. It was his job to travel to Giordani to deliver our butter to the vendors there. He'd start off walking and then travel by bus the rest of the way. On one return trip, he made the acquaintance of the bus driver's wife, Mrs. Campanile, a heavy-set woman who had an armful of clothes she was distributing free to anyone who wanted them. The only item that had any real appeal for Ali was a pair of black nylon woman's underpants. Given the difference in their sizes, it's hard to imagine what use Ali thought he might get from the gift. However, at some point on the walk home, he decided to try them on. Putting the clothes he'd been wearing in the now empty metal container used to transport the butter, he positioned that on his head and continued on dressed only in his new finery. He'd found a stick, around which he'd twisted the extra fabric so that the panties didn't drop to his ankles. Proud of the outfit he'd rigged up for himself, Ali strode by the farm loudly singing an Arabian tune.

When I heard him, I looked out the window. My first impression was of a tall, thin stretch of bare skin with a butter bucket on his head. Not quite able to believe my eyes, I hurried to find my mother. Unsure of how to describe what I had just seen, I tentatively said to her, "Ma, I think Ali is walking back from town naked."

She ran to the front door to check out the situation for herself and, eyes wide with shock, turned to Ada and me. "Don't leave the house," she told us. "Stay away from the windows."

Hurrying to the storage cellar, she seized a burlap sack and quickly cut a hole in the top. Grabbing a length of thin rope as she made her way outside, she starting scolding Ali before the door had even closed behind her. "What are you doing? Have you gone completely mad?" By now she had reached him, snatched the metal container off his head, and was pulling the sack down past his ears. "Have you lost your mind? What would make you do such a thing?"

Ada and I, of course, had been made only more curious by being directed not to watch and were pressed against the window.

Ali protested as Mother adjusted his new burlap garment and tied the rope around his waist. "What? What? What have I done?"

She looked at him in disbelief. "What have you done? Parading around half naked! Don't you know I have an eleven-year-old girl in the house?"

"But this is women's underwear. How can it hurt her to see women's underwear?"

*

Not long after Mr. Marani's widowed sister-in-law and her children moved into the tent next to his, Ali, her thirteen-year-old son, was playing near our house. While I was watching him scratch figures in the dust with a stick, he suddenly let out a muffled little cry. His body went rigid and he fell thrashing to the ground.

"Ali," I yelled, racing over to him. "Ali! Ali! What is it?" But he seemed unable to hear me or to even know I was there. Terrified, I ran to get my mother. "Something is wrong with Ali," I told her, barely able to quiet my own panic long enough to describe what was going on.

She hardly needed to be told. After one quick glance out at the young body convulsing on the ground, she grabbed a cloth and, folding it into a small square as she went, raced to his side. She knelt down next to him and competently slipped the cloth between his teeth. With great tenderness, she grasped his trembling shoulder with one hand while she used the other to hold the fabric in his mouth. When the seizure had passed, she remained with him, calmly assuring him that he was fine, that everything was okay. In order to shield the cloth that she had employed from Ali's sight, she discreetly curled her hand around it. "You just had a little fall," she told him. "Everything is going to be all right."

The Arabs had great confidence in my mother's healing powers. Although we didn't always share each other's customs, there was a basic human understanding between us. As Ashuir, the youngest of Mr. Marani's nephews approached thirteen, the family explained the importance of the ceremony surrounding his upcoming circumcision. In Libya at this time, circumcision was an Islamic ritual associated with puberty. It served as a way of marking Ashuir's adult entry into the wider Arab religious and social community. In addition to undergoing the procedure to remove his foreskin, Ashuir was also expected to be able to recite passages from the Koran. The event was treated as a celebration and was a semi-public affair accompanied by music and special foods. Because our families shared so much, we were invited to attend.

I found it a horrible thing to watch. As soon as the ceremony started, I regretted being there. The moment I saw Ramadam, the imam, pick up a double-edged razor with a wooden handle, I shut my eyes. Only after hearing Ashuir violently exhale, did I sense that the actual cutting was over. In order to stop the bleeding, sand—presumed to be pure because it was obtained from deep below the surface of the desert—was poured over Ashuir's freshly circumcised penis. Trying hard not to show how frightening I found the experience, I was glad when the "celebration" was over and I could return to what felt like the safety of my own home.

A week later, Ashuir, walking with difficulty and looking quite sick, left the family *zeribba* and approached me. "Oh, Rafiq," he said, using the Arab word for friend, "I am not feeling well."

"What's wrong?" I asked. It was clear to me that Ashuir was having a serious problem of some sort.

He looked embarrassed. "I think I need some help."

"What is it, Ashuir? Can you tell me what's wrong?"

He winced uncomfortably and indicated the region of his genitals. "I don't know what to do," he told me.

Now, given that I had attended his ceremony only a week before, I wasn't surprised that he would be in some discomfort. "Is this usual?" I asked him.

Chagrined, he shook his head. "Not so much pain. Not like this." He looked at the ground. "I've had to place a stick in my belly button in order to keep my shirt from rubbing the wound."

Sure enough, I checked, and there was an unusual protuberance jutting out beneath his clothes. "Oh, Ashuir, how can I help you? What is it you would like me to do?" I thought for a moment. "My mother knows how to make a healing poultice."

Ashuir nodded. "Yes, please, could you…" His voice trailed off. "Could you ask her for me?" He finally looked into my eyes, pleading.

It wasn't easy for me to explain to my mother what was wrong with Ashuir. There were words I didn't like to say in front of her, but as we had both attended his ceremony, she grasped the nature of the problem fairly quickly.

He reluctantly followed her into my bedroom. I think he'd been hoping she'd simply be able to supply him with some medicine and send him back to his family, but she was firm. "Ashuir. I have to have a look at it. There is no other way."

Shortly after my mother had taken stock of the situation, Ashuir and I stood together in the kitchen as she began preparations for the treatment she promised would bring him some relief. The first step was to heat a metal rod until it was white hot. Ashuir grimaced when he saw her withdraw the glowing piece of metal from the fire. "No!" He was clearly frightened. "No burning. Please don't burn me. Please, no."

Mother, immediately sensing the nature of his terror, was quick to reassure him. "Not for you, Ashuir." She turned and plunged the heated rod into a jar of olive oil containing some medicinal herbs. When the ingredients had bubbled together and were starting to cool, she and Ashuir disappeared once again into my bedroom where she applied the warm lotion to his infection. After two weeks of her daily care, Ashuir was happy to report that he was fully healed. That incident and others like it filled me with quiet pride at how resourceful my mother was. I understood why the Arabs held her in such high regard. For a woman who wouldn't let anyone say the word *coglione* in front of her or her children, she showed herself to be amazingly competent when it came to dealing with botched circumcisions.

CHAPTER TWENTY-FOUR

Arabian Nights

The sand was once again shifting under our feet. I was eighteen. It was 1950, and things were falling apart. There was increasing talk of Libya becoming a free state. In 1949, the U.N. had passed a resolution mandating Libyan independence from Great Britain before January 1, 1952. We had only another year and a half to try to figure what that independence might mean for our lives here. Relations between the Arabs and Jews continued to deteriorate. One time my father came back from a trip to Tripoli obviously upset. He didn't want to talk about it, but after church on Sunday, he quietly drew Uncle Savino aside to tell him about the things he had seen. I didn't catch most of it, but knew the situation was serious. Hardly a day went by without rumors of the slaughter of still more Jews. "Everyone used to get along," my father said, his voice both sad and bewildered. "What is happening to this land we have come to love?" Not even the brightness of the Libyan sun could burn away our sense of foreboding.

It was as if we were all poised to leave. Guerino already had. Guerino. When the farm could not hold even Guerino, what was there to keep the rest of us in place? There was a gentleman, a Mr. Maiolino, originally from Sicily, who ran a trucking operation out of Tripoli. He hired Guerino to drive a tractor trailer back and forth between there and Cyrenaica. We could count on my brother coming home for Christmas, but other than that, we were never sure when he would show up. Maybe once every three or four months.

With Guerino gone, the cheese business slowed down. I took over the job of picking up the milk from our suppliers, but fewer and fewer people seemed interested in maintaining herds and milking. My mother and Mambruk and our other workers continued to plow, plant, and harvest, but the farm that had produced enough abundance to keep the Palumbos, Del Mastros, and several Libyan families employed full-time gradually saw production drop.

Not six months after Guerino left to work for Mr. Maiolino, Gennaro decided it was time for him to find a paying job. My mother had a cousin in Venezuela who was a contractor. He offered Gennaro employment as a carpenter and, before I knew it, Gennaro was off to South America to build houses.

I'm surprised that Giovanni resisted the exodus as long as he did. After all, he'd been actively missing Marietta ever since he'd returned to Libya early in 1949. By the end of 1950, he could stand the separation no longer and returned to Campo di Giove to marry his longtime sweetheart. "I'll be back," he promised, but we all had our doubts. Marietta was an only child and very close to her family. We couldn't imagine her ever being willing to leave Italy.

With my brothers gone, my parents trusted more and more of the farming to me, but my heart was never in it. As I irrigated the fields, I thought of Giacchino stretching the woolen fabric and wrapping it in wet cloth. I could think of better things to do with water than spray it out over what used to be Libyan desert. Nonetheless, I was a good and diligent son. It was not the work I would have chosen for myself, but I had loyalty to my family and felt I was finally having an opportunity to prove my worth.

One December morning, my father called me over. "Vittorio," he said. "Ali is helping your mother in the fields this morning. He won't be able to deliver the butter to Giordani, and I'd like you to do it instead." Pointing to his bedroom, he said, "Go get the bus fare for Mr. Campanile from my wallet."

When I opened the wallet, I saw a letter all trimmed in black. My heart froze. I knew what this meant. Someone had died. I carefully pulled the letter out and into my hands. It was from Aunt Fiorina, my mother's middle sister. Stealing a glance at the door to make sure my father wasn't coming to see what was taking me so long, I carefully opened it and read the sad news. My grandmother had died. Scarcely able to keep from crying out, I scanned the letter for details of her death. While carrying a copper jug filled with water back from the fountain, she'd slipped on the ice-covered cobblestones and had broken her femur and hip. Confined to bed and unable to recover, she later died as a result of the trauma. I studied the date on the letter. My father had kept it hidden from my mother for a week. I slipped it back into the wallet and slowly walked out to my father.

"I found the letter," I informed him. "Why haven't you told Mother?"

"I lack the courage."

I felt I had no answer for that, and after putting the metal container of butter in the buggy, slowly drove our gelding to the livery stable near the bus stop. The ride to Giordani gave me time to let everything sink in. My grandmother Raffaela had died from broken bones, just as her first husband, the grandfather I had never known, had done before her. Only he had fallen from a horse, and she had slipped on the ice while carrying water. I wondered if my mother remembered her father's death? She would have been only seven at the time. Perhaps concern about triggering all those sad memories had made it more difficult for my father to bring her bad news now. I tried to understand his point of view. However, regardless of the reasons for his silence, I knew someone, probably me, was going to have to tell her before any more time passed.

Mother was washing clothes under the water tank near the irrigation pipes when I got home. Trying hard to think how to break the news, I walked over and stood beside her. She looked up at me and paused in her work just long enough to ask, "What?"

"I found a letter."

She pulled her hands away from the washboard and dried them on her apron. "Go on." When I didn't answer right away, she pressed me. "You found a letter. What letter?"

"This morning when Father sent me to his wallet to get fare for the bus to Giordani."

"Tell me. Tell me," she insisted. She now had moved to face me and her hands were lightly gripping my shirt.

"It was trimmed in black."

"Ohhh." She doubled over slightly as if someone had struck her in the stomach. "Oh, no. Oh, no. My mother is dead." Her voice dropped to a whisper. "My mother has died." Then, as if startled into action by her own words, she turned and ran toward the house, howling with rage and pain. "Roberto, Roberto," she wailed. "How could you not have told me my mother died?"

She was furious with my father. When I saw the extent of her dismay, I understood why he had avoided giving her the letter.

In a clumsy attempt at comfort, my father mumbled, "It is better that she died."

Those words only further stoked her fury, and she turned from him weeping. "How can you say such a thing? How is it possible that you can say such a thing to me?"

Since I'd spent the better part of the day struggling to understand why my father had hidden the letter, I felt more able to try to see his point of view than I might normally have been. I think he may have meant that she was old, a widow, and that it was better for her to die than to live a restricted life. Maybe he meant that she would now be able to join her husband. I'm not sure. I don't know, but he couldn't possibly have meant it the way it came out. After all, Grandmother Raffaela was his stepmother as well as his mother-in-law. At any rate, none of us will ever know what he might have been trying to say, because some combination of my mother's furious sorrow and his own tongue-tied ineloquence prevented him from offering further comment.

The next Sunday we broke the news to Uncle Savino and Aunt Raffaela. Perhaps because we'd had time to think about what we would say to her, Aunt Raffaela had a more measured response on learning of her mother's passing. Still dressed all in black in honor of Umberto, Aunt Raffaela had already suffered the worst blow that death can deliver, the loss of a child. She took news of this additional heartache with seasoned dignity, and the two families set about making arrangements for Father Valerio to conduct a mass in my grandmother's memory.

*

Sometimes it felt as if sorrow were stalking us. One morning early in 1952, shortly after Libyan independence was declared, Mambruk showed up at our house obviously troubled. "What is it, Mambruk?" we asked. "What's wrong?"

"Sciaban Palumbo. La Azusa Palumbo." He struggled to find words beyond the names he usually called my parents. At last he gained enough composure to continue, "It is my father." He drew a deep breath. "We fear that he is dying." He turned and gestured in the direction of the family *zeribba*, which was only about 500 feet from our home.

My parents, Ada, and I went running and, as we did, we noticed for the first time the sad cadence of beating drums blowing in from the desert. Approaching the *zeribbé*, we realized that a large number of Arabs had gathered there before us. They must have heard the drums and traveled by camel through the night. We were all there to pay our respects and say farewell to Marani Ben Maiuf, who was clearly on his deathbed. He died shortly after Mambruk came to summon us. Although he was eighty years old, the news was unexpected. We had not even known he was sick.

There are no words to capture the sense of loss we felt. So much was slipping away, and Mr. Marani's death was symbolic of a bereavement that ran deeper than anything we could articulate. Only the drums seemed able to express the pain that weighed so heavily in my heart, in the hearts of everyone who knew him.

The woeful rhythms that had called members of the nomadic community to Mr. Marani's bedside continued as the family made arrangements for his funeral. Over the next day, the multitude of mourners grew. Only the Arab men were allowed to prepare the body for burial, which by Islamic law had to occur within twenty-four hours of his death. According to the dictates of his faith, Mr. Marani's body was wrapped in a length of white cloth that measured exactly seven meters. The women waited outside the *zeribba* until all the necessary rituals were complete. When the camel that would carry him to the cemetery in the town of Zuara was appropriately adorned in the trappings reserved for such a solemn occasion, Marani Ben Maiuf's body was lifted up onto its back for his final journey. With his feet pointed in the direction of the camel's head, our dear, dear friend traveled the last thirty-five miles that he would ever cover on this earth. His camel led the procession, followed by male relatives and close friends who covered the entire distance on foot.

No women were permitted to participate in the actual burial. They stayed behind to make ready for the ceremonial serving of tea that followed a funeral. As the mourners gathered in the Marani Ben Mauif family's *zeribba*, the custom was for family members to offer their guests tea poured from a pot held high above the waiting cups. This ritual was repeated three times. The first cup was strong and unsweetened to represent the bitterness of death. The leaves were then boiled a second time and a bit of sugar was added to the now weaker tea to celebrate the sweetness of life. The third cup was the weakest of all and was poured over peanuts. I'm not certain what symbolism the peanuts carried, but the gradual weakening of the strength of the beverage seemed an appropriately civilized way to represent Mr. Marani's passage from one world to the next.

My niece Antonietta remembers the sorrowful sound of beating drums continuing for three days. The family members' period of active mourning was much longer. Tumia, Mr. Marani's widow, and the wives of his sons stayed concealed in their *zeribbé* for several months. We did not see them in all that time. The men, although not confined to the tents, were not allowed to either shave or socialize for the same period.

Since Mr. Marani had lived on our farm for ten years, the bond between the families was such that their grief became our own. My parents forbid us to play the radio, and my father put his concertina away on a high shelf. "Who will call me 'Rafiq' now," he said, as he slipped his instrument out of sight. There would be no singing and dancing until the women were free to leave their *zeribbé*.

*

With my brothers gone, Libya had finally turned me into a farmer. However, seeing how much more competent Mambruk, Ali, Saad, and Mohammed were, I began to question whether my contributions were really necessary. The only Palumbos now left on the farm were my father, mother, Ada, and myself. And I began to consider how I might find a more satisfying life. I remembered the stories of how my father had left Campo di Giove for brief periods to enlist in the Bersaglieri. He had used his military salary to purchase the plow and other things that were out of reach of barter agreements. Perhaps I could do the same.

My father surprised me by not saying much when I tentatively put the idea to him. "The government will pay for my transportation if I agree to join the Navy," I told him.

He nodded and stood up. "The Italian Navy has a proud history." He started to leave the room and then turned back to me. "While you're over there, see if you can persuade Giovanni to come back and help us farm."

Although my father agreed to let me join the Navy, the Navy had other ideas. After I'd returned to Italy, reported to the recruitment center, filled out all the application forms, and taken and passed the admittance test, I stripped down for my physical. Only when they'd already checked my heart and lungs, taken blood, and declared me fit for service did they ask me to climb on the scales. "Hmmm," the Navy doctor said, as he slid the weights back and forth across the metal bar. "You're one kilo underweight." He gestured toward my pile of clothes. "Get dressed, go home, fatten up a bit, and then come back to see us."

There was only one home I wanted to go home to. Campo di Giove. As happy as I was to see Uncle Ercole and Aunt Cristina, the hunger I had left in Italy was still waiting for me on my return. There was no way I was going to gain even a kilo living in Campo di Giove. Although no one said anything, I was painfully aware that despite their joy in my return, I also burdened my relatives with another mouth to feed in a land where food shortages remained a daily reality. I stayed for only a month, but in those weeks I was able to persuade Giovanni to make plans to come back to help our parents in Libya.

I think that news alone guaranteed an enthusiastic welcome from my father. "This may all be for the best," he told me. "It may be time for us to diversify a bit, expand what we do. In case things come to a head over this matter of independence, we need to have some piece of our business that we could carry with us to Italy."

Given this line of thinking, I wasn't surprised when my father approached Mr. Messina—a butcher from Tripoli and brother-in-law to Mr. Pelosi of pig-loading fame—about taking me on as an apprentice. I tried briefly to challenge my father, but it was no use. Once his mind was made up, he knew how to turn every argument to support his own point.

"But I don't really like livestock," I told him.

"You like meat, don't you? Where do you think pork comes from?"

"Of course I like meat, but I'm not that fond of cows."

"That's good. Then you should have no problem slaughtering them." He grinned as if he expected me to laugh at his little joke. When I was unable to muster even a weak smile, he continued, "Well, you should be proud. You're the only one of my sons who doesn't faint at the sight of blood. You're the only one I can count on to do this."

Giovanni kept his promise to me, and barely a month later, he showed up at the farm in Giordani. Just as we all had predicted, Marietta, unable to leave her parents, had stayed behind in Campo di Giove with their little daughter, Angela. Before Giovanni even had time to unpack his bag, before he'd even had a chance to hitch the horse to the plow, I was on my way to Tripoli to learn a butcher's trade.

I found a room with an Italian family who lived just a short walk from Mr. Messina's butcher shop. For the next five or six months that small room was my home. After a long day learning the butcher's trade, I would return to my quarters to sleep. Other than an occasional piece of meat with some sauce that Mr. Messina sometimes gave me before I left for the night, I survived on one meal a day. He was not a kind boss. It was as if the brutality of his profession had rubbed off on him. He paid me nothing, nothing at all. I wondered what kind of negotiations he and my father had had? Had he learned his bargaining skills from his brother-in-law? Perhaps he'd pointed out some scar on my hide, some imagined limp that made me worth so little to him.

I worked hard. Yes. Just as my father had promised, I distinguished myself by my ability to kill an animal without fainting. I learned to trim and cut the meat, how to hone the steel blade on a knife to razor sharpness. I wasted no scrap that could be sold for some purpose. I made sauce. I served the customers. I took the money, counted out change, minded the till. Nothing was beneath me. Sweeping the floors, washing out the display trays—I did it all with good humor. No customer ever sensed my unhappiness. I managed a smile for everyone. In short, I learned to be a butcher and resigned myself to returning to Italy with this as my profession.

When my apprenticeship with Mr. Messina ended in the summer of 1952, it was clear to me that my new skills would be put to use in Campo di Giove, not Giordani. Only my father seemed able to hold to the belief that we might somehow be spared any dislocation resulting from Libyan independence. While I was apprenticing with Mr. Messina, he was busy remodeling our house with an eye to having Giovanni and his family take over the farm. What a dreamer he was. He was convinced that fresh paint, a new roof, ceramic floors, and a brand new kitchen in the *casificio* would somehow convince Marietta to leave her parents in Campo di Giove and travel with little Angela all the way to Giordani. I think he also believed that the new government of Libya would look at all he had accomplished and make some exception for our family. Was my new skill as a butcher simply a backup plan in case he and Giovanni failed to adequately convince an independent Libya of its need for Italian farmers? At times it was impossible to know what my father was thinking.

As things turned out, his reading of Marietta was correct. Three months after Giovanni's return to Libya, she and baby Angela traveled from Campo di Giove so that the little family could be reunited. Right as my father was about Marietta, the special favor with which he expected the new Arab government to view his accomplishments carried no guarantees. Just as mandated, Libya had declared its independence from Great Britain on December 24, 1951, and was now called the United Kingdom of Libya. It was only a matter of time. I understood that our days in Africa were numbered. I wasn't sure exactly when the Italian settlers in Libya would have to return to the country of their birth, but I knew that it would happen. My immediate family's orders came much sooner than anticipated. In October of 1952. Rather than being one of the last families notified, we were among the first. We were scheduled to depart on January 2, 1953.

The news traveled over the four square miles of our farm as quickly as if it had been carried by drumbeats almost as sorrowful as those announcing Mr. Marani's death. None of us could find the words to convey the tragedy of this forced relocation. The best that Mambruk could manage was, "How can our new government do this to us? I had hoped they would rule us with more wisdom than this edict implies." His face reflected the sadness I was feeling with the accuracy of a mirror. In the weeks between the announcement and our actual remigration, a heavy silence followed us. We went through the motions of caring for the livestock and working in the fields, but the laughing ease between the Italian settlers and our Arab friends was replaced by an awkward kind of despair. We tried to find the words to tell our neighbors that we knew this was not their doing, but there is no way to explain how helpless individuals are when used as pawns to serve larger political motives.

The actual departures were scheduled over a period of years. Uncle Savino and Aunt Raffaela D'Agostino didn't get their orders until 1956. My sister Giovanna and her husband Salvatore Del Mastro were able to stay until 1960. It was hard to understand the rationale behind the decisions, but there was no challenging them. Those Italian settlers who no longer had homes to go to were assigned to refugee camps. My teacher, Mr. Balsamo, fell into this category. Before he left, we exchanged addresses and promised to write to each other. "Remember, what I told you, Vittorio. It's possible to stay in touch with old friends even when you live apart."

Since we no longer owned a home in Campo di Giove, we could easily have found ourselves in Mr. Balsamo's position, but my father's sister, my Aunt Angela, came to our rescue. This was the same aunt whose gift of an ill-fitting suit had once allowed my hopes of becoming a *sarto* to briefly flourish. In a strange twist of events, she would now play a part in moving me into the butcher's trade. When Aunt Angela emigrated to America, she retained ownership of her home in Campo di Giove. Until she heard of my family's plight, she had rented this property. However, immediately on learning that we had nowhere to go, she turned title of the house over to my father.

"There is no longer any way to farm in Campo di Giove. Not in the manner that we've grown used to," my father said. "We'll go into a new line of business. I've found a partner. We'll set up a butcher shop in our old town."

I must have looked skeptical. After all, on my most recent trip to my hometown, hunger had still been a major problem. "Who will have the money...," I began to ask.

He cut me off. "It's a scenic area. We lived on a beautiful mountain. Now that the war is over, there will be a tourist trade. You'll see."

CHAPTER TWENTY-FIVE

Farewell

We left Libya with only what we were able to carry. More than the material things, we would miss the friends, both Italian and Arab, we had made there. We stood together for one last look at all we had accomplished. Sad and defeated, the seven of us were forced to turn our backs on the white house with the green shutters, on the fields rich with crops waiting for the harvest, on the oleander and eucalyptus, on the sheep, horses, and cows. It would all belong to someone else now, and we didn't even know who that would be. Ada, almost thirteen, was leaving the only home she could remember. I reached for her and wondered if there would ever be a way for her to understand how much I loved her. Suitcases in hand, we walked toward the bus that would take us to Tripoli.

The journey was a routine affair, no fancy former cruise ship, but no battleship either. No dodging explosions in mined waters, but neither were there tours of churches. We had very little to say to each other. Perhaps only Marietta was able to muster a bit of joy at the thought of seeing her mother again. Certainly Marietta's mother was looking forward to having her daughter and granddaughter in her life once more. It was more difficult for the rest of us. My mother had no silken scarf filled with the promise of a better life that I could run between my fingers. Almost dutifully we trudged down the gangplank in Siracusa, Sicily. There we climbed aboard a train to Messina. In Messina, we remained on these same railroad cars as they were loaded onto a ferry headed to Villa San Giovanni in Calabria. The cars were pulled off the ferry in Calabria and moved to a track headed for Naples. It had been 120 degrees in Tripoli. Stepping off the train briefly in Naples before beginning the final leg of our journey home, we shivered in the chilly January welcome our port city offered us.

It was Ada's first hint of what the word *winter* actually meant. We retraced the route we had traveled back in 1939 when on our way to Naples to board the *Piemonte*, the beautiful ship that had carried us to the new land. Only on this return journey, there were no cheering crowds, no patriotic flags and bunting draped along the sides of trains. It was snowing when we arrived in Campo di Giove. Uncle Ercole, Aunt Cristina, and my cousin Luciano were waiting on the platform. And, glad as I was to see them, the faces of all those who were missing—Umberto, Antonio, my grandmother, my grandfather—were so real to me that tears briefly fogged my vision.

My father pulled the brim of his hat down at a jaunty angle. Unable to assume an attitude that matched the confidence implied by his headgear, he gestured toward our meager collection of suitcases. "We left with trunks and return with this," he said softly.

We had left with more than trunks. We had left in the company of family and friends. Where were they now? Gennaro was in Venezuela. Guerino was in Sicily still driving tractor trailers for Mr. Maiolino. Giovanni and his family came back with us, but they would be staying with Marietta and her mother. The Del Mastros and D'Agostinos would return and scatter according to the schedules dictated by the new government of Libya and the challenges of trying to make a life in a country still recovering from the war. Not everyone made it back. Poor Uncle Savino lost so much. First Umberto and then, in 1956, on their return trip from Giordani to Campo di Giove, Savino's wife, my Aunt Raffaela, died on the boat that was carrying them home.

"Hey, Savino," my father had called to him in 1939, "want to go to Libya?"

"Sure, Roberto, we'll go to Libya."

*

There is one photograph from that time that I cherish. It shows Mr. Valerino Del Mastro—the father of Salvatore, Enrico, Vittorio, Elisena, Aquilina, Carmela, Rosina, and Olindo—standing in the middle of a field of wheat, wearing a blue ribbon, his prize for taking first place at the annual village fair held in the city of Sabrata in Libya. That is all the picture shows—one man, the ribbon pinned to his lapel, some family members, and a field of wheat—but it is not all I see. I see the swirling sand that first greeted us on our arrival in Tripoli, and I see the bounty of the fields we left behind after having turned our small piece of the Sahara into productive farmland.

On the October day the snapshot was taken, I had been back in Libya for only three months. All the villages within horse and buggy distance of Sabrata had participated in the harvest fair. With everyone eager to win a prize, it was a festival like none I had ever experienced. The wagons and buggies were decorated with the fruits of our labors. Grapes hung in fat clusters from even the shafts of horse carts. Golden strands of wheat were woven through the spokes of wagon wheels. Animals were groomed to perfection. There was not a tangled mane in sight. Even our horses' hooves were shined. Having rubbed their bodies with curry combs until no dead hair remained, we exhibited them with coats so sleek that every muscle reflected light. Fat cattle were turned to display the gleaming length of their horns. Sheep had their wool carded and trimmed in such a way as to accent the perfection of their conformation. Baskets of fresh produce lined the tables where the judges carefully deliberated before awarding the ribbons we all hoped to win. Even the schoolchildren had put together plays to entertain the settlers. Under the guidance of Mr. Balsamo, our village won first prize for the quality of its dramatic presentation. A blue ribbon for first prize, red for second, yellow for third. The competition was so keen that a ribbon of any sort was a thing to cherish. On the ride back to Giordani that night, the Palumbo family carefully passed the blue ribbon we had won for the best horses from one jubilant hand to another. Giordani had three blue ribbons to mark its success. Horses. Wheat. And drama. Our little town was united in its pride.

*

In 1953 we came back to Campo di Giove with one treasure we hadn't had when we'd left for Libya: Adalgisa. The most joyful part of our return was introducing my sister to all the relatives who, up until then, she'd known only by name. Since the house Aunt Angela deeded to my father required some remodeling before we could really live there, Ada and I stayed briefly with warm-hearted Uncle Ercole and Aunt Cristina. For a change, I was the one who had the easiest time navigating the adjustment to our new circumstances. After all, I'd been back and forth to Campo di Giove a number of times and had a strong sense of place and family there. Not only that, but I also was prepared for the deprivations of life in a remote mountain community damaged by war and its aftermath. Adalgisa was unfamiliar with the kind of hardship our new life carried with it and had a more difficult time, but true to her nature, she didn't complain. However, she was so unprepared for the rigors of a cold climate that she spent her first six months in Italy wandering around the house wrapped in a blanket.

My mother also handled the reduction in her circumstances with impressive forbearance. In Libya, my family had wanted for nothing. In fact, after my parents had been there for only a short time, my father was able to save 350,000 lire he'd earned selling produce to the military units. So confident was he in the strength of the Italian economy and the skill of the Italian Army that he invested the entire amount in government-issued bonds. Had all gone according to plan, that money would have been worth a small fortune by 1953. But all did not go according to plan. Upon our return to Italy my father had just enough money to purchase a few pieces of used furniture, a cow, and a mule.

Every few days, my mother rode that mule to a forested area partway down the Majella Mountain. There she and other women from Campo di Giove gathered firewood in order to warm their homes and fuel the stoves on which they prepared the family meals. Tying the wood into large bundles, they helped each other hoist the cumbersome loads onto the backs of their mules. What wouldn't fit on the mules, they carried on their heads. Mother, often bearing weight of her own, would walk beside her heavily burdened animal on the return trip up the mountain. She had gone from the abundance of the farm in Libya to a life even more constrained than the one she thought she had forever left behind.

Never a man to admit defeat or fault, my father put on a brave show. He set about remodeling Aunt Angela's house. To no one's surprise, especially not mine, the first thing he concentrated on was constructing a place for a butcher shop in the section of the building facing the street. With the help provided by his partner and money from my brothers Gennaro in Venezuela and Guerino in Sicily, my father created a separate entrance for the store, which occupied the entire ground level. We would make our home on the other two floors. The shop offered gleaming testimony to my father's insistence on doing everything first-rate. A mahogany-covered cooler with three doors occupied an entire wall. The floor was tile, and the lower three-quarters of the walls not taken over by refrigeration were faced with the finest Italian marble from Massa Carrara, a city known for the beauty of its stone.

The second story of our new dwelling had a kitchen and small dining area which opened onto a balcony overlooking the entrance to the butcher shop. On the other side of the building was the entrance to our living quarters. My father insisted on a bathroom equipped with the modern amenities we'd grown used to in Libya. Two huge bedrooms filled the third floor. One had doors leading to a balcony far above the bustle of the street. The back bedroom featured a window that framed a perfect view of the Majella Mountains. It was a home that had everything except a family committed to staying together as a family unit.

True to his word, it wasn't long before my father was running a business from the front of our house in the town center. True to my word, I tried hard to help this business flourish, but it was trouble from the start. I didn't like his partner and his partner didn't like me. When the butcher shop failed to thrive immediately, the partner claimed I was taking money from the till. In fact, he was the dishonest one. It was clear to me that he was cheating my father at every turn and was only too willing to blame any shortfalls on me. The thing that outraged me most was that my father seemed so ready to believe the word of his partner over that of his own son.

I guess I can understand why my father would think I might be tempted. After all, he paid me no salary and continued his practice of doling out a small allowance every Saturday night. I was twenty years old and still treated like a child. But, remembering how Gennaro had endured a similar humiliation at age twenty-eight, I realized that arguing with my father would serve no purpose and my only hope was to do what Gennaro had done before me: make plans to leave.

The futility of ever trying to make a point with my father made working with his partner in the butcher shop increasingly difficult. How could my own flesh and blood even consider that I might take money from the till? Had I ever been that kind of son? No. Surely my father knew how honest I was. Why, I'd never once in my life disobeyed him. What made him able to listen to his partner's complaints against me without coming to me to hear my side of the story? I thought back to the day the pigs had refused to climb on the truck and remembered how my father had threatened to shoot everyone except Mr. Pelosi. Was this simply another case of the fatness of someone's wallet lifting him above the level of suspicion? My father must have felt he needed the guarantee of his partner's continued investment in the fledgling business.

But didn't he also need me and my skills? Apparently not. I found myself spending less and less time behind the counter serving customers and cutting meat. However, I continued to help with the slaughtering. Much as I disliked that job, I found it easier than sharing space in the shop with my father's partner. My mother could see me drifting away from the business, and it made her sad. All her sons were leaving. Gennaro had established a life in Venezuela. Guerino had come back from Sicily and stayed just long enough to complete the papers that would allow him to move to Venezuela himself. He left in the middle of 1953, and I never saw him again. Giovanni, who now lived with his mother-in-law, was also making plans to move to Venezuela to prepare for a life with Marietta and their two children. By 1954, only my mother, my father, Ada, and I lived in the house Aunt Angela had given us.

Once I overheard my mother trying to defend me to my father. She cautioned, "You'll lose him. You won't have anyone to help you with the butcher shop."

"Oh, it's too late now. What does it matter? They are all going. Vittorio is already filling out the forms to emigrate to America." He knew this because I had to approach him to get the address of his brother, Antonio Palumbo, who lived in Albany, New York, and who I had hoped would sponsor me. Uncle Antonio and his wife Filomena Antonetti were American citizens who, once I'd written to them, did agree to guarantee their government that they would provide me with a place to live until I was well enough established that I could manage on my own.

I made all these preparations in response to urging from my old teacher, Mr. Balsamo, who had moved from the refugee camp where he'd first been assigned and had found an apartment in the Latina section of

Rome. The two of us had kept our promise to stay in touch, and he began encouraging me to make plans to emigrate to the United States.

Giovanni, who was in the process of filling out papers requesting approval to emigrate to Venezuela, laughed whenever I urged him to come instead with me. "Don't listen to Mr. Balsamo," he told me. "America will come to Italy before you will go to America."

"No, I know we can do this," I told him. "Don't make me go by myself. Bring Marietta and the children and come to America with me." By now Giovanni and his wife had a second child, little Roberto. "We've been together most of our lives. Don't make me go by myself now."

Since we already had two brothers there, Giovanni knew Venezuela was possible. He was completely unable to believe that my American dream had the slightest chance of coming true. Not even showing him the advertisement that sought to recruit 60,000 Italians for relocation convinced him that I was on a legitimate path to American citizenship.

But Mr. Balsamo had built a compelling case. He assured me there were quotas available to those who had relatives who were already American citizens. "Dear Victor," he wrote, using the name he sometimes called me. "I have been to Rome and seen the manifests. Anyone who was a former settler in Libya is eligible to go to America as long as he has a sponsor there."

Mr. Balsamo actually went to the consulate in Rome and picked up the forms I needed to complete in order to qualify for emigration. He urged me to return them to him as soon as I'd answered all the questions, so that he could hand deliver my application to the American Consulate in Naples himself. He did all these things for me.

Once my paperwork was complete, the only step between me and emigration was showing up for a personal interview at the embassy in Naples. Any answers I gave would be cross-checked against the police records in Campo di Giove. This was in 1955. America, at the time, was more worried about the infiltration of Communists than on placing undue emphasis on Mussolini's failed policies. Given that Mussolini's early support was based in part on his opposition to Bolshevism in Russia, the interviewer initially hadn't seemed too concerned about my early exposure to Fascism in Mussolini's schools. Any anxiety I felt about the impending cross-examination was quickly put to rest when I was able to honestly declare that I was not and never had been a Communist.

"Why were you in a refugee camp in Rome?" He tilted his head in a way that indicated a genuine curiosity about what that experience had been like for a young boy. The story flowed out of me. The war years. My family's opposition to the Germans. Our months in the *capanna*. And before that, in the beginning, my family's move to Libya. The frightening journey back to Italy for enrollment in the *Gioventù Italiana del Littorio* boarding schools.

"Yes, the schools," he said. "You were one of the children in Mussolini's schools?"

I nodded. Where to begin? The separation from my parents. The loneliness. The military discipline. The friends I made. Even as I spoke, I realized that if Mussolini's intent had been indoctrination, some combination of sorrow, fear, and disillusionment had neutralized the effect. I remembered Uncle Ercole's answer to my query as to whose side we were on. "Our own, Vittorio. We watch out for each other now." Despite all of Mussolini's efforts, my family remained my single greatest influence.

"How would you describe your personal political views?"

I was silent for a moment. No one had ever asked me this in so many words. I thought of my father and our days in Libya after the war. The success he'd enjoyed there had made him aware of the importance of individual effort. Although he was not particularly democratic in the way in which he ruled our family, it suddenly dawned on me that my father was a great admirer of countries with democratic governments. And so was I. Of course. Of course. This yearning for democracy and all it implied was the reason I wanted to go to America. I looked the interviewer proudly in the eye. "I am a democrat," I answered with absolute certainty.

*

By now, Vittorio Del Mastro was back home and had established a name for himself as a painter of houses. On observing how difficult things were between me and my father, Vittorio offered me a job helping him. When I wasn't busy in the slaughterhouse, this new paying job made it possible for me to set aside the money I would need to finance my passage to America. Around this time a friend of mine, Erberto Sciuba, approached me about whether Vittorio Del Mastro and I had time to take on the job of painting the inside of his family home. Erberto was my age. Our families lived close and knew each other well. Perhaps the Sciubas knew me a bit too well.

When Vittorio and I showed up to discuss the job, Mrs. Sciuba looked at us skeptically. "Will you finish the job quickly?" Some local painters had a reputation of taking on too many jobs at the same time and never really finishing when they promised they would.

"Sure, we're fast," I told her.

"Hmm. Maybe too fast." She looked at me and then at her tile floors. "If I hire you, I think I'm going to have to scatter sawdust everywhere to keep the paint from dripping on them."

When we showed up early the next morning, true to Mrs. Sciuba's word, all the furniture had been moved out of the room and the floors were covered in sawdust. I set to work in my usual manner. The days riding to the movies on the bus with Bevilacqua had taught me the power of music to fill any space with joy. It didn't matter that I was working, I sang as loudly as if I were back in that time. The way my voice echoed in the empty room inspired a tendency toward operatic gusto. The gestures accompanying my song sometimes sent paint drops flying and reinforced the wisdom of Mrs. Sciuba's sawdust. At measured intervals, Erberto's twelve-year-old sister, Rosalba, would stomp through the room, glaring at me with her hands over her ears.

Just as Vittorio and I were applying the final coat, I got word that my application for immigration to America had been approved. "I'm going to America," I cried in my loudest voice as I ran through the streets of Campo di Giove. "I'm going to America! I'm going to America!" Everyone in the town square rejoiced with me, but when I ran into the Sciuba household with my news, Rosalba had her own reasons for celebrating. "Good," she said. "I'm glad you're going. Now maybe I'll have some peace and quiet."

However, I wasn't the only one who had plans for my future. Italy suddenly decided that I might make a fine addition to the Italian Air Force. If I was still in the country on May 7, 1955, I would have to report for duty. In the meantime, I was told to travel to L'Aquila for a mandatory physical. A good friend, who worked as a policeman in Campo di Giove, agreed to drive me. I had no problem with that examination. Everything checked out.

Now I really began to worry about the physical I had to pass before my permission to emigrate to the United States would be final. It was scheduled for the very next day in Naples and would be administered by an American doctor. Given my medical history, I was terrified that this doctor's more demanding requirements would find some reason to make me stay in Italy. After all, a physical administered by the Italian Navy had once kept me from pursuing that career path. The irony now was that unless I passed this American exam and emigrated from Italy before May 7, I would be forced to enlist in the Italian Air Force. I was no longer interested in serving in the military. All I wanted was to seek citizenship in the land of the free and the home of the brave.

I knew from my pounding heart and the flush in my cheeks that my blood pressure was climbing with every step the doctor took toward me. Luckily, the doctor knew fear-induced high blood pressure when he saw it. I actually flinched when he reached to put the cuff on my arm. He stood back and smiled. "Relax. I'm not going to kill you."

Something in his easy-going American confidence calmed me down. He set his medical gear on the table beside him and chatted with me a bit before attempting to resume the examination. After a few shared laughs, he picked up his stethoscope and tried again. When he was finished, he nodded in approval, and I knew I had passed. He looked steadily at me and shook his head, almost in admiration. "Young man, you ought to head straight for Hollywood."

I'd been told that I'd inherited my father's good looks. All the men in my family had heard this said about them at one time or another, but Hollywood? Hadn't I had enough of the motion picture business in Campo Cinecittà?

*

It was late April, 1955. Spring. The time for starting over, beginning again. Giovanni was approved for relocation to Venezuela around the same time I learned I would be going to America. He left Campo di Giove by himself—without his wife and children—just one day before me. As things turned out, Marietta never did find the strength to leave her mother. She and the children remained behind in Campo di Giove. Giovanni periodically returned to spend time with them. It wasn't until many years later that he came back to his ancestral home for good.

At five o'clock the very next morning, with a trembling in my stomach and a suitcase in my hand, I said farewell to a community of people whose lives were imbedded in my bones and in every fiber of my flesh and heart. Perhaps if I'd realized how much I was loved in return, I would have had greater difficulty initiating the steps it took to arrange departure from my native country. It seemed as if the entire town had risen early to wish me fortune in my journey. "Arrivederci, Vittorio." "Addio." Since this last phrase means that the speaker might expect to see you again only in heaven, it gave me pause. I studied the faces surrounding me. Were some of these farewells truly final?

My parents, Ada, Aunt Cristina, Uncle Ercole, and their son Luciano and his wife pressed close against me. "Write," was all my mother could manage. My father stood slightly apart. Behind him, friends and relatives, all waving and all clinging to some piece of my American dream, crowded the town square and the stairs leading down into it. I struggled to find the appropriate words with which to bid them good-bye, but emotion closed my throat and blurred my vision.

Some things you take with you. Some you leave behind. Others you come back for. I left the Majella Mountain knowing I would never forget its people and the struggles we had endured together. I was shaped by my days there in the place of my birth. And despite the loneliness of my years in Mussolini's schools, the physical beauty and the kindness of the people of Fiera di Primiero nurtured some tenderness of heart that makes love possible. Once again, I was uprooted, heading off to a foreign land. I never doubted that I would return. I left carrying the strong belief that I would someday come back to honor my heritage here. However, I also left knowing that my immediate goal was to devote five years to establishing my citizenship in the United States of America. And so I said good-bye to Campo di Giove.

And what of my years in Libya? I remember those nights when my father played the concertina. It rained so seldom there. After the Arabian sunsets had burned across the Sahara and the moon had climbed high, all filled with grace and light, its quiet force settling the dust and erasing the toil from our day's labor, then my father would gather up his concertina and call us to him with an equal grace. Those first few notes built and lifted into song. Drawn by the melody, the neighbors wandered in from the four corners of our little estate in the desert. Beatrice Milano always carried a big stick so she could keep our dogs—Jack, Bosco, and Picchio—away from her, but we never thought to exclude them. The moon and the melody issued the invitation across the eucalyptus-scented air and everyone, even the dogs, responded. My father played the *tarantella*; he played all the old songs. In the beginning, we just listened. But first one voice and then another would join in, and before too long, we were completely lost in the music. Tumia and her daughters-in-law arrived before their husbands, and they would open their faces to us as we sang and danced—each to our own steps, not really together, but nonetheless joined. Not until they saw their husbands following them over from the family *zeribbé* would they reach up and let the veils fall back into place. Music softens rules. When my mother uncorked a bottle of Chianti and poured out small glasses, Mr. Marani, Ali, Mambruk, and the other Arab men would join us in a toast. Even though Muslims usually abstain from alcohol, they drank wine with us. I remember how my father leaned against the stucco courtyard wall as he played, his head inclined over the instrument, his handsome face focused and intent, seeking out some harmony that only he could hear and translate into the music that flowed from him. In those moments, I loved his face, I loved his dreams, I loved that man and everything he tried to create for us. We all do the best we can. We all make mistakes. No person moves through life unburdened by a share of regret and error. But on those nights when my father played the concertina, everything—every single thing—was good.

Epilogue

CHAPTER ONE

America: Land of Opportunity and Ice Cream

On April 27, 1955, I sailed from Naples for America on the *Cristoforo Colombo*, a ship loaded with other Italians who were seeking their fortunes in a new land. An old photograph from that passage captures our hopes and dreams in a sea of smiling faces. We were all so open to adventure, all so sure of happy endings. The reality of the enormity of our aspirations didn't really hit home until nine days later, on May 5, 1955, when we crowded, almost as one, to the side of the ship that afforded the best view of the Statue of Liberty, her torch held high in welcome. This was our moment. We were the huddled masses yearning to breathe free.

Moving slowly past the recently shuttered facilities at Ellis Island, our expressions grew more somber, even as our hearts raced with joy. The Port of New York loomed directly ahead. The docking process, with its cutting of engines and tossing of ropes, added a slow-motion, dreamlike quality to my search for a new world. Once again, I found myself wondering who, if anyone, would be there to meet me. New York's May breezes held more promise than the blistering heat that had greeted me on my return to Libya. Even so, I found myself puzzling over how I would recognize family members I had never seen before. When at last the ship was still and the gangplank lowered, I moved with the flow of the crowd almost as if I had no volition of my own. My fate was set. I was here and had only to wait for my new life to unfold.

My suitcase was a small one. It didn't take the customs officials long to search through the clothes that filled it. A friend, who shared my interest in tailoring, had helped me construct two new suits and two shirts. I had made four sets of underwear without help from anyone. That was it. At the money exchange, I waited while the crumpled lira I pulled from my pocket were converted into twelve American dollars. And then, at last, I heard someone calling my name. Aunt Filomena recognized me. "Handsome, handsome, all Palumbo men look alike," she said, as she pulled me away from the crowd and began rattling off the names and ages of her adult children in hasty introduction. "That's Rose," she said in Italian, pointing to one of two women who were smiling in welcome. "She's forty-three, same age as Salvatore's wife." Both women winced as she gestured to her daughter-in-law, Florence. Even in my confusion I understood that they wouldn't want their ages given as if they were still little kids. Bruno, her forty-year-old son, reached for my hand. He was the only one of Aunt Filomena's children who attempted to speak Italian. "Pleased to meet you" was the one phrase he knew, and he kept repeating it over and over again as he struggled with the pronunciation.

My main impression was of crowds, impossibly tall buildings, noise, and automobiles everywhere. Overcome, I was content to let my cousins chatter among themselves. I heard my name woven through the conversation as they talked over each other and knew that it was spoken in kindness, but there was no way for me to even attempt to do more than smile and nod in acknowledgment of their enthusiastic welcome.

And then we were away from the worst of the traffic and headed north on a smooth highway headed for Albany. It grew as suddenly silent as it had been noisy. And in that silence, I felt my first acute pang of homesickness. What was I doing so far from Campo di Giove?

As if they were as uncomfortable with the unnatural quiet as I was, one of them suddenly pointed to a large billboard and suggested, "Howard Johnson's. Let's stop at Howard Johnson's."

I had no idea who this Howard Johnson person was and wondered if the entire journey to Albany would be similarly interrupted by visits to friends of the family. However, as my aunt pulled into the large parking lot of what was obviously a commercial establishment, I figured out that we were headed for a restaurant. "Have you ever had ice cream?"

Ice cream? I didn't even know what it was, but by the smiles on the faces of my family members, I quickly understood that I was about to be introduced to a particularly American treat.

Aunt Filomena ordered for me. When the waitress slid a huge oblong dish covered with three mountains of whipped cream each topped with a cherry so red that it bore little resemblance to actual fruit in front of me, I was at a loss to know where to begin. My confusion inspired good-natured laughter, a sort of expectant joy in what I was about to discover. Whipped cream was good. Was this the fabled ice cream? No. I was urged to keep going. Chocolate syrup. Butterscotch sauce. Strawberries in a sweet glaze. Nuts. Something firm and cold was sandwiched between the bananas that lined the bottom of the plate. I took one bite of the chocolate mound. Everyone leaned forward as I let it melt over my tongue.

"Well? What do you think?"

"Gelato. Isn't this gelato?"

They all chuckled in delight. I smiled to mask my confusion. Was this what it was like in America? Almost too much of everything, the heart of the matter buried under a mound of decorative excess. I'd never in my life had so much gelato and was unable to finish—something my adult cousins took as a sign of the success of my introduction to American ice cream.

What seemed like an entire brigade of friends and relatives was waiting when we finally pulled up in front of my aunt and uncle's house in Albany. Uncle Tony was nine years older than my father, but there was no denying we were related. By the time I was shown to my bed, I was completely exhausted. Yet just as it had happened on my first night as one of Mussolini's Children of the She-Wolf, I was unable to fall asleep. I had been so many places in my life, had been dislocated so many times before, why did my heart choose this particular moment to long for my father? It would turn out to be like that for most of the first two years I spent in America. Everyone was kind. Everyone wanted to help, but I was unprepared for how difficult it would be to not speak the language of the majority of the people around me. And I was totally unprepared for how much I wanted my father to miss me. At odd moments off and on during those first two years, I would find myself remembering Papá's sadness when Gennaro first decided to leave Libya for Venezuela, his insistence that I convince Giovanni to return to the farm in Giordani, his heartbreak when Guerino left to drive tractor-trailer trucks for Mr. Maiolino. Might my father even now be urging someone to convince me to return to help with the butcher shop? But no one ever sent the letter telling me that Papá wanted me to come back to Italy. From 1955 until 1957, all it would have taken was a single word from my father, and I would have reversed course and headed straight for Campo di Giove. But no such word arrived. After putting so much effort into obtaining a visa to America, I now began to understand that when dreams come true, they don't always feel like answered prayers.

Shortly after my arrival at Aunt Filomena and Uncle Tony's, my cousin John, Aunt Angela's son, drove me to see his mother in Milford, Massachusetts. The timing of the visit seemed appropriate to me. It was Mother's Day. Although I had always thought of Aunt Angela almost as a guardian angel, I realized that in some ways she was more like a loving but geographically distant grandmother to me. Since she was fifteen years older than my father, she had served as a mother figure to him when, at age seven, his own mother died. Even after moving to America, she had kept an eye out for our family. She had sent me the suit that kept my hopes of becoming a *sarto* alive. And if she hadn't so generously turned ownership of her house in Campo di Giove over to my father when we were ordered to leave Libya, our family would have been sent to live in a refugee camp.

One would think that the ride to Milford would have been filled with joyful anticipation, but John had sad news for me. "My mother is quite ill, you know," he told me even before we pulled out onto the highway.

"Aunt Filomena mentioned something, but I thought maybe...I guess I was hoping it wasn't too serious."

John looked sad. "It's serious, Vittorio." He seemed to be paying an exaggerated amount of attention to the road, but I could tell he really was wondering how much I knew and was pondering how to phrase things. "She has cancer," he said at last. "The doctors don't expect her to live much longer."

My eyes filled with tears. It was all the response I could manage at the moment. However, seeing Aunt Angela waiting for me at the door allowed me to pretend for a moment that she was well, that John had somehow misunderstood what the doctors had told him. She welcomed me into her home with as much affection as if she had been by my side since the moment of my birth and we had only recently been separated. Despite my initial impression of health, it wasn't long before I could see her begin to tire. Without interrupting her conversation with me, John propped pillows behind her and eased her onto the sofa. I searched for words to tell her how much she meant to our family, but her own concern about my welfare prevented the conversation from going in that direction.

"And, how are things in Albany?"

"Fine. Uncle Tony and Aunt Filomena are very kind. It was good of them to sponsor me."

"How is it living in the city?"

"Milford has more trees."

John laughed. On the ride through Massachusetts, I had remarked so often on how much I loved the rolling hills that he finally interrupted me. "Mountains, Vittorio, here we call these mountains. The Berkshires."

"But they have trees all the way to the top."

"You're right. Not like home, is it?"

I'd had no answer for that observation, and now John responded to his mother's question for me. "I think Vittorio misses the mountains."

She looked at me sharply. "Albany is very different from Campo di Giove. Have you met many people?"

I shook my head. "Relatives. Mostly relatives. Some other Italians." I wasn't sure how to explore the next topic without sounding ungrateful. "Neighbors don't talk much to each other. It's all mixed in with different races, but they don't really seem to talk much to each other." I tried again. "In Libya, Arabs and Italians all seemed like friends. It's not like that in Albany."

Aunt Angela nodded. "I couldn't live in a city." She pulled a small blanket over her lap. "Maybe it will be better when you find a job. You'll meet more people then."

"I need to find work where my difficulty with English won't be so much of a problem."

"It gets better, I can guarantee. It will get better. Everything is hard in the beginning."

I thought about Aunt Angela's words in the dark car on the ride back to Albany. I was beginning to understand some English. My cousins were struggling to teach me, but I couldn't imagine that I would ever have the easy way with words here that I had had back home.

Albany and I were not a good fit. As it turned out, I wasn't there long. Aunt Angela passed away at the age of 73, only weeks after my Mother's

Day visit. True to her compassionate and generous nature, one of the last things she did before her death was to make arrangements for me to move from Albany to Milford. Aunt Angela's son, Danny, and his wife, Connie, asked me to come live with them in Milford. They helped me find a job making floor tiles in the Stylon factory. Since some of the other workers were also of Italian descent and eased my difficulties with translation, I began to slowly acquire at least a working use of English. My education in American culture was helped along by a young man named Humphrey who was also employed in the Stylon factory and offered to drive me back and forth to work every day in his 1953 Chevy. Those rides were about much more than simply commuting. "Victor," Humphrey told me, "You don't hug men in America. In America you hug women and shake hands with men."

Every sentence began with "Victor." Americans seemed unable to pronounce Vittorio. Since most of them confused it with Victoria, I was only too glad to switch to Victor, a name that seemed to give no one any trouble and made it clear, even before someone had met me face-to-face, that I was a man.

"Victor, you have to stop talking with your hands so much. If you want to be a true-blue American, you have to stop talking with your hands." This was a more difficult habit to acquire than hugging women, especially since I knew so few English words and often needed my hands to help explain my meaning. However, one American passion that came easily to me was the love of the automobile. Humphrey's Chevy inspired me to want to start saving money to buy a car of my own, no small aspiration for a man earning seventy-five cents an hour.

I learned American curse words pretty quickly. How sweet to discover the release of a short outburst that required no understanding of grammar or sentence structure. When children first attempt to mimic adult swearing, they are scolded and quickly acquire a sense of shame to go along with the words. Not so with an immigrant learning profanity on the job. Mine was a happy fluency until I began working side by side with Mary Cicchetti and Ferminda Di Domenico. I manned the compressor that pressed tiles into their flat shape. The job of my co-workers Mary and Ferminda was to take the tiles from the compressor and stack them in a special box that was then carried to an oven where they would be baked.

When something went wrong, using words that meant nothing to me, I joyfully and loudly practiced the American art of swearing.

"Ohhh," Ferminda would yell at me. "Don't use that word!"

Mary, blushing scarlet, tried to explain. "Don't ever say those things, Victor. Those are bad words."

"What do you mean, bad words? How can there be bad words? What am I saying that's so bad?"

Then Mary and Ferminda would huddle together whispering. Since Mary couldn't even hear the words without blushing, it fell to Ferminda to translate what I had said into Italian.

My reaction, carrying echoes of my mother's exchanges with Ali, was immediate. "Don't ever say those things to me!" I cried in horror. "Women aren't supposed to say those words."

*

While I was busy learning what words I could and couldn't say in America, my family back in Italy had their own struggles, news of which reached me through infrequent letters. By the time I learned what was happening with my family, the news was old. That didn't make it any less sad. Sometimes the letters were necessarily brief, and it might be years before I learned the full story behind significant events. In 1956, my father wrote to tell me that my mother's sister, my Aunt Raffaela, had died on the boat on the family's return from Libya. How I hurt for my mother. She and her sister had been so close. How I hurt for Uncle Savino. Our great Libyan adventure had cost his family so much.

My parents had been told the date on which the D'Agostino family was expected back in Campo di Giove, and my mother had prepared a feast in honor of their return. My mother, my father, my sister Ada, and Uncle Savino's oldest son Filippo and his wife Anselma and their children were all waiting to greet the family at the railway station. Imagine their shock when only Savino, sad and broken, stepped off the train. What was to have been a celebration turned into a funeral occasion. Because of the custom that required burial within twenty-four hours of a death, Uncle Savino had had to bury his wife in Siracusa, almost as soon as the boat docked. Following the dictates of a law that requires graves to remain undisturbed for at least ten years after the initial internment, her body would lie there alone for ten years. He could not bring her back to Campo di Giove until 1966. Uncle Savino died only three years later at the age of seventy-nine. He was buried beside his wife who had been sixty-four at the time of her death from unknown causes.

My father wrote again in late December of 1957 to tell me that my mother's only remaining sister, my Aunt Fiorina, had died of cancer on the 5th of that month. By now, I knew that I would not, could not, return to Italy until I had earned my American citizenship papers. It was clear that Papá wasn't going to ask me to come back. Perhaps I'd prejudiced the case against myself by sending him boots and Pendleton shirts from America. How he loved those shirts! His affection for them may have actually helped convince him of the wisdom of my American dream. As for me, that dream was increasingly moving in a direction that left little room for regret. The first two years had been the most difficult. As I became more comfortable with the language and made friends here, I began to feel at home. Still, on learning that another of my mother's sisters had died, I ached for her and wished I could be in Campo di Giove to offer physical comfort.

Sometimes letters brought good news. Antonio D'Agostino found a way of reversing his family's bad luck. I remembered Salvatore Del Mastro meeting me in Tripoli when I was newly returned from the refugee camp. I'd been worried about Antonio who, frustrated with the long wait for official papers, had left Campo Cinecittà in an attempt to find his way back to Giordani on his own. Salvatore had been quick to assure me that Antonio had made it back before I had. "Antonio D'Agostino always finds a way." He had done that once again. On his family's forced return to Italy from Libya, Antonio, still lacking official papers, had been sent to the Caserma Vittorio Emanuel refugee camp in Gaeta, Italy. There he made friends with a man who had been a judge in Libya. This gentleman promised Antonio that, as soon as he was assigned to a new post as a judge in Rome, he would get Antonio a job in the court. True to his word, he made Antonio Clerk of Courts, a position he held until he retired. The remaining D'Agostinos resettled successfully. Caterina, her husband Attilio, and their children Bruno and Maria, went to live in the Province of Noventa del Piave in northern Italy. She remained there until her death in 2005.

VITTORIO PALUMBO

*

After two years of working at making tiles, I finally learned of a job that would move me one step closer to the vision of myself that was first given wings in Campo Straniero. In 1957, I was hired as a stitcher with Anthony Roberts, a company known for the quality of its raincoats. It was piecework, nothing glamorous. But as I competently topstitched the front closure of raincoats, I remembered how proud I'd been when Matilda Farmungari had first assigned me my own sewing machine. Here I was, eleven years later, topstitching once again. However, this time, I saw that my fate was more clearly in my own hands than it had ever been.

The Anthony Roberts factory employed many workers of Italian descent. I was welcomed by them almost as a member of the family. Peter Ventresca and his wife, Elvira, made it plain how much they enjoyed my company. When the upstairs apartment in the home they owned became available, they asked me if I would be interested in becoming their next tenant. I jumped at the opportunity. My cousin Danny and his wife Connie had always made me feel welcome, but I was eager to establish my independence. Mr. and Mrs. Ventresca charged me eighteen dollars a week for room, board, and laundry. It was a happy arrangement for all of us. Even after I married, they never raised it above fifty dollars a month. Of course, once I was married this figure covered rent for the apartment only. Rosalba kept me well fed and in clean clothes. The Ventrescas were more than landlords; they were friends. My job as topstitcher was opening up my world. Elizabeth Mastroianni and her sons also worked with me at the raincoat factory and became an important part of my growing network of friends. I was no longer a lonely immigrant in America.

In 1958, I applied for a job as a tailor at Jordan Marsh Department Store in Framingham. The minute the Ventrescas saw the smile on my face, they knew that I had been hired. From now on, I would head off to work dressed in a suit and tie. After all the years of longing to be taken seriously as a tailor, adjusting the knot in my tie each morning reminded me of how happy I was not to be a butcher!

Jordan Marsh was a huge department store. Its many floors seemed to hold every material thing the human heart could desire. I would be working in the men's department. Since men come in many sizes and shapes, but ready-made suits are limited in their accommodation to that variety, I was very busy making alterations. Every time a gentleman turned in front of the mirror to survey the results of my work, I felt the old thrill that had first touched me back when I apprenticed with Giacchino.

Jordan Marsh held every material thing a man could desire, but with each year that passed, my goal of citizenship was drawing closer, and I began to think of finding a wife. It was hard getting to know someone who felt like the right young woman. There was one Irish girl, the daughter of the local chief of police, who took my fancy. One day, a friend saw me waiting to meet her at the soda shop in Milford and said, "Her father will cut your head off if he finds out she's dating an Italian boy." That remark made me realize I might be pursuing an impossible dream. Even though my English was much improved, there were still so many religious, cultural, and language barriers.

In 1959, I was on my way to a vacation on Martha's Vineyard when a letter from Aunt Cristina arrived. I tucked it into my pocket so I could savor news from home while on the ferry to the island. But rather than the heartwarming updates from Campo di Giove I was expecting, Aunt Cristina and her son Luciano were writing to inform me that my Uncle Ercole had died unexpectedly at age seventy-one. Uncle Ercole! He had been like a father to me. How could this have happened? He'd always been in such robust good health. I tried hard not to let my friends see my sorrow. After all, I didn't want to spoil anyone's holiday, but I found it difficult to realize I would never see my Uncle Ercole again. The only comfort I could manage was that he hadn't suffered long. He'd been out working in the fields when he had a massive heart attack. His friends had carried him home, where he died a week later. He lived just long enough for most of those who'd loved him to say their farewells. I should have been among them.

Campo di Giove. Does one ever really leave his roots behind? I spent a good part of my vacation staring out at the ocean waves breaking against the shore and thinking of Italy. By the time I got back to my apartment with the Ventrescas, I'd made up my mind. America was my home now, but there was nothing to stop me from bringing a piece of Campo di Giove to Massachusetts.

I remembered one girl who'd always flirted a bit with me. I would send a letter to my sister-in-law, Marietta, and see if she could persuade the young woman to write to me. This would be no frivolous correspondence.

I was ready to take a wife. I trusted Marietta, my brother Giovanni's wife. We were very close and not simply because I'd financed so much of their courtship. She was more sister than sister-in-law. Marietta would serve as my matchmaker.

CHAPTER TWO

Letters Across an Ocean

Marietta's first letter contained disappointing news. My old flame was already married to someone else. However, Marietta was nothing if not enthusiastic about the task I'd assigned her. Her letter helpfully contained a fairly long list of all the eligible young women in Campo di Giove. Near the top of the list of her recommended candidates was a name I remembered well. Rosalba Sciuba. Rosalba, that funny little kid who'd complained so much about my singing when we were painting her parents' house? Just remembering the way she stomped through the room with her hands over her ears brought a smile to my face. I quickly did the math. She would be fifteen now. Sixteen by the time I had my citizenship and could return to Italy to claim her as my bride. That was marrying age. The families lived close and knew each other. I was good friends with her brother. I'd write to Rosalba.

Only later did I learn the reaction Rosalba had to my first post. After opening it and studying the contents, she went to her mother. "Hey, Ma," she said, handing her mother the photo of myself I'd included with the letter. "I got a letter from America. From Vittorio Palumbo."

Her mother took the picture. "Wow. He used to be so skinny. He turned into a handsome guy." Her eyes went from the photo to the letter still in Rosalba's hand. "What does he want?"

"He wants to be my boyfriend, Ma. He wants to get married to an Italian girl."

"You're too young."

"I'm fifteen. I'll be sixteen by the time he gets his citizenship and can come back to Italy for a wedding."

Rosalba's mother continued to study the photo. "He is a handsome guy. We know the family. The families know each other."

"Can I write to him, Ma?"

"Fifteen is too young."

"I know how to make pasta. I can do all the things. I've been taking care of my grandfather since I was ten."

"Go talk to the nuns. See what they have to say."

Rosalba hurried over to the church and sought out one young nun who was her special favorite. She handed her the photo. "He is a handsome guy," the nun said. "What does he want?"

"He wants to get married."

"You can't do that, you're too young," the nun answered in alarm.

Rosalba stood her ground. "What do you mean too young? Look at you. You're only five years older than me. You became a nun when you were even younger. And you're a beautiful woman. You drive all the guys crazy."

"We won't talk about that." The nun tried to stop the direction the exchange was taking.

But there was no stopping Rosalba. "Look at you. Look when you decided. Look what you did. How can I be too young?"

Next, Rosalba went to show the letter and my picture to her girlfriends. By the time she got back home, her mother had had time to do some thinking. "Lots of girls get married at sixteen." Since Rosalba's father and brothers were working in Venezuela, the decision would be Mrs. Sciuba's to make.

"I know, Ma, but I've never been away from you. I'd have to go all the way across the ocean to make a home with my husband in America."

"Rosalba, write to him. See how you like this guy. See how he likes you. We know the family. They live right down at the corner. Good people." She held out her hand for one more look at the photo. "Go ahead. If that's what you want, write to the guy. I've lived my life. I brought you up. Now it's your life to live."

And that's how Rosalba and I became engaged through the mail. Every time I wrote to her, I put a two-dollar bill in the envelope so she would be able to buy the stamps to answer my letter. Letters were really the best way to communicate, as there was only one phone in town and it was in the local bar. In order to use that phone, you had to make a special appointment stating the time and date when you were expecting a transatlantic call. In addition to being very expensive, such an arrangement didn't allow for much privacy, since word of the anticipated event quickly spread through town.

When Rosalba and I got engaged, her life began to change almost immediately. She had always taken part in a performance the church put on every year at Christmas to raise money. When she showed up to play her part, the nun in charge looked at her in shocked disbelief. "Rosalba, you're an engaged woman. You can't do this anymore."

Rosalba's mother told her the same thing. "Rosalba, you're an engaged woman. You can't do this anymore."

When my mother got wind of Rosalba's plans, it was the same story, only told in a louder voice. "Rosalba, you're an engaged woman. You can't get up on that stage."

The stubborn little girl who'd protested my singing didn't give up easily. She wrote to me saying, "Vittorio, you have to send a letter to my mother telling her I have your permission to do this. And then you have to write a letter to your mother insisting that I be allowed to take part in the play. Remind her the nuns will be with us. There won't be any funny business."

Well, I must have written a pretty persuasive letter. First I won Rosalba's heart and hand, and then I was able to convince both mothers that Rosalba had my permission to take part in the performance with the others. Even the nuns relented after reading my carefully constructed words. When the group from Campo di Giove won a regional competition and was awarded a tour of sanctuaries in Rome, St. Anthony, and Padua, Rosalba jumped for joy. She had never been to any of these places and now she would have a chance to see them before leaving Italy to make a new life in America.

Meanwhile, I was loving my work with Jordan Marsh. They were so pleased to discover the extent of my skills that when I told them I wanted to return to Italy to get married as soon as I'd qualified for citizenship, they agreed to grant me a three-month leave of absence. In order to save money for my flight over there and all the expenses associated with the wedding, I put in increasingly long hours. Flights were quite costly, but travel by ship was too slow for my purposes. Three months was not a long time to conduct a proper in-person courtship, reconnect with relatives, and make the arrangements for a reception at the Hotel Zeus, a brand new hotel in town. Ours would be the first wedding reception they had hosted.

Until then, wedding receptions had always taken place in the family home. I also wanted to take Rosalba on a honeymoon to the places I had come to love in my native land, especially Fiera di Primiero.

A friend from Campo di Giove was coming to America for a visit. I asked her to take Rosalba's measurements and give them to me, so that I could arrange to buy a wedding dress for my bride. Mrs. Ventresca and Mrs. Mastroianni, my landlord and my friend, offered to come with me to the House of Brides in Worcester to help me pick out a dress. She knew all the other items Rosalba would need—the corset and things like that—so with her help, we purchased those as well. The dress was beautiful, and I took it back to the bridal department at Jordan Marsh so they could tend to the alterations to ensure a perfect fit. I was more used to working on men's clothing and felt it would be better to let those experienced with wedding dresses handle this part. Once the purchase was made, I happily described the dress in a letter to Rosalba. The next thing we knew, Nikki in the bridal department got a call from Rosalba's dressmaker in Campo di Giove.

Nikki sent a young Armenian girl who worked with her down to tell me that the priest wouldn't marry Rosalba in a scooped-neck dress; they would have to design a lace insert in order to make the dress more modest.

I couldn't understand what she was talking about. "What's a scoop neck?" the young girl kept asking me.

"Scoopnik?" I looked at her puzzled. Hadn't she been listening to the news? And what did all of this have to do with a wedding dress? "What's a scoopnik? Why, it's that thing they shot up to the moon!"

Everyone around us burst out laughing. It took a while for my friends to calm down, but a guy in the department eventually explained the difference between a scooped neck and Sputnik. When they finally told Nikki the story, she just shook her head. "One's dumb, and the other's dumber," she said with true affection.

*

On July 11, 1960, I became a citizen of the United States of America. As soon as the judge announced that it was now official, I turned to him and asked if there wasn't some way I could arrange to get a passport that very same day. As I explained my reason—my desire to return to Campo di

Giove to marry my sweetheart—he smiled, reached for the necessary forms and directed me upstairs.

Two weeks later, I boarded a plane in Boston for the eighteen-hour flight to the Ciampino Airport in Rome. My future brother-in-law, Rosalba's brother Erberto, was waiting on the tarmac to take me back to Campo di Giove by train. My old childhood friend and I went from the railway station directly to my home, which was crowded with relatives who hadn't seen me in five years: my parents; Gennaro's wife Ilde, who had returned from Venezuela to wait for her husband to come back to permanently resettle in the town where he had been born; Aunt Cristina; cousin Luciano and his family; but most important, Marietta. I'd no sooner walked through the door than Marietta ran to the balcony and called down to the corner, "Rosalba, Rosalba, he's here. Vittorio is here."

Rosalba's mother wasn't at home when Marietta cried out the news of my arrival, but since there were so many potential chaperones crowded into our family living room, it was okay for her to come over. She told me later how scared she'd been. Her palms wouldn't stop sweating. Marietta leaned out over the balcony and, as soon as she saw Rosalba walking across the cobblestones, she raced down the stairs to pull her up to meet her fiancé.

Everyone got quiet as Rosalba stepped into the room. We just stared at each other. She wasn't a little girl anymore. I was going to marry this beautiful young woman, but now that the words had to flow from my mouth instead of a pen, I struggled to express my feelings.

Rosalba hadn't been there five minutes, we'd not yet had the courage to say much of anything to each other, when another knock came on the door. It was the local policeman, an old friend of mine, the very guy who'd driven me to L'Aquila to get the military physical before I left for America.

"Okay," he said. "Vittorio, you are under arrest for evading the Army. I have to take you down to the jail immediately."

Everyone stopped talking, but I was calm. "Oh, no," I told him, as I searched through my papers. I held my passport proudly in front of him. "You can't touch me. I am an American citizen now."

"You son of a gun," he said. "I guess you thought of everything."

By the time we'd all stopped laughing, Rosalba and I didn't feel so shy with each other anymore.

Courtship in Campo di Giove was different from the way it happened in the United States. Every evening I would go over to Rosalba's house and we would sit next to each other while her mother positioned herself across the table, tried to keep the conversation going, and watched us like a hawk. Every now and then I would start to put my arm across the back of Rosalba's chair, but a stern look from her mother would stop the movement in mid-flight. Sometimes we reached our fingers toward each other under the cover of the table, but her mother was alert to any change in body posture.

Once when Mrs. Sciuba had to run some errands while I was there, she had Rosalba's cousin come watch us. "Don't let them out of your sight," Mrs. Sciuba said as she made her way toward the door.

"Why not?"

"Just don't."

As soon as she left, I held out some money to the boy. "Don't you want to go buy a pastry?"

The kid shook his head. "She said not to leave you alone."

"Okay," I told him. "Stay here if you want, but you don't have to keep staring at us."

So, he kind of put his head down and covered his eyes with his hands, but he did it in such a way that he could still peek through his fingers.

After a couple of weeks of watching us so closely, Rosalba's mother finally decided it would be okay for the two of us to go out walking together. Just before shutting the door behind me, she said with a meaningful glance, "You know what to do." Of course, what she really meant was that I knew what not to do. I hardly needed to be reminded. All the women in Campo di Giove were on the lookout and were all too ready to report back should I fail to act like a gentleman.

Meanwhile, wedding plans were in full swing. By the time Rosalba's family, my family, and Rosalba and I had issued word-of-mouth invitations, over two hundred people were scheduled to celebrate with us. The Hotel Zeus was off to a good start. Their first wedding reception was going to fill the hall. Hiring a hotel for the reception was the only place where Rosalba and I broke with the wedding traditions of our hometown. We followed local customs for everything else.

The first thing on the morning of our wedding, my family prepared their gifts for the bride: a necklace, a bracelet, a watch, things she was expected to wear that day. Next they put them on a tray and brought them to the bride's house. Once the gifts were delivered to Rosalba's house, she got dressed in her gown. Meanwhile, Rosalba's family arranged my wedding band, and a shirt and a tie on the tray they carried to my home. Only after these items were exchanged, did I get dressed for my wedding. Shortly after that, all the guests from my side showed up at the Palumbo family home for a traditional offering of food and drink. Then, lining up two by two, the entire party went to Rosalba's house where they joined with the friends and relatives invited by the bride's side of the family. There everyone was offered more food and drink. After this initial breaking of bread together, it was custom for the bride's father to accompany his daughter to the church. However, since Rosalba's father was working in Venezuela, she took her brother's arm so that the two of them could lead the procession to the altar, where we would be married by Don Giovanni Di Placido. (The priest who performed our wedding ceremony turned ninety years old in 2010.)

All the invited guests, except for two, followed Rosalba and her brother the one-and-a-half-mile distance from her home to our church. I walked a few steps in back of Rosalba. Who were the two people who were left behind when the rest of us headed for the church? The mother of the groom and the mother of the bride. As soon as Rosalba and I were pronounced man and wife, we left the church and went directly to my home to pick up my mother. As tradition dictated, she was waiting to give us little gifts of almonds, confetti, and coins to throw to the children who clamored about us. Rosalba and I then led my mother to Rosalba's house, where we urged her mother to join with us. Once again, we were given candies and coins to throw to the neighborhood children. The two families were now officially one. It was August 28, 1960. Rosalba and I were man and wife. We hurried to the hotel for the reception followed by a crowd of two hundred loved ones who were eager to celebrate with us. It was a beautiful sunny day, and I felt that all my dreams had finally come true.

We started our honeymoon in Venice. My godfather, Mr. Gino Simion, affectionately known as Espedito, worked at the Hotel Luna, a very famous and expensive resort that was beyond my budget. However, he knew the city and helped me make arrangements to stay at a smaller *pensione* that offered us three meals a day and laundry service. With the housekeeping details taken care of, Rosalba and I were free to spend our time exploring

Venice. However, the sights that were most precious to me were those of the faces of my old friend and his wife, Gemma. How fine it felt to be able to introduce him to my bride. Rosalba and I both enjoyed getting to know Gino and Gemma's two children, Margherita and Fabrizio. Watching Rosalba interact with my godfather and his family made me proud to have a family of my own that I could share with him. Neither years nor geography had diminished the strong bond between us. I was no longer a child. I had grown into the man my godfather had hoped I would become.

After leaving Venice, Rosalba and I headed for Fiera di Primiero. Was it only because I was finally getting to share the Dolomites with someone I loved that they seemed even more beautiful than I had remembered them to be? The last three days of our honeymoon were spent in San Martino di Castrozza, also located within the Dolomite Mountain range. I was so taken with Rosalba that my affection became obvious to a general in the Italian Army. Because she looked so very young, his protective instincts were aroused. After watching me for a while, he introduced himself and asked who the young lady beside me was. "Oh," I told him happily, "this is my wife, Rosalba."

He shook his head skeptically. "I don't mean any offense, but would you mind showing me your marriage license?"

Perhaps I appreciated the fact that someone else was as concerned about Rosalba's welfare as I was, perhaps it was the kindliness of his manner, or perhaps it was the authority granted by his uniform, but I took no offense and proudly produced the document.

After an initial moment of embarrassment on his part, a moment softened by my obvious pride in my married state, we laughed with each other. Before we knew it, we had formed the kind of friendship that enabled us to spend the last two days of our honeymoon sightseeing with him and his wife.

By the end of October, it was time for me to head back to the United States. How could three months have gone by so quickly? After sadly saying good-bye to Rosalba in Campo di Giove, and before heading to the airport, I stopped by the consulate in Rome and applied for Rosalba's visa. All our money had been spent on the wedding and my plane fares. Rosalba would be traveling by ship when it was time for her to join me in what was no longer my apartment in Milford. From now on, I would think of it as *our* apartment. I returned to Milford and began preparing a proper home for my bride.

Since the wait for the visa meant we couldn't travel together even if finances hadn't influenced our choice, Rosalba decided to stay in Campo di Giove until my brother, Gennaro, returned from Venezuela. Given that he had been away for so long, she wanted an opportunity to get to know her new brother-in-law.

By the time she'd met Gennaro and booked passage on the *Leonardo Da Vinci*, it was April. My days of counting the days were almost over. I didn't see how my new life could hold anything but happiness. Unfortunately, fate was about to throw a few complications my way.

CHAPTER THREE

Tears and Laughter

I had a car. I had a job as a tailor. I had a wife. Eager to bring Rosalba home with me, I readily agreed when a co-worker asked me if I could give her a ride to Brooklyn on my way to meet Rosalba at the Port of New York. That meant we would leave the day before her ship was due to dock. We set off in a rainstorm. I didn't mind. My car had windshield wipers and my heart was filled with enough sunshine to make up for the bad weather.

As we approached New Rochelle, rain washed across the highway in front of us. With the power of the water forcing the automobile out of control, all I could think of was some way to stop the spinning so that I could be standing on the dock waiting to greet Rosalba with open arms. As it happened, I was unable to steer my way out of the impending crash. It was a tree that suddenly brought the vehicle to a sudden halt. I was thrown out of the car. The next thing I knew I was in the recovery room of the New Rochelle Hospital. I'd had to undergo major surgery and had no idea where I was or what day it was. Nurses hovered around me as I regained consciousness. They could tell me the extent of my injuries but no one had any news about Rosalba. My passenger, whose injuries were less extensive than mine, was also hospitalized. I drifted in and out of a narcotics-induced sleep, panicked and absolutely powerless to make anyone understand that a seventeen-year-old girl who spoke no English was waiting on the dock, wondering why her husband wasn't there to greet her.

I suppose it's lucky that the crash was serious enough to make the news. My landlords, Mr. and Mrs. Ventresca, back in Milford heard about the accident on the radio. Because they were such good friends and I had told them so much about Rosalba and her family, they knew that she had Italian-speaking cousins who lived in Walpole, Massachusetts. Mrs. Ventresca put in a call to Charlie and Adriana, who was herself new to this country. She and Charlie had also become engaged through the mail and were married in Italy about the same time as Rosalba and I were. However, since their honeymoon had resulted in a pregnancy, she had arrived in this country with her husband.

As soon as they got word of my accident, Charlie and Adriana made arrangements to travel by train to New York to meet Rosalba's ship. By the time they finally got there, they found a broken-hearted young woman who'd been waiting for over two hours for a husband who wasn't anywhere to be found. Only a fellow passenger kept her company. He'd vowed not to leave her until someone had claimed her. Rosalba had been very sick on the boat ride to America and had lost over fifteen pounds, making her look even younger than her seventeen years. Her innocence and youth were such that no one had been able to believe she was a married woman. And now, here she was, a deserted married woman.

Adriana, six months pregnant, rushed toward her. Not wanting to alarm Rosalba, she claimed I was sick with a cold.

Rosalba knew me better than that. She was certain no mere cold would have kept me from her side, and Adriana was finally forced to reveal the truth. "But, it's okay. He's alive. He's in the hospital. We'll take you right there to see him."

Lugging Rosalba's trunk with them, they traveled by rail to New Rochelle. Given the limited connections, they were able to spend only a little over an hour with me, before having to catch another train to take Rosalba home with them.

I was hardly the bridegroom Rosalba had been expecting to find. Flat on my back and completely immobilized in a full-body cast, the best thing we could find to say about me was that I was alive. One leg had been badly twisted, the other broken, the kneecap so smashed that there was a question about whether or not I'd be able to walk without a serious limp. I had a broken nose and stitches in my arm, and was in so much pain that I was heavily drugged. But, drugged or not, my overwhelming reaction was one of relief. Rosalba was safe. She was in the hands of Italian-speaking relatives, and we would find a way to get past this obstacle. I had no car. No money. No job. How could I work when I couldn't even move unaided? I was in a hospital too far from home, but somehow we would find a way to get by. All the money I had in the world was in my pocket. Two hundred dollars. For that time it was a lot of money, but not a lot for someone who could no longer count on a regular paycheck. Before Rosalba left that night, I had Charlie help me locate my hidden store of cash, and I forced one-hundred-fifty dollars into her hand.

I might not have been able to count on a regular paycheck, but I very quickly found out I could count on my friends. Everyone rallied around us. Eileen O'Driscoll, my boss at Jordan Marsh, made the long drive to come see how I was doing. Two childhood companions from Campo di Giove—my cousin Pasquale Palumbo and Vittorio Del Mastro—now lived in New York and came to visit me in the hospital. More than broken bones needed mending. While under treatment for pain, I had become seriously addicted to morphine. The sweating and terror resulting from withdrawal from those drugs was perhaps the most difficult part of my recovery. After three months in the hospital my body was healed, and I no longer relied on those nightly injections in order to be able to sleep. However, as the doctor handed me instructions about coming back in six weeks to have the body cast removed, he stressed more than anything else that I was not to take any medication for pain, not even aspirin.

I was out of work for almost eight months. But I was not out of the mind of my friends, co-workers, and employer. Rosalba stayed with Charlie and Adriana for only two weeks before Mr. and Mrs. Ventresca insisted she come move in with them. Jordan Marsh, wanting to find a way to help us through this difficult time, had offered Rosalba a job sewing and had made arrangements for her to commute with another employee who lived in Milford. Rosalba had voiced initial concern, "But I can't speak English. I can sew, but I can't do what Vittorio does."

"It's okay," Mrs. Ventresca told her. "Victor has told everyone at work about you. They know what to expect."

So, Rosalba became the family breadwinner, hemming pants at Jordan Marsh. Mrs. Ventresca insisted Rosalba occupy their grown daughter's former bedroom and live downstairs with them until I was well enough to return, and we could begin our lives together in the apartment I had prepared to welcome my bride to America. During that time, my landlady not only refused to accept any rent from Rosalba, but she also packed a lunch for her every morning. I'm so glad the Ventrescas spoke Italian because no one at Jordan Marsh did. Unfortunately for Rosalba my immediate boss, Eileen O'Driscoll, the one who had planned to take Rosalba under her wing, was on vacation the first ten days that my wife was on the job. When lunchtime came, all her co-workers left their sewing machines and went out into the patio to eat. Rosalba didn't understand that she could go with them, and so she quickly ate her lunch at her machine and then continued hemming pants. When Eileen came back from vacation, she asked how Rosalba was doing.

"Oh, great. She's doing great. Very hard worker. She never leaves her machine."

"What?" Eileen turned to the guy who was in charge of the piecework department. "Didn't anyone show her around? Does she even know where the ladies room is?"

"That's not my job, to take a woman to the bathroom," he answered.

"Oh, my God," Eileen said, as she grabbed Rosalba and gave her a quick tour, starting with the ladies room. When she got home after work that day, Rosalba told Mrs. Ventresca that she had never in her life been so glad to see a restroom.

Well, Rosalba wasn't the only one who had a little trouble with toilet facilities. After I got out of the hospital, we enjoyed making each other laugh with shared stories about the difficulty of learning to communicate in a new language.

One time, before I'd married Rosalba, I was walking through the department store to deliver a newly tailored suit to the customer. It was almost Christmas and holiday decorations were everywhere. As I paused to admire them, a woman with a little boy and a girl approached me. "Excuse me," she said. "Can you tell me where the toyland is?"

"Which one you want?" I asked her, looking at the children. "For the men or for the ladies?"

She got really mad. "If I had wanted that, I wouldn't have asked you!"

I hurried to find my friend Andy. "Andy, Andy, can you tell me what this toyland is?"

When he explained that it was the toys department, I expressed my frustration. "Why couldn't that woman talk more plain? Why did she have to get so mad?"

Vittorio Palumbo

*

I was home from the hospital, but still not back to work. I don't know how Rosalba and I would have managed without the network of family and friends that supported us through this time. My brothers sent money from Venezuela. One good thing about my recuperation at home was that all the people who'd wanted to see me in the hospital and were eager to meet Rosalba were finally able to stop by. Our evenings were filled with happy laughter among friends. I felt proud that there was this community of affection surrounding my wife and me. It was a neighborhood of sorts. Many of these people spoke Italian and Rosalba was able to join in the conversations. I wasn't going to let her be as lonely as I'd been during my first two years in this country. We were finally at home in our apartment in America. Our friends would often give us an envelope containing money as they were saying goodnight. "Just a belated wedding present," they'd whisper.

One Saturday evening, Mrs. Mastroianni's son and daughter-in-law stopped by. "Come on. You've been cooped up in your apartment too long. Let's go get a pizza. I've heard they have good pizza at the Italian Vet's Hall. Let's go there."

This was a new one on me, but as soon as we walked through the door, I understood what was going on. "Surprise!" a roomful of people hollered in unison. Our friends had arranged a Jack and Jill party for us. A Jack and Jill party was common in America back then. Most often it was held before a couple got married, kind of like a wedding shower, only both men and women were invited. In order to attend, people purchased tickets. About two hundred people were there. Angela and Joseph Niro and their sons, Tony, Michael, and cousin Leo. The folks from Jordan Marsh. Danny and Connie. All our pals from the Italian-American community. It was hard to imagine how they had gotten everyone together and organized all this. After paying the expenses associated with the event, our friends proudly handed us three-hundred-fifty dollars—a lot of money at that time. At long last, we would be able to buy a small couch, a chair, and a Eureka vacuum cleaner. Eureka. We were at home. I was feeling better. The tough times were almost behind us.

CHAPTER FOUR

Pieces of the Dream

At last I was fully rehabilitated after my accident and was able to return to my job at Jordan Marsh. Rosalba had established her own circle of friends there and planned to continue working until it was time to start a family. What we had lost in earning power during that rough year, we had gained in friendships. When my pal Tony Niro joined the Army and was about to head off to Korea, he pulled me aside. "I don't think it's such a good thing for my car to just sit idle during the four years I'm away. Why don't you keep it going for me?" We finally came to an agreement whereby I would give him so much money every month, until I had paid for it in full.

After the trauma of my accident, I was nervous about driving, especially a car that was still technically someone else's, but I knew this was something I was going to have to get over if I was to make it in America, the land of the automobile.

These were happy years for us. Rosalba and I were both working, I'd finally gained enough confidence in my driving skills to offer rides to my co-workers, Rosalba was getting more comfortable with English every day, and we'd discovered the joys of summer vacations. We traveled to Virginia Beach, Virginia; to Montreal, Toronto, and Ottawa, Canada; to Lake George, New York; and enjoyed exploring the nearby New England beaches and mountains. In the years before we had children, we traveled back to Italy a couple of times and experienced the pride our families felt in all we had accomplished.

We were finally living the American dream. During this period of time, we met a lot of Italian people in Milford and spent our free time with them, swimming and playing on the beach, having picnics, heading to the drive-in movies, and going out to dinner. Rosalba and I cemented the bonds of our marriage by doing many things together as a couple. We were even managing to save some money. By 1964, I had paid Tony Niro in full for the car, and we traded it in for a brand new white Pontiac LeMans with a red leather interior, a car that we kept until 1967.

Much as I loved my job at Jordan Marsh, I found it difficult to resist the offer from a new Sears store that was opening up in the first mall to be built in Massachusetts. It was flattering to have my skills as a tailor in such demand. It was 1965, and Rosalba and I were beginning to dream of starting a family. Sears was talking about a much larger salary than I was earning at Jordan Marsh. I went to my current employer in hopes that they could match what I was being offered at Sears. However, they were unable to come even close. I felt I had no choice but to try to better myself. I left Jordan Marsh with regret, but knowing that I had their well-wishes. If owning a car was central to life in America, being able to save enough money to send one's children to college was even more important. The job at Sears would make this possible, as would Rosalba's continued employment with Jordan Marsh. There were no hard feelings, only an appreciation for what I hoped to accomplish.

In 1966, we were taking a Sunday drive with friends and dreaming about how nice it would be to have a home of our own. Suddenly, we wandered into a neighborhood that made us feel we could be happy living there. "Oh, look at that sweet house on the corner," one of our friends said.

"The driveway is too steep," I told her, and in that moment I realized that I was already picturing Rosalba and me raising our children here. Just down the street, we paused before a house still under construction, but complete enough that a "For Sale" sign had been pounded into what would be the front yard. I pulled my car into the level space in front of the garage. "Let's have a look."

The four of us tentatively opened the front door and stepped inside. It was love at first sight. Seeing Rosalba's joy at the layout reminded me of watching my mother explore our new home in Garibaldi, on that first night in Libya. Rosalba moved almost as if in trance, afraid to touch anything, but reaching her hands out in appreciation of how well this home was designed to accommodate a family. She saw me watching her, and forced a more critical look and attitude. Rosalba knew when I was ferocious in pursuit of something I wanted, and she was afraid we weren't yet ready to take this step.

As we were leaving, Rosalba was quiet, but our friends chattered excitedly as I wrote down the name and telephone number of the builder. "It doesn't hurt to ask how much it costs," I told them. "It never hurts to make a phone call." I looked around. "What's the house number?"

"Sixteen."

"And the name of the street?"

"I guess we'll have to drive down and read the sign on the corner."

My friend had the best eyes and the most skill at reading English. But even I could have figured this one out. "Di Vittorio Drive."

I glanced over at Rosalba. She just folded her hands and took a deep breath.

The house on Di Vittorio Drive is the first and only home Rosalba and I have ever owned. We paid $19,900 for it in April of 1966 and moved in over the Memorial Day weekend. (We celebrated our fiftieth wedding anniversary there on August 28, 2010.)

A good job, a good wife, a car, a house, a college savings account. All we needed now were the children and the pieces of our American dream would be complete.

On July 30, 1968, we welcomed Cristina Angela into our family. Literally the answer to our prayers, we named her in honor of my Aunt Cristina and my mother, whose name was Angela. Completely enchanted by her, Rosalba and I could not believe our good fortune. We marveled at the sweet perfection of her tiny fingers and toes. Generations are linked by little things. As a child I'd been fascinated by Ada's hands. Now my own daughter's made me understand the power of a parent's love, and I vowed to shelter my family from all harm.

I was thirty-five years old and had lived long enough to know that periods of happiness are often punctuated by tears. Later in the same year, Rosalba, who had left her job to devote herself to motherhood, became pregnant. Our joy was cut short when Rosalba lost that baby boy in a miscarriage at seven months.

On June 5, 1970, Rosalba traveled with me and a close friend to Worcester, Massachusetts, where we witnessed her earn her citizenship in the United States of America, a ceremony that made official what she had long felt in her heart.

We had much to celebrate, and we chose to mark the occasion with a trip to Italy where plans for a different celebration were in process. Our cousins Danny and Connie, the ones who had invited me to live with them when I first moved to Milford, had not been to Italy and decided to accompany us. We couldn't wait to share our little girl with all the relatives who were equally anxious to embrace the two-year-old they knew only from photographs. It had been fifteen years since I'd seen my sisters, Giovanna and Ada, and almost twenty since I'd been face to face with Gennaro and Giovanni.

This turned out to be a wonderful family reunion, marred only by the absence of Guerino. "He has his own business in Venezuela," my father said. "There's no one he can trust to watch out for things while he's gone."

I heard my father's words for the excuse they were and knew that, no matter what rationale he gave, he was deeply hurt by his son's failure to mark the celebration of fifty years of marriage between him and my mother. It was the reason the rest of us had coordinated our visits. Still, laughter is hard to suppress and we all talked over each other, sharing the old stories and learning new ones. Before returning to the States, Rosalba and I journeyed once again to Fiera di Primiero, the place that had once rendered my heart so open to love.

Toward the end of 1970, Rosalba became pregnant again, and we cautiously embraced the hope that we were on the verge of welcoming another child into our family. Hope was soon replaced with more sadness. Rosalba went into labor when she was seven and a half months pregnant. Our baby boy lived for only a day. Rosalba felt those losses so deeply that I was helpless in the face of her grief. It would be another five years before the birth of a healthy and robust son, Steven, finally put our sorrow to rest.

CHAPTER FIVE

Parents and Children

Even adult children have the power to wound a parent's heart. My mother and father had not seen their son Guerino since he first left for Venezuela in 1953. All of their other children made frequent visits back to Campo di Giove, but Guerino never came. He did write. He did send money, but it just wasn't the same as seeing him in the flesh. Once when the pressure to return was too great for him, he wrote to me, offering to pay my fare if only I would take a trip back to Italy so that our parents' need to see an adult son might be satisfied.

"Oh, Guerino," I told him by return post. "It's not me Papá wants to see. It's you. I could never take your place in his eyes. It would only sting him further to see one son so devoted while the other stayed so far away." It was a difficult letter to write, especially since I had spent much of my life trying in vain to win the affection my father showered so readily on Guerino, who seemed not to want it and to have done very little to earn it.

Then on the morning of December 8, 1972, we received an early morning phone call from my niece, Rosanna, Giovanna's now-adult daughter. My brother Guerino had been killed in an automobile accident in Venezuela.

Guerino. How can a life end so suddenly? All hope of reunion and reconciliation destroyed in a single violent crash of twisted steel and broken glass. I was devastated and overwhelmed, both by my own sorrow and by awareness of the agony my parents must be suffering. However, not in my wildest imaginings was I prepared for the tragedy delivered in a second phone call from Rosanna the following morning.

Unable to comprehend the sudden loss of his favored son, my father had paced back and forth in ruined despair. Completely broken by the news of Guerino's accident, he cried out, "Guerino, what have you done to us?" and turned, staggered, and fell to the floor, dead. Papá had suffered an apparent heart attack. Just that quickly it was all over. His longing. His pain. His life. He and his son were finally joined in some cruel twist that left the rest of us struggling to make sense of it all. Two deaths in two days. My mother had lost a husband and a son. I had lost a father and a brother.

There was no Christmas tree in our house in Milford that December. Poor little Cristina, only four years old, couldn't understand why it was impossible for me to celebrate the holiday in our usual way. I still feel guilty for my inability to move beyond my own sorrow and tend to my daughter's innocent desire.

*

Life goes on. We simply move forward. There is no other choice. Perhaps we lose ourselves in our work. In 1973, when Cristina turned five, Rosalba decided she would start doing alterations at home. I still had my full-time job at Sears, but also was open to an offer to work part-time for Jordan Marsh. I'd enjoyed my employment there and had stayed in touch with my many friends. Before I knew it, I had two jobs and was putting in sixty hours a week, a schedule I held to for the next thirty-seven years. When at home, I spent my time planting flowers, raking leaves, and watering the lawn.

At least we now had the money to travel to Italy, but finding the opportunity to do so became more difficult. However, in 1974 we managed to get away. We'd been in Campo di Giove only three days when Rosalba became sick. Fearful of the tragedy that sometimes appeared to be stalking our family, we all agreed that she needed to see a doctor immediately. Rosalba's Uncle Torindo was both a radiologist and a pediatrician. After examining her thoroughly, he came back smiling. Rosalba wasn't sick, she was pregnant! However, given the difficulties she'd experienced with her last two pregnancies, Uncle Torindo insisted that she remain in bed for the rest of our visit.

Cristina was now an engaging little six-year-old. I'd been working so hard that I hadn't really had much chance to simply have fun with her. So, despite my concerns about Rosalba's health and fears for the life of our unborn child, there was a bit of magic in having three weeks to devote to my little girl. Rosalba's mother was completely taken with Cristina. Before we left to return to the States, she was already talking about coming to live with us in America in order to help Rosalba with what we were hoping would soon be two children.

Her plans became concrete when she learned that the specialist we'd visited as soon as we got back to the States informed us that if Rosalba hoped to carry this pregnancy to term, she would have to stay in bed until her due date in March of 1975. That's all a grandmother needs to hear. Mrs. Sciuba arrived at our home in Milford in November of 1974 and promptly took over all care of Rosalba, Cristina, the household, and me. It was a long four or five months. My mother-in-law's willingness to help was a gift for which I'll always be grateful. But having already lost two babies, Rosalba and I carefully monitored every kick and worried if more than an hour or two went by without Rosalba feeling the baby move within her.

Finally, on March 17, Rosalba went into labor, and, aware of each bump in the road, I carefully drove her to the hospital in Boston. Steven Joseph made his official appearance on the next day, March 18, 1975. This time we had a happy ending. However, our worries weren't completely over. A day after I brought Rosalba and Steven home, she developed complications from the surgery she'd had. I rushed her back to the hospital where she was diagnosed with blood clots and pleurisy. The risk to her health was serious enough that she remained hospitalized for two weeks. I don't know how I would have managed without the devoted help of my mother-in-law. It was becoming obvious that the joys of parenthood came with potentially high costs. We're lucky that Cristina and Steven turned out to be the sort of kids who make their parents proud. All the anguish happened early. Once Rosalba returned home and was feeling better, our happiness at being the proud parents of a little boy and a little girl slipped the final piece of our American dream into place.

Steven's christening was scheduled for May. Rosalba's father traveled from Italy for the ceremony and stayed with us until June. Mr. and Mrs. Sciuba were no sooner reunited than she began to express concerns about his smoking. In Italy, the floors were all tile and it was usual for a man to put his cigarette out by dropping it on the floor and stepping on it. Mr. Sciuba could not do that in an American home without damaging either the floors or the carpet. He refused to learn to use an ashtray. This became a bone of contention between my in-laws and Cristina decided to join forces on her grandmother's side of the argument.

"You should just stop smoking," Mrs. Sciuba told her husband. "Now's a good time to quit that habit. You can't put your cigarettes out on the floor, and you won't use the ashtray. Time to quit."

Mr. Sciuba offered no argument and simply nodded. For a brief period, Rosalba's mother thought her logic had prevailed. There were no cigarette butts to be found anywhere. Cristina continued to keep a careful eye on her *Nonno*. She followed him around, repeatedly reminding him that her *Nonna* didn't want him smoking. Once again, he didn't bother to give his little granddaughter any argument, but nodded his head as if he was in agreement with this pint-sized police officer.

He would have gotten away with his ruse had not his generosity and the Italian custom of keeping sweets for the little ones in the pocket of his trousers enabled Cristina to blow the whistle on him. One day she reached in for a piece of candy and instead pulled out a handful of cigarette butts. "*Nonna*," she cried as she headed straight for her grandmother. "I found out where *Nonno* has been hiding the evidence. He hasn't stopped smoking at all. His pockets are filled with cigarette butts."

Shortly after my father-in-law arrived in our household, we were invited to a wedding. Because I was scheduled to work on the day it was being held, I would be unable to attend. And so I asked Mr. Sciuba if he could please represent the family by accompanying Rosalba to the event.

"But I don't have anything to wear," he told me.

"Never mind. I have a dress shirt, coat, and tie that will fit you."

I'd never seen my father-in-law look quite as distinguished as he did when heading off to the wedding. Happy that I'd been able to help him out, I went to my job at Jordan Marsh well satisfied with the arrangement.

When June arrived, Mr. Sciuba decided it was time for him to return to Italy; he had difficulty speaking English and was eager to resume playing cards with his friends back home. Although we understood his reasons, we all knew that we would miss him. He was not the only thing I missed. Shortly after he left, I went to put on the jacket I'd lent him and couldn't find it anywhere. Hmm. That was a puzzle. Rosalba helped me look through all our closets. "It must be here somewhere," she said. "A jacket, shirt, and tie don't just get up and walk away."

Well, a few months later, we discovered that they had done just exactly that! Someone back in Campo di Giove inadvertently solved the puzzle of the missing clothing when they sent us a photo of a family get-together. There was Rosalba's father, front and center, and looking very dapper in my jacket, shirt, and tie!

*

One never becomes accustomed to the loss of loved ones, but I was learning to accept that one generation replaces another. Now that I was experiencing the joys of being a father, I was also having to learn to live with the death of those who had served almost as parents to me. First Uncle Ercole in 1959. Then my actual father in 1972. Three years later, Aunt Cristina died, at age eighty-nine, on July 6, 1975 in Sulmona, Italy. She had outlived her much-loved son and her husband, but made her final resting place beside them back in Campo di Giove. She had been like a mother to me for so much of my life. I told myself she lived on in my daughter. And she does.

Rosalba's mother devoted herself to helping her daughter and grandchildren. Without her help, the pregnancy that gave us Steven might never have gone to term. She stayed on after Mr. Sciuba returned to Italy, joining him only when she had confidence that Rosalba was strong enough to care for two young children. After her husband died in Campo di Giove in 1982, Mrs. Sciuba waited a few years and then came back to live with us in Milford. She treasured our success and did all she could to make sure our children had both love and the opportunities for full lives. My mother-in-law not only watched over the children, but—understanding both the expense and the importance of a college education for her grandchildren—she urged her daughter to return to work outside the home. Because of her support, Rosalba was able, in 1985, to accept a job with the U.S. Navy Clothing & Textile Research Facility as a sample maker, constructing uniform items and experimental items. Rosalba's contribution made it possible for Cristina and Steven to graduate from college without any student loans or other debt. We owe so much to Rosalba's mother.

Rosaria Massarotti Sciuba passed away on June 23, 1986. She was seventy-nine years old. On being admitted to the hospital in Massachusetts, her main concern was that Rosalba would lose her job if she had no one to help her with the children and the household. She died thinking of others. Rosalba has so much of her mother's strength that she was able, even while mourning her mother's death, to carry on with all the things that had been so important to the generous woman who had been a central part of our lives. Mrs. Sciuba's last wish was to be buried next to her husband in Italy. We made sure this was done.

Families help each other through hard times. In the summer of 1987, I got word that my brother Gennaro was very sick. Getting back to Italy to see him was complicated both by airline strikes and missed connections. Although I'd told my family members what flight to meet in Milan, I ended up having to fly into Torino. The bus that was supposed to transport us from the airport in Torino to the one in Milan suddenly dropped us off alongside the highway at a little station nowhere near the airport. I doubted that those who were scheduled to meet me would even begin to know where to look. It was dark and felt like the middle of the night. This was well before the days of cell phones. I was so rattled by the turn of events that I couldn't remember my own area code. My brother was dying, and I had no way of letting anyone know how to find me. Pouring money into the payphone, I kept dialing the wrong number. By some miracle, I finally was able to remember my own area code and got through to Rosalba. She, in turn, relayed the message to Borsano.

By the time it was all straightened out, I had only a couple of days to spend with Gennaro before I had to return to the United States.

"Ah, Boccetto," he greeted me, using the old term of endearment that I knew was mine alone.

Boccetto. Little One. I offered no correction as I had done back in Campo Cinecittà. The name had never felt more accurate. Just hearing it spoken in a voice too frail to belong to my brother rendered me a child again, a child who needed this man perhaps above all others. Unable to trust my own voice, I just nodded in acknowledgment of the salutation.

We spent the next two days together. Occasionally, eager for reassurance, he would turn toward me and say, "How do you think I look, Boccetto? How do you think I look?"

"Just like Caesar Romero," I told him. "Just like Caesar Romero." Gennaro was used to having total strangers approach him with this observation, and he seemed satisfied by my answer.

Even my mother sensed that he was dying. When we were alone together, she said sadly, "A mother should not have to bury her children before her."

Gennaro surprised everyone by holding on until November 1, 1987. He was only sixty-six years old when he passed away. I continue to carry him in my heart. My sister Giovanna's husband, Salvatore, passed away on January 17, 1989, about two years before my mother.

My mother did not outlive Gennaro by long. Ninety when she lost her oldest son, she survived him by only three years. Angela Pensa Palumbo was born on February 16, 1898 and died on December 27, 1991. She was very ill when she passed away in Borsano in Province Varese, Italy, and her body stayed with my father's in Borsano.

The older generation was gone. Even my generation was falling to the travails of time and illness. Giovanni, my only surviving brother passed away at age seventy-four also in Borsano, Province Varese, Italy, in 2002. Of our original family, only my two sisters and I remain.

*

Birth. Death. And, between the two, all the milestones and accomplishments we crowd into our years on this earth. Cristina and Steven kept Rosalba and me focused on the joys life offered. They were good students who made us proud with their inductions into the National Honor Society. After graduating from high school, they both received partial scholarships that covered their college tuitions. How I wished Mr. Balsamo, the teacher who had helped me complete fifth grade so many years before, could have witnessed all my children went on to accomplish. Cristina graduated in 1990 from the University of Vermont with a Bachelor of Arts degree. Steven graduated with a degree in Bio-Medical Engineering from Vanderbilt University in 1997.

On September 15, 1996, Cristina married Paul Hurley at the Sacred Heart Church in Milford, Massachusetts. Watching them exchange their vows, I couldn't help remembering my friend's warning in the Milford soda shop back in the mid-fifties. "Her father will cut your head off if he finds out she's seeing an Italian boy." And now, wedding bells were ringing. At last. It may have taken a generation, but there was finally peace between the Irish and the Italians!

They became husband and wife on a gorgeous sunny day, with the kind of clear blue sky that sometimes happens in September. Steven invited four of his friends from college to his sister's wedding. Being from the south, they had seen depictions of Italian weddings only in the movies and were eager to experience the real thing. We didn't disappoint them. Over two hundred guests witnessed the ceremony and celebrated with us at the reception afterward.

Five years after they were married, Cristina and Paul blessed us with our first grandchild. Olivia Vittoria was born on September 16, 2001. Life was moving full circle, one generation replacing those that had gone before. On August 6, 2003, Caroline Elizabeth, our second grandchild joined our family. How could we be so lucky? Two adorable little girls. Still, it seemed only yesterday that Cristina and Steven were themselves babies. How swift the passage of time. How rich the store of dreams and memories.

*

We were a true Italian-American family, with deep ties to both places. Rosalba and I made sure our kids got back to the place of our birth as often as we could find the time and money to make such trips. When Steven graduated from high school, his friend Dustin accompanied us to Campo di Giove and Fiera di Primiero. My godfather, Mr. Gino Simion, had died since our last visit. Only his wife, Gemma, was still living. Eager to entertain us in style, she had made plans to serve a big Italian meal in our honor. However, her dreams had outpaced the limits imposed by her years. Rosalba and my sister Ada quietly set the table and took over most of the actual cooking.

During our stay in my favorite region of Italy, Gemma's daughter and her son-in-law gave us a tour of the area. Perhaps the high point of the trip for the kids was the journey to San Martino di Castrozza. Margherita and Luciano took their automobile as far up the Pale di San Martino, the highest mountain in the area, as it was possible to drive. After they parked the car, we climbed to the very top and sat at the base of the cross placed there by the town. The view alone inspired religious awe. A vast panorama spread before us. We looked down over green forests giving way to valleys dotted with tiny towns. The expansive reach of so much beauty in one place left us awestruck and speechless, until one of the kids remarked that he finally understood what it had been like for Julie Andrews in that first scene from *The Sound of Music*.

Before we left Fiera di Primiero, we visited the Transaqua Church where I had received my first communion while a child in Mussolini's schools. It was also here that I had first met Mr. Gino Simion—Espedito, my godfather—and it was here that I said my final farewell to him. He was buried in the cemetery behind the church. As I stood before his gravestone, I silently thanked him for all he had done to make my life whole.

Mr. Simion's wife, Gemma, passed away only a year after this visit. We remain in touch with Margherita, who will always hold a special place in our affections.

In July of 1999, we traveled once again to Italy, this time with our close friends Lucia and Vincenzo D'Aloia, who originally came from the Puglia section of Italy. Before Mussolini turned our lives upside down, the Palumbo family had driven sheep to the winter pastures in the Puglia. Now, Rosalba and I were going back with another couple, not as shepherds but as tourists. Our itinerary was crowded with the names of cities we wanted to explore: Rome, Florence, Pisa, Venice, Verona, Stressa, Sorrento, Capri, and Naples. During our lives together, Rosalba and I had met so many people who, on hearing we were from Italy, recounted tales of the vacations they had taken in our home country. Some of the places they mentioned we had never seen for ourselves. All that was about to change. As part of an organized tour, we even got as far as Lake Lugano in Switzerland.

For two fabulous weeks we wandered Italy with our friends, new and old, staying in wonderful hotels and feasting in restaurants with well-deserved reputations. During our stop in Stressa, our families surprised us by suddenly showing up at the hotel. The commotion caused by this unexpected reunion filled the hotel lobby with loud conversation and laughter. The desk clerk, smiling widely, came over to ask if this was our entire family. I think he was trying to get a head count. When told that no one else was expected, he offered us a small room where we could reconnect with our family members in comfort. The gesture was typical of the hospitality we encountered everywhere. At the end of the two weeks, we bid a temporary farewell to Lucia and Vincenzo so that each of the two couples could return to their home cities for a brief visit before reconnecting in Rome and flying back to America. Of all the wonderful trips we'd taken to Italy, this one stands out in our minds as the happiest.

If the trip in 1999 is remembered for its happiness, the one Rosalba and I took with Cristina and her husband Paul in 2000 resonates with the memory of the honor I felt at my reception by the Mayor of Transaqua. He received me in the town hall almost as if I were a visiting dignitary. His interest in the story of my years in this region was genuine. Since he was filled with questions, the visit lasted longer than I had expected. Before bidding each other farewell, he presented me with a collection of beautiful books which I have since read and display as an important part of my personal library. Just as the generations have come full circle, so have I. From the Apennine Mountains to the Sahara Desert and finally, to America, the land of opportunity.

CHAPTER SIX

Tailor Made

In America I finally became a tailor. That first job topstitching raincoats was followed by work at Jordan Marsh, Sears, and two exclusive men's clothing stores. In 1987, I accepted an offer from Ara's in Wellesley. I worked there until 1989, when I decided I might be happier at Milton's in Framingham. Every advance gave me a chance to demonstrate the range of my skills at turning something ready-made into a garment that appeared to have been tailor-made. However, when working at smaller exclusive shops, I realized something was missing. The clientele had a way of treating me almost as if I were invisible. I needed to feel myself part of a larger whole.

In 1991, I decided to make that happen. I readily accepted the offer when the Natick Research & Development Engineering Center (NRDEC)—later renamed the Soldier Systems Center Command (SSCOM)—offered me the opportunity to work on uniform and equipment design at Natick Labs in Natick, Massachusetts. During my years working in military design, I have been involved in projects for the Army, Navy, Air Force, and U.S. Marine Corps. Barbara Quinn, the research facility group leader, recognized my design skills at a time when almost all of the actual design was facilitated by the computer. She saw the magic that occurred between my eye and my hand. I could look at a piece of fabric and understand, almost without conscious thought, where to cut in order to achieve the desired effect. My scissor was my pencil. I never wrote anything down. The material and I carried on a conversation, and when I was finished, Barbara would measure the final dimensions of my pattern and enter it into the computer. Her ability to recognize my talent and know how to translate it into computer-generated designs enabled us to work closely together on a range of projects: coveralls, backpacks, ballistic vests, interceptor vests, helmet covers, and neck protectors. I also redesigned battle dress uniforms, camouflage dress uniforms, chemical/biological joint service uniforms, and—under the Heritage Program—the U.S. Air Force's dress coat. Although designing prototypes for dress uniforms most clearly recalled the ambitions I'd had when watching Giacchino at work, every project was vitally important. I knew what I was doing went beyond mere fashion; I was designing clothing that was going to save lives.

Because Major Gabe Patricio was the military contact with the NRDEC, he worked closely with Barbara Quinn. Sometimes I would sense him watching me while I fashioned his requests into a prototype. He was always a gentleman and treated Barbara Quinn and me as respected professionals, as his equals. I guess I shouldn't have been surprised when he one day waited until I'd put my scissor down and then walked over to me in a way that indicated he had something important to say. "Victor, how would you like to work directly with the Marine Corps?"

"Sure," I told him. "I like military design and will work for whoever wants to give me the money."

He laughed and we shook hands.

Well, as soon as the word got out, one of my bosses—I won't mention his name—came and told me I wasn't going to be working on the project with Major Patricio. "I've recently hired a young man who has advanced training in computer design. I want him to take over this assignment."

Well, when Major Patricio heard this, he hit the roof. "Oh, no. I decide. It's all settled. I want Victor and will work with no one else."

Gabriel Patricio—Gabe, he told me to call him—is the man who made me. Starting in 1995, I was his trusted consultant on design projects. He took me with him to military bases all around the world, to Puerto Rico, Washington, DC, and even Japan. Everywhere I went with him, people got to know me. Quantico was the base where the officers actually greeted me by name. "Hey, Victor," they would call out. "Good to see you."

We were involved in designing a modern dress uniform for the Marines. This is no simple project. Just the beginning stage can take perhaps six months. Put the pocket over here. No, no, it might look better moved down and to the side. I worked to turn their dreams into an actual garment. When we finally had a finished uniform, I traveled with Major

Patricio to the Pentagon. It was there that he introduced me to four-star general James Jones, who has since served in the administration of President Barack Obama.

General Jones was staying in the Ritz Hotel where one-hundred-forty generals of lesser rank would have to approve this new dress uniform before it went into actual production. One-hundred-forty! Who might have guessed that there would be so many? General Jones waited with me in the lobby while they reached a majority decision approving my prototype as the new dress uniform for the United States Marine Corps. All those generals liked what I had done. I even got to meet some of them. One was a fellow who spoke Italian, very nice guy. During this time, I made repeated trips to the Pentagon to do uniform fittings.

When I retired, I was presented with a plaque featuring a photograph of General James Jones wearing the uniform I designed. I am especially gratified by the words inscribed on the brass panel below the photo:

Mr. Victor Palumbo
United States Marine Corps Team Natick

In appreciation of your friendship, professionalism, and
devotion to duty in support for the United States Marine Corps.
Over the past decade you directly contributed to and improved
the survivability, mobility and sustainability of Marines
in peacetime and war. Your work will forever be a part of a
long and illustrious history of distinguished
Individual Combat Clothing and Equipment worn by Marines
and will remain a visible presence and global identifier
of Marines for decades to come.
You exemplify the work "Semper Fidelis" and I wish you
"Fair winds and following seas"

Presented by LtCol Gabe Patricio USMC (Ret)
6 December 2005

Yes, I have a photograph and a nice letter of appreciation from General James Jones, but I have something even more important: the memory of a young Marine's proud posture when he dressed himself in one of my designs.

One of the most difficult assignments I had during this period was to adapt the uniforms of the soldiers at Walter Reed Army Hospital to their particular injuries. I guess I'm not as strong a man as I had thought. Upon returning home from my visits with those who had been so grievously injured in service to their country, I found myself unable to sleep for weeks. It's the same old story. History books recall the wars, the political upheavals, while forgetting the names of those ordinary people on whose backs such movements are carried. I met too many of those ordinary, truly extraordinary, people in Walter Reed Hospital.

Missing arms. Missing legs. I can fashion a uniform that makes a man feel whole. And perhaps that is enough. We all carry scars. Some visible. Some not. It is the getting on with our lives that counts, the moving forward. I am a tailor. I can help in the only way a tailor knows. One young Marine was eager to return to duty, despite the fact that he had lost both arms. The metal appendages at the end of the prosthetic devices he wore weren't facile enough to enable him to master the buttons on his dress shirt. A Marine is nothing if not proud. He wanted to be able to dress himself without assistance. I took his shirt and fashioned the front plait—remember I am very good at topstitching—with all the buttons neatly aligned, already buttoned it would seem. This finished precision look was accomplished by slender bits of Velcro. I handed the young man his shirt, "Try it on," and stood by while he slipped effortlessly into it. With one swift motion, he pressed the shirt closed, smiled briefly, and then stepped in front of the mirror. Once there, he assumed that stern, courageous Marine posture, the one so familiar from all the commercials on TV. Shoulders erect, he surveyed his reflection in the mirror. After a long moment of silence, he nodded his approval. Who would have known that a man could look this good?

Overcome, I lowered my head. Even after all the years that have passed since I first saw a gentleman turn in just that way back in Giacchino's shop in the Quadraro section of Rome, something in the momentarily unguarded nature of this young man's appraisal caught at my heart, and I felt fulfilled by my choices and the opportunities life has given me. My name is Vittorio Palumbo and I am a tailor.

Afterword

Return to Libya

Of all the trips Rosalba and I have taken together, the most recent one, in October and November of 2010, is one that became more pilgrimage than mere vacation. We traveled to Libya with other Italian former residents of that Arab country, including my sister Giovanna's two daughters and son. We were all in search of our childhood homes, our roots in what is now foreign soil. Foreign, but not unfamiliar.

Remains of the Roman Empire are apparent in old archways, marble columns, and ancient towns unearthed through ongoing archeological digs. We visited the Apollonian fountain where water has been flowing since the time of Christ. The area is marked by caves where they used to bury the dead. At the cemetery in Tripoli, the graves are of more recent origin; some members of our group still had family members buried there.

Evidence of my generation's time in this Arab nation is found preserved in a museum near Cireni and crumbling in the settlements constructed during Mussolini's claim on the region. The names of the towns the Italians built and occupied have been changed. What was once known as Garibaldi is now called Al Dafniyah. Giordani has become Annasiria. Almost all of the buildings and former shops have fallen into disrepair. Our beautiful church in Giordani stands completely empty—no altar, no pictures, no bell. However, it still holds my memory of the statue of St. Joseph shattering the steps leading up to it.

I was surprised that the buildings hadn't been razed, since almost none of them is occupied or used for much other than storage. All around the remains of our former lives, modern homes have been erected. Sometimes these incorporate a bit of the old into the new, but it almost seems as if they are waiting for time to erase what came before. Tents no longer dot the landscape. A camel is an unusual enough sight that our bus stopped along a major highway so that we could take photographs of one being transported in a truck. This is a twenty-first-century Libya.

However, there are living remains of the lives we touched in our time in a place that we once called home. The Arabs of my generation still can speak quite serviceable Italian. We were amazed by this. Surely, the words had been locked away, for years unused, in some region of the brain. How quickly language can pull the past into the present. Whenever men and women of my age heard us speaking Italian, we were greeted with warmth in our own tongue, still so fluent in their hearts after all this time.

When we were in Giordani, now Annasiria, an old childhood friend of my nieces Rosanna and Antonietta heard their voices and knew them immediately. Ramadam, Antonietta, and Rosanna hugged each other, all the while marveling at how quickly they were able to recognize each another after forty-one years apart. We were all overcome with emotion and all included in an invitation to lunch in the beautiful three-story home where Ramadam lived with his two wives and his brothers and their families. The windows of the former D'Agostino farm may have been boarded up, but the Italian and Libyan hearts were wide open.

Two days after this fabulous reunion, our tour group returned to Giordani in the hope that others might also be able to locate the houses where they had once lived. At last, I found myself standing in front of farm #100. As we stood there reminiscing about the old days, a number of Arab people poured out of their own homes and made their way to greet us. We wondered if any of them remembered the Italian families who had lived here in the 1950s.

Among all these young people, one older gentleman, dressed in the traditional Arab style, began to translate our words for his countrymen. There was such a tumble of language and conversation that it was hard to stay focused. While I moved slightly away from the main group and stared at my old home, someone asked this gentleman if he remembered any of the families who had lived here during his childhood.

"Yes, the Palumbo family lived right there." He pointed to our old farm. "I knew Signore and Signora Palumbo. She was a very nice lady, very hard worker; you never find a lady like that anymore." He paused before continuing, "I also knew their son, Vittorio, and their daughter, Ada."

At that point, my nephew Valerino began screaming for me, "Uncle Vittorio, Uncle Vittorio, get over here, he knew you!"

I walked up to him and he proceeded to tell me all about my family. Although I introduced myself as Vittorio, there was so much excitement that he missed what I was saying. A few seconds later he began telling a story about Vittorio, and I interrupted him, "*I'm* Vittorio."

He grabbed my hand and stared into my eyes. "*You're* Vittorio?"

"Yes, I'm Vittorio."

"Your father and my father used to buy and trade animals together. I'm Hadi."

I had never expected to see anyone from those old days again. Hadi and I both started crying and had to walk a bit away from the group to compose ourselves. We might as well have stayed among them, because everyone else was also in tears. Memories just came flooding back.

Hadi then took me by the hand and led me to the house we both knew so well. He showed me the room where we made cheese and the courtyard where I used to tend to the landscaping. He said, "This is where you planted the flowers." At that, he bent down and touched a small walled circle of rocks. "I never removed the stones that bordered your flowers, because this is where I come to get away from the stress of daily life and reminisce about the days with your family. I remember all the good times I had with you and them." Hadi smiled at me. "Do you remember your three dogs? You named the smallest one Picchio. One day you decided he would be cooler if you trimmed his coat, and you asked me to hold him while you went to work with the shears." He started laughing. "By the time we were finished, he looked just like a little lion."

We had so much to say to each other that Hadi agreed to travel with us while we toured for several more hours. The only sight I needed to see was Hadi sitting beside me on the bus. The two of us fell to sharing memories from our teenage years, and it was as if we had never been apart. Without any prompting from me, he talked about the time the Marangone daughter had run away with an Arab man. We compared details about the lives of the Michelone and Milano families, but most important, he was able to give me information about the family of Marani Ben Maiuf. I was happy to learn that Hadi had remained in touch with Mambruk, now eighty-five years old. Although Mambruk lived too far away for there to be time for us to arrange a meeting, Hadi assured me that he would carry my good wishes and news of this visit to my old friend. At the end of our time together, Hadi and I cried and hugged each other. He touched his heart and looked heavenward. "Vittorio, now I can die and go to *paradiso*."

Italian Days, Arabian Nights

On the first day of November, on what would be our last full day in Libya, the tour guide made special arrangements to take us to Garibaldi to see what was left of farm #32, our first home here on the north shore of Africa. The Arabian family that now occupied the property welcomed us with offers to kill a lamb in honor of our return. They wanted us to join them for the feast they would then prepare. Unfortunately, our time was short. All we could accept of their generous hospitality was shared drinks and a tour of what had been our house. Their home was built next to the one that had been ours.

So much was gone, but so much remained. Emotions flowed through me like the six-year-old child I'd been. I had lived here for only nine months, but I had clear memories of Ada's birth, of our prosperous farm, and of all the happy times we'd shared as a family before I'd been taken away to return to Mussolini's boarding schools. The same tiles were on the floor, the original green shutters still hung from the windows. Only bits and pieces of our lives here were left. The rusting skeleton of our old stove was pushed into one corner, and I suddenly saw my mother standing there cooking, everything new and in its place. There was the stable. We found the metal rings we'd used to tie the animals. I saw the stall where we kept the pig, and what was left of the windmill that pumped our water. How proud we were of the bathroom on the outside wall of the house. Our first flush toilet! The pedal and the chain we'd pulled were still in place. Parts of the roof were gone and the sun had faded the paint on the walls, but nothing could fade my memories.

Outside, all the olive trees my parents and Giovanna had planted were fully grown and still producing. Wanting to present me with something I could take back to my sister, our host family handed me two red hot peppers and an olive-laden branch, the symbol of peace. Holding these in my hand, I wandered to the front of the house. There, on the outside wall, number "32" was still engraved in red stucco clay, clearly visible after all these years. Ever since leaving this home in Libya, I had dreamed of returning. Some destiny had brought me back to this place exactly seventy-one years after I had first stood before our new house in an unfamiliar land. November 1, 1939 to November 1, 2010. I knew my trip was complete. More than that, my dream had been fulfilled: the ancient longing for home finally satisfied.

www.ingramcontent.com/pod-product-compliance
Lightning Source LLC
Chambersburg PA
CBHW050458110426
42742CB00018B/3290